DOES GOD CARE?

War, Natural Calamity, Disaster, Disease, Plague, Birth Defects, Human and Animal Suffering?

GEOFFREY E L BENNETT

Prime Seven Media
518 Landmann St.
Tomah City, WI 54660

Printed in the United States of America

Table of Contents

Part 3

Twenty-First Century Answers to
Natural Suffering, Pain and God

Preface

My First book, **Is God Incompetent?**, was published in 2003. So much has changed in the last 21 years, that I felt it necessary to bring it up to date with a new title,

Does God Care?

Science, astronomy, chemistry, biology, geology and medical understanding have all developed greatly in the last twenty years. I have also experienced much suffering myself, as well as caring for my sick wife.

With two lots of cancer, I have been burnt internally by Radiotherapy treatment; while I also fell very badly and was hospitalized with two cracked vertebrae in my neck. My wife developed dementia and total paralysis from her two brain tumours, and subsequently died in 2019.

I have sought to find an answer to the major questions about suffering. Is there a God? If so, is God Caring, Callous or Incompetent? Why is there pain, Illness and Disease? What about Natural Disaster? Why do good people suffer? Numerous other questions are also examined.

I hope you will find this new revised edition of **Does God Care?** both challenging and thought provoking. May you find your own answers, as I believe I have found mine?

Acknowledgements

I would like to thank my son Neil Bennett, whose work as a European translator made him an ideal person to review, criticize and suggest many minor alterations. He proved of immense help in finalizing the style of the book.

The initial review by Reverend Doctor Geoff Walters, Chaplain to the Canterbury Hospice Movement was both helpful and encouraging.

I also wish to thank Reverend Phillip Gathercole (Retired Baptist Minister) for his helpful comments on the early Biblical sections, and Canon David Knight for his review, encouragement and suggestions regarding the chapter on Hell and Judgment.

Humphrey Smith, previous Director of Time at Greenwich Observatory and Herstmonceux Observatory; and Tom Buscombe, Physics and Mathematics teacher at Bexhill High School, both reviewed my Science sections part 3 and offered helpful suggestions. Also, my membership of

Christians in Science, and The Hastings Geological Society both helped my thinking

I wish to dedicate this book to Christine who suffered permanent injury from brain tumours for over twenty years, leading to vascular dementia and total paralysis before her death in 2019.

Introduction

My Dilemma: What Sort Of God Allows Suffering and Pain?

*I*s it possible for an intelligent, thinking person, educated in the Scientific thought process of the 21st Century to believe in an all-powerful, loving "God" when the evidence of Natural Disaster, Disease and Human Evil suggest otherwise?

If "God" is a meaningless concept, then there is no problem. If "God" does not exist, then all human existence is arbitrary and purposeless.

Perhaps "God" is in all things. He/She/ It/ may be the inner strength, the life force, the essence of all- a Pantheistic being personified as "Mother Nature."

Or, "God" may be a limited power, either because the Chaotic nature of the Universe has outsmarted such a concept; or because an equally powerful Evil force, like a "Demon" constantly opposes such a "God".

Perhaps competing "Gods" exist, who limit each other's powers.

Worse still, "God" may be a vindictive, callous and Evil force that needs to be appeased by sacrifice or worship, or "It" might treat all life in an arbitrary manner.

My dilemma is this: if there such a being as a "God," I cannot conceive of him/her/it being inadequate, incompetent or powerless. To me, such a Being would not be worthy of the status of "God."

For me to believe that "God" exists, then I have to conceive of Him/Her/It as both Creator and sustainer of the entire Universe and Cosmos, in Ultimate Control of all Creation-Galaxies, Stars, Solar Systems, Planets and this Earth.

Equally, I see "God" as the Creator of all life and the ONLY force in Nature and the one that is the Mind behind all the laws of Biology, Physics and Chemistry and behind all Science – the master mathematician whose Mind is over All.

Anything less, then "He" cannot be "God" to me – for that seems to be what "God" is, the Creator of all. I readily accept that others conceive of "God" in quite different forms from myself.

But here is my dilemma, because I believe "God" is Almighty and All- Powerful (Omnipotent) and because Christians believe "Him" to be loving and kind, I wonder how such a "God" can possibly allow pain, misery, disaster, disease and evil to exist in this world of ours.

Not just human evil and social ills caused by Free Will and failure; but other evils such as Natural Disasters brought about by Earthquakes, Storms, Viruses, Bacteria, Genetic Disorders, Pestilence and Plague.

What sort of "God" allows all this?

This book seeks to answer the questions raised.

PART 1 Tells of my own suffering and pain, experienced both personally and as Hospital chaplain and my own search for meaning. It also reveals how different groups attempt to answer the problems raised by either accepting that suffering does not exist, or else in believing that pain and suffering are the fault of an inferior vindictive or callous "God."

PART 2 Examines how some ancient Biblical writers come through an evil megalomaniac "God", yet who paradoxically comes through as a caring, loving and competent being revealed in the **Psalms** and other **Old Testament books**, and as a loving Father Figure by Jesus Christ.

PART 3 Seeks to understand physical disaster and human disease in terms of 21st Century Science and human experience. Is there a reason for Natural Disaster, Hurricanes, Tsunamis, Cliff falls, volcanic action, Earthquakes, Disease and decay, inherited genetics, intense pain, mental illness, and disasters? Why is there pain? In addition, how do religious concepts like Hell, the Devil and life after death, make sense in this scientific age? Can the meaning of pain and suffering in terms of future judgment and the afterlife make any sense from the mindset of a modern, rational and scientific 21st Century Christian? What is the role, if any, played by "God"? Doesn't He Care?

Part 1

The Problem of Natural Suffering, Pain And God

Chapter 1

To Hell and Beyond

I stared at my father in horror. Four thick black crusts stood out from his pale skin like two sets of tramlines stretching from each shoulder to each heel. There was no gap from top to bottom.

Early that morning Dad had undergone surgery to fit a heart by-pass valve. It turned out that the anesthetist responsible for the operating theatre had decided to place an electric blanket under my father to keep him warm during his open-heart surgery.

The heart operation had gone smoothly, but the blanket had overheated, caught fire and burnt right into my father's flesh. The surgeons maintained that the air extraction fans were in operation so the theatre staff did not smell the burning through their masks.

Even when they did manage to turn off the current, the blanket continued to smoulder. They were unable to lift my father off the table or remove the blanket, as he was still undergoing open-heart surgery. The result was that he also continued to smoulder.

His burns were unique. Normally, one would expect the whole area to be burnt, but my father's whole back, buttocks, legs and ankles were seared right through to the bones in just four straight lines each an inch(2.5cm) wide. What seemed strange, though, was that my father felt neither pain nor discomfort.

"The first I knew of it was when I saw my back in the bathroom mirror!" he said softly.

The consultant explained that the burns were so severe they had destroyed all the nerve endings in my father's skin leaving him devoid of feeling.

Unfortunately, freedom from pain was not to last.

During the next months and years my father received numerous skin grafts. Thin slices of epidermis, the outer skin, were skived off the inside of my father's thighs, to be replaced in the burned areas. Four square feet (over 3,600cm2) of skin removed and placed on the scar tissue.

Then his pain sensors cut in!

I watched him struggle with excruciating agony at Odstock Burns Unit in Wiltshire. He wept, screamed, cried, prayed for death and then wept, cried and screamed some more. The torture was unendurable.

"Son." he groaned, "I've been to hell and beyond. I can't stand this pain any longer."

But he did. Yet again and again relentless. Agonizing. Tearing the screams from his throat.

And then some more.

No let-up. His nerves held him in the rack, sending pain messages to his brain. He shouted, screamed, clenched, and gasped. To Hell and beyond! Then a relapse. New skin grafts – and Hell dragged him screaming to itself once more.

You may forgive me if I ask where God was during these years of trial.

Is God cruel or callous? Does He not care? Could He do nothing? Does God answer prayer, or does he hide Himself from our view? Why did my father suffer so much? Was he being punished for wrongdoing? Was burning his back a reasonable punishment? Why is God so unfair? Or is it preferable to ask if there even is a God? Does God really exist, or is he a figment of human thought?

And the same numbing questions are still being asked by millions the World over.

I am only one person concerned with just one unique accident at one particular time. Yet such perplexing problems have bewildered human beings since they first began to reason.

MY OWN HELL

At this point, may I reveal a little of my own personal and secondary experiences of suffering.

As a young child, I lived throughout the war, sleeping in air-raid shelters, under beds, under dining rooms tables, in cupboards, but never in a bed. Like many war children, I was unsettled, afraid of the siren, fearful of wearing my gas mask, yet unaware of the gravity of the situation.

The death of my father's brother in Belgium, early in 1940 affected the whole family, and I Participated in the mourning of Uncle Tom's death

A fighter plane hit my junior school at 11:45am one school morning, Killing the pilot, and injuring almost thirty of my friends. We had fourteen weeks off school while the building was made serviceable again. I saw my friends with scar tissue and fractured limbs.

My parents separated three times during my early years and finally divorced. I lived with father in lodgings, with my father's new partner and her children, with my mother at my grandparents' home; and my grandparents and a spinster aunt, while my mother was hospitalized.

By the time I was nine, I had learnt both to fear and hate my father, and lost complete touch with him for six years.

When I was just thirteen, my grandfather died at home. As I possessed a bicycle, my mother sent me to register the death with the coroner, as we had no car or telephone. We had nursed my grandfather for a number of years, and his death meant the loss to me of the only male member of the family I both loved and respected. His slow, lingering death left an indelible mark in my memory.

One year later my father met my mother and sister, Brenda, on the beach, and regretted not knowing his daughter. He wanted to re-join the family in order to look after Brenda, who was a lovely ten-year old. Eventually he returned to my grandmother's home to be with my mother again, but she never properly accepted him.

I returned home from a boys' camp and cried with joy to meet my father, but my mother's rejection of him caused me to feel ambivalent towards him, making me feel even more guilty and uneasy.

At the age of seventeen I joined the Army to train as a medical orderly and medical clerk in the Royal Army Medical Corps. Over the next three years I worked in a surgical ward in Glasgow, and also in Kinrara, near Kuala Lumpur, Malaya.

My training in anatomy and physiology, together with nursing patients on the surgical wards, gave me an insight into the pain of others. Not just physical pain, severe as that sometimes was, but also the mental agony suffered by survivors when they learnt of the death of friends and colleagues.

I had to spend some time nursing a soldier rescued from the sea whose companion had been bitten in half by a shark. It was impossible for a sensitive person like me, not to be profoundly affected by such experience.

I began to understand the pain mechanism, how nerves transmit their pain signals, and how inflammation is an essential part in the healing process. But I also learnt to sympathize and empathize with patients in their own suffering. During my army career I also worked for a psychiatrist at Tidworth Military Hospital as psychiatric receptionist and typing the doctor's notes for medical boards.

My post as duty-clerk led me to interview five men who had survived the unimaginable horror of being run-over by two tanks on Salisbury Plain. The tanks broke away from a slippery hillside-parking place during a night of torrential rain and ran over a tent containing nine soldiers.

One was unharmed, three died almost immediately, and I was sent to interview the five remaining soldiers in order to obtain statements about the incident. Two of the men subsequently died. At the young age of eighteen I found this a harrowing experience, which was to stay with me for many years.

I also had to both "coffin" and bury dead soldiers on one occasion at Tidworth, so death was no stranger to me.

Still only nineteen, I was posted to active service in Malaya, where I served with two field ambulance units providing medical cover for the SAS, Parachute Regiment, Rifle Brigade, and various Commonwealth troops engaged in jungle warfare. I was not involved in actual fighting, but in serving men who were. Again, I worked in a surgical ward, dealing with soldiers recovering from various operations.

On resigning from the RAMC, I studied theology for two years, passed university entrance examinations for teacher training, and obtained a teacher's certificate. Later I took two further courses in Youth Counselling, and became a schoolteacher and County Youth Service leader, helping young people with personal and family problems.

My parents separated again, and later divorced and I once more relived the hatred I had of my father for almost eleven more years. The very problems I helped my young people to overcome were the same problems that took over my own life.

Eventually I became Head of Year 10 in a state high school, where I attended pupil funerals, took part in social services case conferences concerning abused children in my year, and counseled both parents and pupils involved in a whole range of traumatic experiences.

There were times when I had to take school assemblies following the death of either another teacher or a pupil. Such occasions were pregnant with emotion and questioning. Why does God allow this? Is there an answer?

On retiring after 26 years of teaching, I was accepted as a Baptist Minister by the Baptist Union of Great Britain. As a result, I was appointed as a Chaplain's Assistant at a large Hospital Trust in Kent, where I had sole chaplaincy responsibilities for the hematology ward, where patients suffered from blood-disorders, including cancers,

It was here, over the next five or six years that I met young people with HIV and AIDS. Many were in homosexual relationships, and it was a privilege to befriend and minister to them. Many failed to survive the illness brought on by their collapsing immune systems, so their time in hospital was often short and lonely.

Other patients were in various stages of leukemia, or hepatitis. Some were as young as sixteen, a few had been friends from school and church, and some were ex pupils of mine.

It was painful to see so many whom I came to know and minister to, go home only to return with more severe symptoms in a matter of months or a year. They would again return home after their second, third or even fourth term of chemotherapy.

As months came and went, so more came in for the final time.

Brian had returned for his third dose of chemotherapy. When I greeted him and his girlfriend, Doreen, he retorted that he had nothing to be happy about as he was dying. I remember asking Brian how he felt about that, to which he replied angrily, "How would you feel?"

I told him that I did not know how I might feel in his circumstances, which was why I had asked him. "Bloody angry, that's how I feel," he exploded. We talked at some length, Brian shouting in anger and bitterness, and my listening with an attempt to understand. All I could do was listen. Brian was having difficulty controlling his rage, and my task seemed to be to attempt to calm his anger just by being the willing listener.

Eventually I left Brian, but his girlfriend, who had not uttered a word, caught me up. She wanted to talk about Brian's behaviour and rudeness to me.

I told her that Brian's reaction was quite normal. And as chaplain, I often took the brunt of patient's anger. It was so much easier for them to swear and curse me as a representative of God, than to swear and curse the hospital staff. I was a good sounding board.

Then we turned to her own problems. She needed help to deal with Brian's impending death. She was a Christian, needing the help and comfort that I had not been able to provide for Brian. We spent an hour or so in the hospital chapel and in the patients' common room, talking about God's love, God's forgiveness, and the meaning of Christ's Gospel of Salvation. It was my privilege to be able to help Doreen to see some kind of meaning in her life.

That night was the last I saw of Brian. When I next went to visit him, he had died.

After five years with the Chaplaincy department, I felt it was time for a change. With previous hospital experience behind me, including nursing, I trained as a chiropodist and podiatrist with Scholl's at their London School of Chiropody.

Fifteen months later I was practising as an Associate Member of the Institute of Chiropodists and Podiatrists.

Much of my chiropody was with elderly people in nursing homes and secured wards, often senile or suffering from some form of dementia. Much of their suffering was unknown to themselves, but was a source of constant upset to their families.

Dealing with surgical chiropody, it is easy to see how individuals react to pain in such different ways. Some accept it, hardly ever complaining, while others become hysterical at the mere suggestion that I examine a foot.

Often, I was able to ease pain by surgical techniques. I felt a warm glow inside myself when a patient expressed relief and told me how much better he or she felt. With many patients I was able to discuss spiritual issues, and even hardened atheists discussed my Christian beliefs with me.

Then four bombshells hit me!

First, I had undergone a simple routine operation on my nose, which had meant a one–night stay in hospital. On returning home, I received an urgent telephone call from my General Practitioner, who directed me straight back to hospital for blood tests, There, I was informed the tests were positive for diabetes.

It took a while for the news to sink in, I knew a great deal about Diabetes Mellitus, as a chiropodist, and had treated many patients with the disease. Some were unable to feel pain at all, others had limbs amputated and I could think only the worst for a few days.

Now I control my diabetes with insulin injections. I take my own blood pressure, check my own urine and blood sugar, and accept it as a normal part of my own life.

But secondly, the worst was to come. My wife of 32 wonderful years developed two brain tumours which have been removed, unfortunately with part of her brain.

She began to suffer with vascular dementia. I spent years caring for her at home; then I came down with my own prostate cancer and the social services had to take over both our care for some time. I had internal burns from my radio-therapy, from which I still haven't recovered.

Thirdly, my cancer returned after eight years, so I could no longer care for my wife. I had to hire care workers to come to my apartment and dress, bathe and put Christine to bed. She reached the stage where they could no longer cope with her.

Christine was transferred by Adult Social Care to a care home, and finally to a nursing home where she could not move herself in any way. She was fed by teaspoon, washed daily, and just slept. It was so sad to see her in that situation. It is my greatest pain. She finally died with all her family by her bedside on 23 April, 2019. There were many tears in my eyes, and also at her funeral in May.

Then fourthly, I tripped and fell headlong into a closed door and broke my neck! I was hospitalized for some time with a very uncomfortable collar around my neck supporting my head. After hospital I was visited by a team four times daily to dress and wash me, prepare meals and supervise my morphine and other medication. Eventually the team supervised my own meal making and gradually helped me become independent again.

This brief outline of my life will, I hope, enable you to see that I have a special stake in the problem of suffering and pain. And as a Christian, you can understand how and why I have the temerity to challenge God and ask if he really cares.

Fortunately, my life is well rounded. I have two sons, one working abroad. I also enjoy an excellent relationship with my sister, Brenda and her family, whom I love deeply; and I have been greatly blessed by my second marriage to Diane, a wonderful lady friend who knew Christine.

My bitter relationship with my father was stabilized after my own children were born, and he and I became great friends. He remarried, and I loved his wife, Betty, who was a kind grandmotherly figure to our two boys.

Together my father and I fought for compensation from the Dorset Hospital Trust, which was finally settled. Of course, it did not compensate him for all his suffering – nothing could compensate for the agonizing pain of third degree burns and their aftermath.

The Search for Meaning

*I*s life "a tale told by an idiot", as Macbeth believed? Is there meaning and purpose in life, or is each of us a unique accident of evolution brought into existence by mere chance?

Why do the innocent suffer? Why does God allow pain? How can a good God let His creation be destroyed and broken by unendurable horror? Is there even such a being as God?

The whole of history is filled with such questioning. Such probing of the unknown, with questions like these, was of equal importance to the Ancient World.

Ancient literature clearly reveals that suffering and divine cruelty to lesser mortals are the substance of myth, legend and story.

"The Epic of Gilgamesh", written on twelve clay-tablets in Babylonia, deals with legendary heroes of the ancient city state of Uruk. In the eleventh tablet, the story of the

"Great Flood of Enhil" deals with the problems of life and death.

It asks why the gods destroyed the world and gave Utnapishti – the Far Distant One – eternal life. The ancient gods destroyed all human beings without discrimination - both evil and good – in a great flood, because of a crime apparently committed by Ishtar, their mother-goddess. Only Utnapishti was saved with his family and a few animals, in a huge six-story ark requiring 30,000 baskets of pitch, just like Noah in the **Bible**.

In ancient Greek myth, Prometheus had his heart daily torn out by predators as a punishment for bringing fire to human beings. He was then cruelly resurrected each night, only to be re-tortured to death the next day in a continuous hell devised by the gods. My father felt the same fate had befallen him.

Perhaps the most famous ancient story is that of **Job**, in the **Old Testament**. Satan dared God to call Job's bluff. If Job were to lose his family and personal wealth, and at the same time be stricken by a painful complaint that covered his entire body in puss-filled sores, he would lose his faith in God. Job did suffer all this and more, and cried out to God for the reason behind it.

Job found, however, only total silence as he sought an answer to his prayers.

In his introduction to **The Pocket Canon Version of the Book of Job** (Canongate Books Ltd), Louis de Bernieres suggests that God is cruel and capricious. In fact, deBerniere states that God "comes out of the story as the most morally tarnished...looking like an unpleasantly sarcastic megalomaniac." He writes: "God is revealed as a frivolous trickster who offers no justice to the servants or children of Job who he kills off for a bet with Satan."

Not only does de Bernieres suggests that **Job** shows God as a "botcher" by his crudity, but he believes God is revealed in a bad light many times in the **Bible**, such as when he commands Abraham to slay his son Isaac, or orders Saul to destroy the infants and sucklings of the Amalekites.

His conclusion is that "God is a mad, bloodthirsty, and capricious despot, or that all this time we have been inadvertently worshipping the Devil."

Seeing my father in writhing agony made me wonder if God really is a cruel despot.

For me, pain and suffering are a problem, a mystery, a numbing puzzle – a problem to be solved, a mystery to fathom and a puzzle to be explained.

I clearly understood the impossibility of both watching my father suffer the most horrific tortures on a daily basis; and also, at the same time believing that God could be loving and gracious on one hand, as well as being all-powerful on the other. The two completely contradict each other.

Yet those very apparent contradictions, which seem self-evidently absurd, may in fact be really true.

Rather than contradict each other, the real truth may be more of an anomaly, a paradox, and an enigma that may perhaps be answered in a way that is both possible and plausible.

Does God care about human torment and pain? Despite my own experiences as both a recipient and an observer of suffering, my answer is a resounding "Yes."

The atheist or humanist does not have the same problem with pain and suffering – "Problem" is the wrong word; anguish and agony are merely facts of existence. God has nothing to do with it. For the atheist sees life as meaningless with no purpose, and pain as a reflex caused by the brain's reaction to the varied stimuli of pain receptors.

Like all Christians, however, I face a serious difficulty in my own attempts to deal with suffering and pain. My problem lies in my belief in three contradictory ideas, I believe that suffering exists, that God is all - powerful, and that God is both loving and good – He does care.

These three notions appear to deny each other's validity, seem to be in opposition to each other. If I accept only two of these beliefs, then there would be no problem.

I could perhaps understand and accept a good God who was not powerful enough to prevent pain. He might be in conflict with another equally-powerful god or devil, or in conflict with another evil force.

Or if I were convinced that suffering does not really take place in the minds of positive and goodly people; or that God is fickle and is not a loving force, then the problem might be seen as a meaningless illusion.

But Christians don't believe in just two, but in all three notions at the same time, and herein lies my dilemma.

Despite the horrors I have witnessed both in my father and in other aspects of my life, I have nevertheless come to believe very much in a good, loving and gracious God, whose one concern is for the people he has created.

The latter part of this book will explain exactly why I have come to this conclusion.

Chapter 3

Does Suffering Really Exist?

*P*eople educated and raised in a modern, scientific world may be forgiven for thinking that no sensible individual could really believe that suffering doesn't exist. Its destructive force seems self-evident.

But many argue either that suffering does not really exist, or that it can be controlled or overcome as to be almost irrelevant.

Religions deal with the problem of suffering and pain in numerous ways, and I wanted to discover their different attitudes to suffering and pain to see what I might learn.

THE ANSWER OF THE CHRISTIAN SCIENCE

Mary Baker Eddy, Founder of Christian Science, thought that suffering and pain do not actually exist but only appear real. Prayer, she said, can heal sin and disease.

Over 3000 Christian Science churches proclaim the message that sin, suffering, pain and evil are all illusions. Two thirds of all Christian Science meetings take place in the United States of America. There are fewer than a thousand congregations in the rest of the world.

As a child, Mary Baker Eddy suffered from convulsive hysteria. Her first husband died, and the second left her because of her fits. In 1862, she met a hypnotist, Phineas Quimby, who cured her. It was a case of "Mind over matter"; her own mind had shown that her suffering was an illusion. Both her knowledge of Christianity and her hypnotic cure led Mary Baker Eddy to believe that the mind could overcome all negative and alien emotions, including suffering and pain.

Her book, **Science and health with a Key to the Scriptures**, which she claimed God had dictated to her, explained her new concept of the Divine Science of Healing. In it, she explains that there is no reality in life except "Mind" or "Spirit".

God is Spirit – that is, He is Mind, Truth, Power, Life, Goodness and Love. This is reality. On the other hand, evil, sin, sickness, suffering, pain, material and death are unreal. Mrs. Eddy taught that Jesus Christ did not die and rise again. He overcame death knowing that no one can really die. When we each come to realize the illusory nature of suffering and death, then we shall each be saved from its unreal nature. Unfortunately for Christian Scientists, their beliefs appear to be neither Christian nor scientific – no scientific experiments have been undertaken to prove the illusory nature of suffering and death by the Christian Science membership, and no sermons may be preached in the Christian Science meetings. Only readings taken verbatim from **Science and Health** may be used for their services, while discussion of the text is not allowed.

Thus, no one can question the book that Mary Baker Eddy claims to be given by God. In fact, the whole scenario seems no more than a delusion imposed on gullible people! It certainly does not answer the question for me.

THE ANSWER OF BUDDHISM

Siddhartha Gautama, an Indian prince living during 6th Century BC, was appalled by death, decay and disease in his princedom.

He left his palace to find enlightenment, which he claimed to have found while meditating under a Bodhi Tree. Later known as "Buddha", meaning "The enlightened one", he taught that all forms of suffering have their source in the mind.

All suffering is the consequence of human thought and can be overcome by using various spiritual methods which help people to overcome their delusions. Gautama Buddha laid down four noble truths:

1. Life is suffering-which must be understood.
2. Suffering is caused by desire – which must be abandoned.

3. Ceasing to desire results in the cessation of suffering – which must be realized.

4. The Eight-fold path leads to the end of desire.

It is this Eight-fold Path that enables the Buddhist to train his mind to gain liberation from all suffering.

Following the path involves knowing the difference between good and bad actions, having the right motives, speaking without harm, accepting the suffering of other people or animals, striving to perfect one's own spiritual path, living in harmony with the world, and meditating to find Nirvana.

Nirvana is the highest state in which the true follower is able to overcome all desires and affections and be freed from the cycle of reincarnation itself, thus while the Buddhist accepts the fact of suffering, he sees it as the fault of his own selfish desires that may be completely overcome through following the right path.

It is very difficult for women to follow the path because of prejudice. There are many lay women who follow Buddhism though, and a number of women nuns, but it is difficult for women to beg or live a solitary life or to live other than as a mother and wife. In fact, it is often assumed that for a woman to reach her Nirvana, she must be reincarnated as a man.

As I see it, Buddhist teaching on suffering gives very little hope. Pain may take numerous lifetimes to overcome. And there is not much incentive for women, whose lot is often worse than their men.

THE ANSWER OF NORTH AMERICAN NATIVE CULTURES

Many of the Native American beliefs are based on the concept that pain and suffering are meaningless.

We often call Native American men, "Braves". When a boy reached manhood (puberty), he would be initiated into "The Company of the Brave" by undergoing various tortures in which the true "Brave" had a vision of their god, Manitou.

Apache youths, for example, had holes drilled in their pectoral muscles just under their armpits. Cords were threaded through, and the youth hung from a tree branch. He would be twirled round until he went dizzy and had his vision. Subsequently, Braves accepted pain as a norm. They perceived it as a fact of life, which a man could overcome by his superiority over the child. It was the North American Native equivalent of the "stiff upper lip" attitude of the hardened British Public-School boy.

If a boy were not "man" enough to undergo such torture, he was designated a "woman-man". As such he was accepted by the tribe as effeminate and served as a shaman or witch doctor, He also advised the Braves on how to be fertile with women, providing potions ad spells for childbirth.

When Apaches captured white settlers, the prisoners would often scream in dreadful agony under torture. Often women and children of the tribe might torture a prisoner. Apache men would not scream. They accepted their pain as part of life.

In the film, **Savage Innocents**, a policeman whose frozen hand is placed into the body of a slaughtered husky dog, screams in pain as blood flows back into his freezing arteries.

The Eskimo (Inuit) who rescues, him asks the question, "What's wrong, man are you afraid of pain?" The implication is that the Eskimos do not fear pain.

THE ANSWER OF MYSTIC CULTS

Fire walkers are also religious groups who walk either through fire, on burning coals, or across stones heated in a wood fire. Found mostly in India, Japan, Mauritius, Fiji, Tahiti and Trinidad, Priests and people walk barefoot through heated areas, on red-hot stones or burning coals without apparent burns or pain.

No satisfactory explanation has been made as to why the adherents are not burnt. Some suggest that the ecstasy brought about by high-spinning dances produces temporary insensitivity to pain. Dancers are so intoxicated with their own adrenaline "high" that they feel nothing.

I certainly have great respect for initiates, but am most happy not to be included in such ceremonies. It is not merely cowardice on my part, but a realization that when I suffer in mind or body, my pain and suffering are real.

And my experiences of others in hospital beds, on the chiropody couch, or grieving over suffering or the loss of loved ones, makes their pain and anguish real to me.

Chapter 4

Is GOD's Power Really Limited?

any people accept the reality of suffering and pain, but believe that God is not always able to assist His people because of limits to His power and authority.

THE ANSWER OF ZOROASTRIANISM

Zoroaster or Zarathustra (who appears to be contemporary with three or four Hebrew prophets, and possibly Buddha and Confucius) lived in Persia in the 6th Century BC, where he developed a dualistic religion.

Because he believed that the gods were cruel and evil, he argued that the cruel gods, called "*daevas*" (from which we get our word "devil" or "demon") are constantly fighting against the true supreme God, Ahura Mazda.

The *daevas* are under the control of the spirit of Evil, a Devil named Ahriman.

In the world, human beings are called to fight on the side of Mazda who is involved in an age-long struggle against the forces of evil, and will one day be assisted by a messiah- like figure, the Saoshyant.

After a 6000-year struggle the victory of good over evil will come, when the resurrection and judgment will take place. Zoroastrianism, as Pierre Bayle in his 1697 Dictionary calls the religion, reveals the key to the problem of evil.

The beliefs in a resurrection, in angels, the Devil and the Messiah in Zoroastrianism predate Christianity, and are also found in the literature of the Essene Community near the Dead Sea.

The righteous and pious go straight to Paradise (a Persian word), while the wicked visit Hell to be purified. The entire human race will eventually be in Paradise after the resurrection takes place.

Zoroastrian priests were called "Magi", the name given to the wise men from the East who followed the star to Bethlehem.

Few Zoroastrians are found today in the West. Indian Parsees (just over 125,000) are modern followers of Zoroastrianism, although much of their belief system has changed over the years. Approximately 18,000 Gabas still live in Iran in the Persian regions of Yazd and Kerman; and a further 5,200 live in Karachi, Pakistan. As a child I could have imagined the world to be under opposing forces of good and evil, and might have leaned towards the views of Zoroaster. Not now.

THE ANSWER OF WITCHCRAFT

A number of fundamentalist Christians appear to believe in the idea of Satan and his demons limiting God by their habitual temptation of human souls. Again, I find it difficult to conceive of God fighting with a rival throughout the vast period of human history and before (but I will return to this later).

Belief in the Devil, demons and various forms of witchcraft is prevalent throughout the world. Evil spirits, the occult, "medicine men" or Shamans, all form part of primitive religious belief. Without going deeply into the plethora of animistic beliefs, it is sufficient to record that from earliest days people have believed in evil spirits and the power of magic to restrain them.

In England, a very detailed study of Paganism and Witchcraft was undertaken by Anthony Kemp in **Witchcraft and Paganism Today** (Brockhampton Press) in which he concludes that Paganism and Witchcraft are not to be confused with Satanism.

Paganism in England is concerned with reverence for nature, and a belief in the existence of a God and Goddess. Modern Druidism encompasses a range of beliefs from ancient Druidism, North American Indian Spirit Worship and ideas from both the Vikings and also from the philosophies of the Far East.

Few in the West think similarly, although there is a surprising increase in witchcraft and paganism today.

MY DILEMMA

If there is a God, then I cannot conceive of Him being inadequate, incompetent or unable. Such a being would not be worthy of being called, "God".

If God does exist, then He must be the creator and sustainer of the entire Universe. He must be in ultimate control of all creation – galaxies, stars, solar systems, planets and this Earth.

He must be the creator of all life and the only force in nature. He must be the mind behind the laws of biology, physics and chemistry, and behind all science. He must be the master mathematician whose mind is over all.

Anything less, then He cannot be "God", for what I believe as a Christian is that God is all the above, the Creator of all.

So here is my dilemma. Because I believe God is almighty and all-powerful (omnipotent), and because Christians believe him to be loving and kind, I wonder how He can possibly allow such pain, misery and evil to exist in this world of ours.

Not just human evil and social ills caused by individual free will and failure; but other ills such as natural disasters brought about by viruses, bacteria, earthquakes, storms, pestilence and plague. What sort of God allows all this?

Chapter 5

Is God Really Vindictive and Callous?

In Shakespeare's master tragedy, **King Lear**, the Duke of Gloucester, whose eyes have been plucked out by Lear's daughter, utters those words, "As flies to wanton boys, are we to the gods; they kill us for their sport."

Sometimes it does seem that God is teasing us - playing with us for sport in a cruel, callous way.

Jerry, a friend, lost his first wife with cancer. After some years he remarried a lovely vivacious woman. Within a few years she also came down with cancer and died.

Talking on the telephone, Jerry shared his feelings with me. "I feel that God is playing games. Why do I have to go through two lots of grief like this?" I spent an hour talking with my friend, and felt his grief deeply.

Jerry was a Christian whose faith in God had been sorely tempted. "Why?" he kept asking. I had no answer.

Some religions see God as a malevolent being that must be appeased by human or animal sacrifice. In Aztec,

Societies human sacrifice was made to stay the hand of God.

The same was true in the Biblical world. Moloch required burnt children who were placed on his heated hands -- "Passed through the fire" is the phrase used.

THE ANSWER OF ISLAM

Islam, the religion of the Prophet Mohammed, sees human suffering as God's punishment for sin or wrongdoing. All that happens is "the will of Allah".

There appears to be a certain amount of fatalism among the faithful. All men must be subject to God, and divine retribution is paid to those who fail to give Allah his due.

In the Past Muslim mythology, demons and evil angels caused suffering and pain. Jinn (Genies) are mythical spirits – good or bad – who can assume human or animal form and influence humans by supernatural means.

Modern Islam pays little attention to these myths, taking the teaching of Allah as recorded in the **Qur'an** as its authority.

Mohammed is believed to be the last of God's prophets, following on from Abraham, Moses and Jesus as well as over a thousand others.

The Angel Gabriel is said to have given Mohammed the words to recite ("Qur'an"), but, as he could not read or write, he was able to remember all the words and recited them to his followers who wrote them in **The Qur'an ("The Recital").**

While pain and suffering are inevitable, Muslims are to do their best to bear them with patience and fortitude. Hardships and suffering are seen as times of testing.

Pain should be endured with humility as true life for the Muslim begins only in the Kingdom of Allah. Life on earth is only a prelude.

Heaven and Hell feature often in Islamic teaching. Life on earth is a period of testing, during which the angels record human goodness and evil. A man must endure the trials that befall him, behave in a good way, help others in need, and trust in the mercy and justice of Allah for his future reward.

Heaven is a garden of flowing streams, luscious fruits, richly covered divans and beautiful maidens to serve men and grant them pleasure. The description of both Heaven and Hell in the **Qur'an** is similar to that in the **Bible** and the **Apocrypha**.

Many modern Islamic scholars see the teaching of Hell with its horrendous tortures, and the wonders of Heaven with its sensual attributes, as symbolic of the punishments to be inflicted on the unfaithful and the rewards to be bestowed on the faithful.

These punishments and rewards are beyond human understanding. Only Allah, who can do no wrong, understands the human condition. His justice and wisdom will ultimately give the answer to human tragedy.

In the **Qur'an**, Mohammed said that to "those nearest to Allah will come rest and satisfaction and a garden of delights, and…peace; but if you are of those who have…gone wrong, then your entertainment will be boiling water and hellfire" (surah 56).

Muslims believe that disabled or incomplete bodies are merely vehicles for perfect souls. Allah is perfect, fair and just, so no one endures anything that has not been pre-ordained. The Hadith, a supplementary tradition written about Mohammed, uses words similar to those used by the Apostle Paul: "Eye has not seen, and it has not entered the human heart what things Allah has prepared for those who love Him".

THE ANSWER OF ANIMISM

Animist Groups believe in numerous gods of the trees and hills who must be appeased by gift or sacrifice.

Intermediaries, shamans, "witch doctors", priests, or talisman, help primitive people to accept the awe-inspiring powers of nature by sacrifice, gift offerings or other forms of placation. God is a power to be reckoned with. He must be humoured in some way.

Some see the story of **Job** in this light – servants, animals and Job's children die, while Job suffers lingering and horrible agony purely for the sake of a wager.

Such a god is not worthy of our worship. Truly free human beings with moral feelings would rightly defy such a god and refuse to offer their obedience and worship.

Or if they did worship that creature then they would surely learn to hate it in their hearts. Certainly, I would not wish to accept a cruel, impartial god; but at least I would see suffering for what it is – the partial whim of the master of the Universe.

Again, that fails to answer the question of suffering in a world, which is the creation of a God whom I believe to be both all-powerful and all loving.

Chapter 6

Is There any Value in Suffering?

Most thinking people can see some limited value in small doses of pain or suffering. If pain identifies a solvable problem, is limited both in duration and intensity, and there is hope of it subsiding or disappearing entirely, then pain can be seen to be an asset.

When its agony is unrelenting, the pain constant, unbearable and hopeless in its outcome, however, no meaning can be deduced from it. Terminal cancers, chronic arthritis or other painful conditions, loss of loved ones, watching a lover waste away, giving birth to a deformed or seriously ill baby, or emotional and mental breakdown bring unanswerable questions.

Similar problems that challenge the idea of a loving God occur when natural disasters (often called "Acts of God") cause loss of life and suffering.

Every year at least 20,000 people are killed by such disasters according to **Great Disasters** (Readers Digest).

Doctor Basil Booth, in **Earthshock** (Dent), also suggests that while 20,000 is a minimum number, it is often millions who lose their lives each year through worldwide natural disasters.

Natural disasters are not just physical "Acts of God" like avalanches, floods, volcanic eruptions, earthquakes, tornadoes and hurricanes. They also include plague, AIDS epidemics, Covid and famine.

What possible value do these disasters have for humanity? I can think of no value at all. Disease has always been with us. Even Neanderthal Man who lived 100,000 years ago suffered from deformity and arthritis.

A Neanderthal skeleton discovered at La Chapelle-aux-Saints revealed an old man crippled with arthritic joints who, while unable to hunt, nevertheless survived.

The skull and right arm of a Neanderthal man was also found in Iraq. The arm was not only withered, but had been amputated above the elbow, an operation that he successfully survived.

It appears that 100,000 years ago, illness and suffering existed among primitive people who cared for family members. It is not just a modern phenomenon. There are numerous causes of disease. Bacteria are vegetable forms of life, which multiply in minutes to produce toxins and disease.

Fortunately, penicillin and other drugs destroy many lethal ones but many are becoming resistant to such drugs.

Protozoa are tiny animal organisms, which cause disease such as malaria carried by anopheles' mosquitoes.

Viruses are even smaller "systems" (they are not really living organisms because they cannot reproduce unaided). They need to find a human, animal or vegetable host in which to "procreate" themselves. Viruses are parasites that frequently lead to diseases such as herpes, the common cold or AIDS.

Poisons, which enter the body through food, skin, cuts, bodily openings, or through the simple act of breathing, cause sickness and sometimes death. So too do radiation and ultra violet rays.

Birth defects, problems brought about by difficulties in delivery, or occurring while the foetus is in the womb, are all areas where pain and suffering are caused by natural phenomena. Again, I can find no worthwhile meaning for such random occurrences.

In addition, a range of suffering and pain is caused by human evil and stupidity. People cause war, famine, exploitation, slavery, fraud and other crimes. Obesity, drug addiction, alcoholism, chronic gambling and poverty are responsible for just some of the suffering caused by human beings to themselves.

Why doesn't God stop crime and wars, and remove human evil? After all, I pray for the governments of this world, and for my own king and country, as do thousands of other Christians. Why doesn't God answer our prayers?

* * * * *

So far, I have attempted to discuss the questions that others and I have found difficult to answer. To ask the questions, then glibly say that "I do not have an answer, but God does," is to "sit on the holier than thou fence."

I believe Cowper was right when He wrote:

> Blind unbelief is sur to err
> And scan His work in vain.
> God is His own Interpreter,
> And He will make it plain

Christians are not to be "head in the clouds – pie in the sky" believers. We are urged repeatedly in the **Bible** to "gird up the loins of our mind" – in modern parlance to "put on your thinking cap." (**1 Peter** 1:13 KJV).

In the call of Isaiah, the word of God invites Israel: "Come now, let us reason together" (**Isaiah** 1:18 KJV)).

Jesus, himself, asked the religious leaders of his day, "Why do you not judge for yourselves what is right?" (**Luke** 12:56 KJV)).

And Saint Peter urges his readers "to be ready to give an answer of the faith that is in you, with modesty and respect." (**1 Peter** 3:15 KJV).

It is my purpose to attempt to answer the many questions I have raised.

In the next section I shall examine certain Biblical writers who appear to have a contribution in attempting to explain suffering, starting with **Old Testament** writers and then proceeding to **The New Testament** writers.

Then, in the third section I will attempt to answer the questions from the viewpoint of twenty-first century scientific and cultural knowledge.

The new discoveries in medicine, human psychology and animal psychology, biology, oceanography, meteorology, geology and astronomy that were unknown to the Biblical writers have helped me to answer some of these questions to my own satisfaction.

I hope the insights provided will help you to understand how I came to believe that God is not only all powerful (omnipotent) and all knowing (omniscient); but also, at the same time is loving, kind and gracious in a world where suffering exists.

Part 2

Biblical Answers to Natural Suffering, Pain and God

How to Interpret the Bible in the Light of Twenty-First Century Scientific Knowledge

Before examining some passages in The **Bible** that deal with suffering, there are two difficulties about **The Bible** that I believe need to be faced.

The first is this: **The Biblical writers had no knowledge of modern science**. They did not know about plate tectonics, Max Planck's theory of quantum physics, Einstein's theory of relativity, modern meteorology and astronomy. Modern physics, chemistry and psychology were unknown to them. Neither did they know about modern genetics and DNA coding, the longevity of the Earth with its fossil remains of dinosaurs and other extinct forms of life.

They knew nothing about prehistoric people - Neanderthal, Sinanthropus, Cro-Magnon or even

Palaeolithic Homo sapiens, or that human life already existed in the Americas, Northern Europe, the Far East and Oceania.

In other words, the biblical writers were extremely limited in their understanding and knowledge of our world. I realize that to seek answers to the questions I have raised about the apparent lack of power and the apparent cruelty or callousness of God, I must understand the **Bible** only as it makes sense according to my knowledge as a twenty-first century Christian.

Closing my eyes to recent discoveries, working theories and modern insights will undermine any answers that I might attempt to give.

I hope, therefore, to examine the Biblical evidence to see what the **Bible** has to say about suffering in this section. Then I intend to examine the questions raised in the light of twenty-first century scientific and cultural thinking in the next section to see if there might be any correlation between the two.

My second difficulty concerning the Bible is to decide how I am to understand or interpret what I read.

Does the **Bible** make sense in our modern world? What about its numerous contradictions? Are some parts more important than others?

Is the **Bible** true? Is it relevant to the Twenty First Century?

I have no desire to read a book like the **Bible** and just accept it uncritically. As an educated person brought up in a scientific society, I believe that all evidence must be based on experience, reliable testimony and logical deduction. And while this is true of Scripture, I believe the **Bible** must also be interpreted in accordance with the culture of the times in which it was written.

One thing is clear about the **Bible** - it has been interpreted in different ways by each generation. The early church was more concerned with which **New Testament** books to actually include, as were Jewish scholars with their "canon" of Scripture. I have used three versions of Scripture, although I have eight different translations at home, including a **Greek New Testament** and a Greek copy of the **Jewish Septuagint**.

My English church uses the **New International Version** (NIV), my school uses the **Good News Bible** (GNB), and some still use the **Authorized** or King James version of 1611. They are three I have used.

During the Middle Ages the authority of the Holy Catholic Church took precedence over the text of the **Bible**. Church authority took Biblical material as "allegory".

Protestant reformers saw the **Bible** as "God's words", although Martin Luther did not think much of the **New Testament letter of James**, which he called "a right strawy epistle". Martin Luther also dropped the books of the **Apocrypha**, which were in the Greek Version of the **Hebrew Old Testament**, and part of the Catholic Scriptures. He also questioned the books of **Esther** and **The Apocalypse**. (The Catholic Church calls the last **New Testament** book, **"The Apocalypse"**, while Protestants call it **"The Book of Revelation."**)

Puritans believed the 1611 King James' Version so literally that John Owen claimed it to be "dictated by God – even the quotation marks".

Later eighteenth and nineteenth century scholars saw the **Bible** as a human book, a search for religious experience, and a record of human attempts to find God.

Fundamentalism believes the **Bible** to be "verbally inspired" or "inerrant" in all matters of history, science, biography and factual detail. In 1909 a series of books entitled, **The Fundamentals**, introduced the church to the title "Fundamentalist", meaning someone who believes every part of the **Bible** to be verbally inspired by God and literally true. Fundamentalism sees the **Bible** as "God breathed" or "breathed out by God", according to Professor Paul Enns of Dallas Theological Seminary in his **Moody Handbook of Theology (Moody Press).**

Other Christians, such as Professor A.H. Strong in his **Systematic Theology (Pickering and Inglis),** suggested that the Bible is not properly a revelation, but a record (or history) of God's revelation of Himself, culminating in the coming of Jesus Christ.

They conclude that the **Bible** is partially or "dynamically" inspired, so that God inspires only those parts relating to faith and practice, whereas history, science, chronology or other non-faith matters may not always be totally accurate.

* * * * *

The first thing that struck me about the Biblical writers, both in their different accounts of creation and in their different interpretations of suffering, is the remarkable absence of any anti-science. While none of the Biblical writers is scientific in what he or she writes, neither is any one of them non-scientific. The writers do not write about magic spells, of tortoises or elephants or giants such as Atlas carrying the world on their backs.

They are clearly pre-scientific in their expressions, but write about things as they appear to the senses, such as "the Sun rises and sets", or "the winds blow from the four corners of the earth".

Many passages of scripture present masterpieces of description in poetic form.

In the King James Version, the writers use imagery and metaphor in a bold way – "the clouds are God's chariots", "the trees and the stars shall clap their hands", "the Lord is my shepherd", "the hand of the Lord is not shortened".

These are the words of the artist, the songwriter, the seer or prophet, and the poet.

My purpose has been to examine scriptures that were clearly written to include some sort of answer to human suffering. Thus, I have deliberately omitted the writings of Moses, who predicts calamity on those Israelites who fail to keep the Law.

Instead, I have included pertinent Wisdom literature, prophecy concerned with suffering, the relevant teaching of the Gospel writers, the Life, teaching, death and resurrection of Jesus, Paul and the writer to **The Hebrews**, together with that of the **Apocalypse** or **Book of Revelation.**

It also seems obvious to me that whilst the writers are unique in their individual presentations, their messages show some similarity.

I found this surprising, for the **Bible** is not really one book: it is a library, comprising sixty-six books, written by forty or more authors over twelve hundred years in three continents.

Among the writings are poems, dirges, songs and prayers, together with stories, parables allegories, legends, drama and debate. Formal laws, rules and regulations occupy four books, while histories, biographies, and gospels occupy twelve or more volumes. Special forms of Hebrew writing like prophecy, apocalyptic and Midrash are also found in the **Bible**. (A Midrash is a story or legend spun around a prophecy or a religious story.)

The **Bible** is written by diverse human beings in the languages and cultures of their times. Hebrew, Aramaic and Greek are the main languages used, and the vocabulary and style differs from author to author.

As I read the **Bible**, I recognised human weakness and error, which required me to thoroughly examine and interpret each genre of writing, just as I would any other piece of literature.

Chapter 8

Answers from The Wisdom Literature

(PSALMS, PROVERBS, ECCLESSIATES AND JOB)

I searched for a meaning to the problem of suffering in the Wisdom Books of the **Old Testament**. Where better to find an answer?

As a history and religious education teacher, I was aware of the training given in the ancient world to young pupils in the temple schools.

From the early days of written records, men and women were trained in the arts of writing and thinking.

Sumerian records of the fourth millennium BC indicate that teacher-priests in schools attached to the temples educated wealthy men and women. Their lessons included reading, writing and arithmetic, study of patriotism, the lives of kings, and respect for Sumerian religion, based on Moon worship.

The elite of Ancient Egyptian society were also educated in temple schools in the civilization, arts and crafts and religion of the Egyptian people. Written records of medicine, surgery and simple anatomy were kept, a decimal system of mathematics developed and observations of the planets and stars were made.

In addition, written accounts found in cliff tombs suggest that children learnt the religious legends of Egypt, and that good men could hope for a happy life after death.

No wonder that Moses, who was brought up as the son of an Egyptian princess, is described as "educated in all the wisdom of the Egyptians" (**Acts** 7:22 KJV).

So, I studied the Hebrew wisdom, first at Avery Hill College, London, where I submitted a special year paper on the **Book of Job** in place of my second examination in Divinity for my Teacher's Certificate.

My studies surprised me. I did not find my answer then. Instead, I discovered a cruel God who gambled on the life of a good man, by making a bet with Satan. The **Old Testament** seemed to have no message of hope in a cruel world.

It was to be many years later, as I came to see each separate book of wisdom in its own context that I began to change my mind and see the first glimmer of hope in finding a solution. In the Wisdom books of the **Hebrew Bible,** much is made of the sayings of "the wise".

By the sixth century BC, students learned through dialogue and argument between the teachers, "the wise", and the disciples or learners.

"The wise" were priests, judges, treasurers and administrators, ambassadors and kings, who taught young men from wealthy backgrounds, who might be princes, sons of scholars and merchants, or sons of priests. The training was more like a religious management course in Hebrew administration. The wisdom referred to was a "moral wisdom" based on following the ways of Yahweh or God.

The **Book of Proverbs, Ecclesiastes** (also known as **The Words of the Preacher),** the **Psalms** and **Job** form the Wisdom Literature in the Hebrew Scriptures.

Their format takes two forms: proverbs and speculation. Proverbs are short striking observations about practical living such as those found in the **Book of Proverbs** itself, and in certain of the **Psalms**.

Proverbs describes the happy and blessed life of the righteous man and the judgment placed on moral fools. It seems to indicate that suffering and pain are experienced only by the wicked.

Foolish individuals, who are moral defectives before God, are punished and cut off from normal relationships with good people. The Righteous Ones, on the other hand, receive happiness and wealth as part of God's blessing.

The book commences by stating its purpose and theme: "The proverbs of Solomon son of David, king of Israel:

> for attaining wisdom and discipline;
> for understanding words of insight;
> for acquiring a disciplined and prudent life,

doing what is right and just and fair;

for giving prudence to the simple,

knowledge and discretion to the young—

let the wise listen and add to their learning,

and let the discerning get guidance—

or understanding proverbs and parables,

the sayings and riddles of the wise.

The fear of the LORD is the beginning of knowledge,

but fools despise wisdom and knowledge" 1—6 NIV)

In addition to the name of Solomon, King Lemuel and his mother, Agur the son of Jakah, and the "the wise" are mentioned as authors of particular sections. While scholars cannot identify these individuals (apart from Solomon who gained a reputation for his own wisdom), they do suggest that much of the book uses material from other countries.

Solomon, who married an Egyptian princess, may have known **The Teaching of Amenemope**, as there are close similarities between the Egyptian wisdom of Amenemope and parts of **Proverbs** 22 and 23.

Proverbs teaches that good, righteous people will always be happy and contented. The righteous will be rewarded for their morality and avoid the suffering that comes to the wicked or foolish. The wise will live long lives and accumulate wealth and honour.

"Misfortune pursues the sinner, but prosperity is the reward of the righteous" (13:21 NIV), "The righteous eat to their hearts' content, but the stomach of the wicked goes hungry" (13:25 NIV).

Hard work, high morals, moderation, support for the weak, loyalty to one's parents, humility and kindness were the marks of "righteousness". The good were the old pupils from the temple schools.

As I read **Proverbs**, I realized the naivety of "the wise". The book was written at a time of Hebrew prosperity and peace, when Solomon had earned himself an international reputation for his trade, technology and foreign treaties.

Many of the proverbs actually contradict each other. My own mother, I remember, also used contradictory proverbs to suit the occasion. If she needed help, she would say, "Many hands make light work."

When, she didn't require assistance she would respond with "Too many cooks spoil the broth."

In my own career choices, I was never sure whether to invoke, "Fools jump in where angels fear to tread," or "He who hesitates is lost."

I found the same contradictions in the Biblical proverbs. One example is the two-fold prohibition, "Do not answer a fool according to his folly or you will be like him, yourself." and the opposite maxim, "Answer a fool according to his folly or he will be wise in his own eyes." (**Proverbs** 26:4-5 NIV).

Which is correct? I realized that each of them makes sense only in given contexts. They represent maxims that are true in any society at any time. They are a kind of universal wisdom, vague generalisations, equally true in any society at any time, but unable to account for the many exceptions which make up human life.

Like the wisdom of Egypt, China or a hundred other countries, Hebrew wisdom is based on human experience, especially on the observations of one particular class.

It is essential to realize that the "wise" who wrote down their pithy sayings were not ordinary people - or poor people who might suffer as individuals. They were priests, teachers, national traders and administrators living in particular times and cultures, who were writing about the behaviour only of the rich and wealthy.

They were people who lived in large, safe palaces and noble houses with their own water supplies and covered courtyards.

Slaves and servants ran their homes and estates; hired hands toiled in their fields, tending crops and herds. They had accumulated wealth and lived in opulence.

And if they saw a colleague who fell or lost his possessions, it was so easy to assume that pride, foolish behaviour or evil meant that he was being punished for his own lack of wisdom.

Not all the "the wise" lived so luxuriously and free of trouble.

King David, writer of many psalms, knew personal suffering. He was an outlaw in hiding from King Saul for a number of years. Then, when he came to the throne, his own son, Absalom, who wrestled the kingdom from his father, betrayed him. David, therefore, knew that the righteous do not always get their own way. He still believed, as other sages before him, that the wicked will eventually be punished and the good rewarded.

In **Psalm** 37, possibly written at the time of Absalom's revolt, David states that wrongdoers will wither like grass, and that soon the wicked will be no more. The righteous, though, will dwell in the land and enjoy safe pasture where they will be given their heart's desire.

Although David suffered, he believed it to be a transitory state of affairs that God would eventually bring to an end.

Asaph (the leader of King David's choral group) also realized that things were not always rosy for the wise ones. In **Psalm** 73 Asaph envies the arrogant, wicked men who prosper, have healthy bodies and live violent and deceitful lives.

He asks, "Does the Most High have knowledge?" as he observes the carefree, wealthy lifestyle of evil people. "Surely in vain have I kept my heart pure." (NIV)

Asaph feels guilty for questioning God. He explains that he entered God's sanctuary feeling oppressed, and had an awareness that the final destiny of wicked men will be judgement and ruin. If justice does not appear to take place in this world, Asaph realizes that it will in the end, for God will reward the good and condemn the sinful.

Such sentiments are part of the childish belief of primitive people. They are clearly not in accord with the plight of the modern world. God is not a "heavenly babysitter" of the kind pictured by these "wise" men. He doesn't smack naughty children and cuddle the good ones.

Such ideas may have been needed to establish the Hebrew clans and unify them into a nation.

Their God, Yahweh, was a patron god, a clan god, a family deity, and the one who led the tribe.

By the time of Solomon, the "wise" were beginning to think of Yahweh as their national god, although there were other voices struggling to be heard.

These were not to be found in proverb and riddle and pithy saying, but in the reasoned speculation of profound thinkers. Such speculation is revealed in monologue or dialogue in **Ecclesiastes**, many of the **Psalms** and **Job.**

The writer of **Psalm** 8 acknowledges that God is not the tribal or national God, so much as the creator of the sky, moon and stars, creation culminating in humanity itself.

"When I consider your heavens, the work of your fingers, the moon and the stars, which you have set in place – what is man that you are mindful of him…?" (NIV).

Similar declarations of God's glory in all creation commence the 19th **Psalm**: "The heavens declare the glory of God." (KJV)

Heman the Ezrahite writes a complete cry for help in **Psalm** 88. He prays day and night because "my soul is full of troubles and my life draws near the grave." (NIV).

Poor Heman is abandoned in the pit of despair, both by his friends and by God, and he is quickly going blind. The psalmist is forlorn, with no hope of relief. Here at last, my mind snapped into focus! In a flash I recognized the first psalmist who told life as it truly is – apparently hopeless, gloomy and meaningless. Yet he was a sufferer who still prayed in the hope that God might do something.

Here was a psalmist who voiced my own prayer and asked my own questions. Why doesn't God do something? Can't He, or won't He?

The pop-song recorded by Bony-M, "**By the Rivers of Babylon**" was a favourite of mine in the late 1970s. It was based on the lament of Hebrew prisoners in Babylon – slaves – who remembered their city "Zion" (another name for Jerusalem).

The lyrics come straight from **Psalm** 137, telling of the Hebrews plight as they weep, and feel unable to sing their songs. The bitterness of feeling comes at the end as the poet hopes Babylon will be destroyed: "happy is he who repays you for what you have done to us—he who seizes your infants and dashes them against the rocks." (NIV).

Once more, I detected in the cry of the psalmist, unrequited suffering - the agony, the pain, the bitterness, the anger and the hatred. At least two of the psalmists were seeing life as it really is, in all its stark reality.

Some years ago, I watched a cassette filmstrip, produced by Scripture Union, concerning the worthlessness of human endeavour. The soundtrack used Simon and Garfunkel's song, "**The Sound of Silence**", to portray the meaninglessness of **The Words of the Preacher – Ecclesiastes**.

Interspersed with photographs of affluence and dire poverty, childbirth, adolescent romance, marriage and divorce, came the music of **"The Sound of Silence"**, together with readings from **Ecclesiastes**.

In his monologue, the preacher attempts to confront difficult philosophical and religious questions such as the problem of evil and the prosperity of the wicked.

Unfortunately, he fails to understand evil. He views life as a paradox, seeing man as the greatest enigma, limited by his finite knowledge while pursing hopes and expectations that have no meaning or purpose.

"'Meaningless! Meaningless!' says the Teacher. "Utterly meaningless! Everything is meaningless!" His theme is the meaninglessness of man's efforts apart from God.

Even wisdom has no meaning: "I applied myself to the understanding of wisdom, and also of madness and folly, but I learned that this too is a chasing after the wind. "For with much wisdom comes much sorrow; the more knowledge the more grief" (1:17-18 NIV).

To the preacher, there is nothing new under the sun. Pleasure has no purpose; hard work has no meaning, and neither does wealth.

He sees the tears of the oppressed and observes no comforter, and suggests that the dead are happier than the living (4:1-2). In the first chapter, the preacher discusses the vanity of everything, including wisdom itself. He then asserts the meaningless nature of pleasure, wisdom and folly and work or labour in the second chapter. There is a time for everything:

"a time to be born and a time to die

a time to kill and a time to heal...

a time to weep and a time to laugh...

a time to mourn and a time to dance...

a time to love and a time to hate...

a time for war and a time for peace..." (3:2-8 NIV)

Furthermore, he sees the oppression, toil and friendlessness of all people under the sun: "I saw the tears of the oppressed – and they have no comforter; power was on the side of their oppressors – and they have no comforter. And I declared that the dead, who had already died, are happier than the living who are still alive." (4:1-3 NIV).

Promotion and advancement, together with wealth, are all condemned as vanity

The preacher is an old, disillusioned sage, who urges young men to seek God in their youth. He realizes that without God, life will never have any meaning. The Preacher almost understood the vacuous nature of existence. His book is a melancholy poem of anguish and despair. Yet even he states that everything will turn out all right in the end if only young men will trust in God. It seems to me, however, that the writer merely adds this adjunct almost as an after-thought.

Thus, it seems that the sages of Hebrew culture almost all accept that the righteous or good will eventually prosper while the wicked will suffer loss, pain and heartache.

The message of "the wise" seems to be pragmatic, often religiously neutral, encompassing a common sense approach to life – a sort of universal wisdom. Trust in God and all will be well.

This is quite different from the two Psalmists, who believed otherwise.

One thing became clear to me – **Old Testament** wisdom is *human wisdom*, not God's. It was the best attempt of human thought, ingenuity and reasoning to understand God's world and their place in it.

Nothing bad was to be said of good people, and nothing good was to be said of the foolish and wicked.

It was a kind of "religious fence-sitting" still in vogue among many Christians who feel unsure whether they ought to question why the good suffer.

"All things work together for good to those that love God" (Romans 8:28 KJV). "Trust in the Lord and all will be well," they say.

In my own church, people never speak about church--members dying or having a funeral service. Christians have "gone to be with the Lord," or received a "home-call", and a "special remembrance service" will be held to "thank God for their lives."

A book by Revd. Dr. Geoff Walters, **Why Do Christians Find it Hard to Grieve?** (Paternoster Press), explains some of the reasons why Christians are afraid to grieve over the loss of loved-ones. They see grief as a denial of faith, and often feel guilt at feeling angry with God for daring to ask, "Why?" So many Christians believe that death is not real – only the body has died, but the real soul lives on.

This is not, according to Dr. Walters, true Biblical teaching. Only God has immortality, not mortal human beings. Christian belief is in something quite different. It is faith in the resurrection from death, through the sacrifice and resurrection of Jesus Christ.

I remember being with a family on the death of their father. The family talked of Dad being still with them. His wife felt that he might be an angel in the skies. Dad had not gone. They wished me to conduct the funeral, at the local crematorium.

In my address, I started by telling the assembled congregation: "We are here to say "goodbye" to Charles. He has died and gone from us. And we are all sorry and grieving at such a loss."

Only when people face the truth can they deal with its realities. And facing the truth was precisely what most Wisdom writers failed to do. Clearly the good do suffer and prayer is often not answered. The wisdom of the wise men today is no more reliable than that of the past.

As I read the Wisdom literature, I could not help noticing how frequently the writers make statements like, "As I have observed" (**Job** 4:8 NIV); "Go to the ant" (**Proverbs** 6:6 NIV); "I devoted myself to study" (**Ecclesiastes** 1:13 NIV), "I was young and now I am old, yet I have never seen the righteous forsaken or their children begging bread." (**Psalm** 37:25 NIV).

Unlike the ancient prophets, the "wise" do not appeal to God, or to God's law, or to revelation. Their observations are their own. And they are very different observations from mine!

Chapter 9

The Cosmic Drama of Job (Part 1)

*W*hen comes the shock! One wise man rises above the accumulated knowledge of his day to dare to challenge God. He has been described as "The Greatest Poet of all."

In **"The Poetry of the Old Testament"** (SPCK Commentary), Professor T.H. Robinson describes **The Book of Job** as the "supreme literary masterpiece of human genius."

The **Book of Job** is different from all other wisdom literature.

It is a long, carefully sustained discourse, written in the tradition of a dialogue. Job and his friends make long speeches to each other, each speaker apparently discoursing three separate times.

The author and date of writing are unknown. Scholars generally agree that the prologue and epilogue were part of a folk tale or legend, which had an oral history before being committed to writing.

A story of some kind was known to Ezekiel who mentions Job twice (**Ezekiel** 14:4 and 20).

Some see the words of Jeremiah, "Cursed be the day I was born" (**Jeremiah** 20:14 NIV) as indicating that Jeremiah knew of Job's cursing his own birth.

There is no mention of the Law of Moses, and even more surprising is that all the characters appear to be non-Jewish. Job lived "in the land of Uz" (1:1), which is usually identified with Edom, or possibly located south of Damascus.

Eliphaz is a Temanite, also identified with Edom.

Bildad the Shuhite is believed to come from Arabia, east of Southern Lebanon, as does Elihu the Buzite who appears towards the end of the discourse.

God is called "Yahweh", the national God of the Hebrews, only once in the dialogue of Job.

Over thirty-one times He is **"El Shadai"**, God Almighty. I could not help noting the artificial construction of the **Book of Job** - the sacred numbers three and seven occur so frequently. Job has seven thousand sheep, seven sons, and three daughters all killed in the prologue.

Then God restores to him a further fourteen thousand sheep, six thousand camels, and gives him another seven sons and three daughters in the epilogue.

His three friends sit on a dung heap in complete silence for seven days and seven nights before speaking.

There are three speeches given by each friend, and at the end of the story, the friends are ordered to sacrifice seven bulls and seven rams so that Job might pray for them.

Job speaks nine times in answer to each of his friend's speeches, and Elihu speaks in three forms – his own prologue, his poem and his epilogue. (Most scholars believe that Elihu's speech was added later).

Without it, there are twenty-one sections to the book (Prologue, eighteen human speeches, the dialogue of the Almighty, and the Epilogue), or twenty-four if Elihu's speech is included.

There may even be a hidden meaning in Job's name. In their **Critical and Explanatory Commentary**, Jamieson, Fausset and Brown (Marshall, Morgan and Scott) suggest that the word, "Job," may come from Arabic, meaning "to return (to God)" or "Repent".

Job may be an ancient Semitic character. If so, he seems to have belonged to a time before the wisdom literature. His wealth in camels, sheep, donkeys and cattle seem to be more reminiscent of Abraham's day.

Job served as priest (1:5) by purifying his sons and offering burnt offerings to God in case any of his children sinned. Such patriarchal sacrifices belong to the literature of Abraham's time, before the Levitical Priesthood developed under Moses.

Furthermore, his wealth was taken by Sabean and Chaldean raiders (1:15 and 17), which better fits the patriarchal period, before Moses.

The mention of the "kesitah" as a unit of money (42:11 KJV note) also suggests the second millennium BC, as later Hebrew coinage was based on the "shekel".

Yet the views of the poet and his style of writing are far more modern. The dialogues in their didactic form are similar to Greek discourse like Plato's dialogues between Socrates and his disciples.

The poet has a wide-ranging knowledge of geographic features. He discusses various types of storms, wildlife ranging from the crocodile and hippopotamus to the ostrich; he includes detailed descriptions of deserts, snow, mountains and deep mineshafts, but he never mentions any historical data.

In the prologue and epilogue, but only once in the poetic section, he uses the Hebrew name, Yahweh, for God. Throughout the remainder of the drama (from chapters 3-41) he shows an amazing comprehension of the universal God, whom he refers to as "The *El Shadai*", translated literally as "God the Almighty".

Perhaps the **Book of Job** was written very much later, when Hebrew life seemed hopeless - when Jeremiah cried to God over the horrific exile of his fellow Jews to Babylon? No one knows, but date and authorship are unimportant.

The argument is as relevant in the twenty- first century as it was whenever Job lived, or whenever the book was written.

Wherever the ancient sages expressed their views, they taught that the righteous prosper and the evil perish. Job curses his birth and cries out that God is cruel and unjust. To the writer, everyone is on trial – including the Almighty, Himself!

In her book, **The Cruel God** (Beacon Press, Boston), Margaret B Crook interprets **The Book of Job** in a stunning and original way.

She reveals the poet-author as an innovative "university professor" of the fifth century BC, dealing with questions raised by his post-graduate students, suffering in Babylon and rebelling against the traditional contemporary thinking of Hebrew wisdom.

She sees these post-graduates arguing with their teacher, the author-poet, and transforming "patient Job" into the impatient spokesman for the problems of their day. Job's three friends represent the conservative schools of Ancient Israel whose opinions the poet and his students must examine and reject.

According to Margaret Crook, this new academic centre for higher learning employs new techniques of free questioning, original thought and creative dialogue to attempt to understand the realities of the Almighty God, and human destiny.

Using the basic story of a good man who suffers for his piety as the result of a wager between God and the Accuser, she suggests that the author-poet uses arguments raised by past students to produce a textbook for future discussions.

Perhaps the arguments of Job were the work of students or of the poet- teacher himself. Certainly, she sees the final intervention of *El Shadai*, God Almighty, as the supreme insight of the teacher into the power and majesty of God as he inserts his most daring and innovative finale.

Job is an exceptionally prosperous farmer, known and honoured as a godly sage. People respect his piety, seek his help and acknowledge his justice and wisdom.

In heaven, Yahweh points to Job as a model of holiness, but the "Accuser", the "Satan", claims that Job's piety stems only from his wealth. The Hebrew word "Satan" originally meant an Adversary in the Court of justice. "Accuser" and "Adversary" are variant translations of "Satan".

God gives permission for the Adversary to strip Job of his assets and within twenty- four hours, Job loses his oxen, asses and sheep, while his ten children and servants are slaughtered.

After worshipping God, Job utters the words, "Naked I came from my mother's womb, and naked I shall depart. The Lord gave, and the Lord has taken away; may the name of the Lord be praised." (1:20-21NIV).

The accuser then asks permission to test Job's faith by "striking his flesh and bones."

Job is afflicted with painful sores from head to toe, sits among ashes and scrapes his body with broken pottery.

Even his wife regales him to "Curse God and die!" (2:9). She is suffering also - her children have died; her security has gone and her husband is a sick man.

He tells her not to be a foolish woman but to accept trouble as well as goodness from God. In addition to his wife's reproach and condemnation, his own friends turn against him. He suffers nightmares (7:14), seems to choke with neck swellings (7:15 and 19), his skin becomes loathsome and foul with broken sores, parasites and worms (7:5) and he becomes aware of imminent death (16:22NIV)).

Job's three friends go to sympathise with and to comfort their friend, but when they meet, he is hardly recognizable, so they just sit in silence for seven days and nights.

It is at this point that the various debates or dialogues begin. Each speech is given in the form of poetry. Perhaps the teacher takes the part of Job, or one or more students play his role.

Job curses the day of his birth (3:1) and wishes he had been stillborn. He wonders why light is "given to those in misery, and life to the bitter of soul, to those who long for death that does not come" (3:20 NIV). It is clear that everyone is on trial – even God.

Eliphaz begins his first challenge. God is holy and just, he insists. Job has instructed many people in trouble and now he is overcome. Eliphaz is appalled at Job's audacity in charging God with cruelty.

He has observed "those who sow trouble reap it". Troubled dreams make his "hair stand up", for he knows that "those who live in houses of clay, whose foundations are in the dust, who are crushed more readily than a moth…die without wisdom" (4:19-20 NIV).

Clearly God must be the author of Job's misfortunes; He destroys the wicked and their families. If only Job would seek God and commit to Him, then he would live a prosperous life. "Blessed is the man whom God corrects; so do not despise the discipline of the Almighty" (5:17).

Eliphaz expounds the teaching of the Wise men at its best. The world is superbly ordered, God is in His heaven providing the fruit of the earth in its season and punishing the evildoer. "We have examined this, and it is true. So hear it and apply it to yourself." (5:27 NIV)

Job counters by protesting his innocence. He wants his deeds weighed on the scales of justice, and cannot understand why God's poisoned arrows pierce his body (6:4). He would hope for death, so he can die without denying his God (6:10), but he feels that God is abandoning him, as are the friends he so desperately clings to (6:14).

Job also accuses his friends of seeing the awesome possibility that his fate might befall them – "You see my fate and draw back in fear", he declares. Then he challenges them to tell him his faults and to stop being unjust (6:21-29 NIV).

He talks about the scabs and worms in his body, and the end of his life coming shortly, the nightmares and visions that terrify him and make life meaningless. Then he quotes from **Psalm** 8:3 "What is man that you make so much of him, that you give him so much attention, that you examine him every morning and test him every moment?"

Job declares his innocence, asks why his offences are not forgiven (7:17-21), and calls on God to hear his case before it is too late.

It is now Bildad's turn. Job is a windbag. How dare he claim that God perverts' justice? God is perfect and never rejects a blameless man. If Job returns to God then God will "fill your mouth with laughter and your lips with shouts of joy" (8:21 NIV).

Job agrees that he cannot as "a mortal be righteous before God", but he wants to meet God to argue the case for his innocence. Realizing the power of the Almighty, Job describes God's creation of the stars and concludes that God would not deign to give him a hearing, "Even if I summoned Him" (9:16 NIV).

Further, Job discards the current ideas of reward and punishment, for he realizes that God destroys both the pure and evil (9:22). God "mocks the despair of the innocent", and "blindfolds the judges". If Job were to "wash with soap and his hands with washing soda," God would drop him into a slime-pit (9:30-31 NIV). He challenges God to tell him the charges and asks if God "smiles at the schemes of the wicked" (10:3 NIV).

Job expects to die and end up in "the land of gloom and deep shadow, to the land of deepest night…where even the light is like darkness" (10:22 NIV).

Zophar calls Job a liar for challenging God (chapter 11), and insists uncompromisingly on Job's sin and his need for repentance. He is much harsher and dogmatic than his companions and suggests that Job deserves far more punishment. How dare a deceitful and witless man like Job challenge God.

Poor Job rejects his friends as comforters and tells them that wisdom will die with them (chapter 12-14). He has become a laughing stock, though he is righteous. In fact, he states, "I have a mind as well as you. I am not inferior to you. Who does not know all these things?" (12:3 NIV).

Job points out that the tents of marauders are undisturbed and those who provoke God are secure (12:6). Even animals, birds and fish know God's protection, but wisdom is found among the aged. Job knows that "to God belong wisdom and power; counsel and understanding are His" (12:13 NIV).

Even though "He slay me" Job will still trust God and plead his innocence. Job wants only two things from God – a removal of the terrors that frighten him, and a summons to speak before God in order to justify himself.

Most of chapter 14 seems to hint that Job may believe in the possibility of resurrection. Perhaps God will hide him in a grave (*Sheol*, the place of the dead) and conceal him until His anger is passed. "If a man dies, will he live again?" asks Job (verse 14 NIV).

From chapter 15 to 31 Job's three friends have nothing new to add to the debate. They continue to challenge Job concerning his sin, insulting and abusing him. Eliphaz explains that Job's wickedness is evident by what he says: "Your sin prompts your mouth: you adopt the tongue of the crafty." (15:5).

Job knows nothing that his colleagues don't, for they learnt all their wisdom from elderly men who were even older than Job's father (15:9-10).

They each speak twice more, and Job increasingly appeals to God to help and hear him. Job cries to God to protest His innocence. "I've been wronged! I get no response;

though I call for help, there is no justice. He (God) has blocked my way so that I cannot pass; He has shrouded my path in darkness" (19:7-8 NIV).

When it seems that Job's life cannot become any worse, it does! Job's brothers and family forsake him, his servants refuse his requests, his wife cannot stand his smell, and local children laugh in derision (19:13-20 NIV). Job is at his lowest.

Then with a leap of faith Job suddenly realizes that God is on his side. He knows that his "Redeemer lives and that in the end He will stand upon the earth, and after my skin has been destroyed, yet in my flesh I will see God" (19:26-27 NIV).

He knows there is someone who will come at last to his defence. Job knows nothing of redemption in the Christian sense, nor does he know anything about resurrection. His "redeemer" is the God who will come to listen to his charges and explain himself to Job.

Zophar is upset by Job's insulting about the Almighty and reaffirms that God will destroy all wicked men (chapter 20).

Job pleads with his friends to listen and give him a chance to explain. He tells them all that has happened to him and asks, "Why does God let evil men live, let them grow old and prosper? They have children and grandchildren, and live to watch them all grow up…their cattle breed…and they die quietly without suffering" (21:7 – 13 NIV).

Job can only wonder that the wicked do so well while the righteous perish. He is completely reversing all the known wisdom of his age. His own summary of the situation is that

"Some men stay healthy till the day they die; they die happy and at ease, their bodies well nourished. Others have no happiness at all; they live and die with bitter hearts. But all alike die and are buried; they are all covered with worms" (21:23-26 NIV).

Job continues to complain about God. He wishes to know where to find the Almighty in order to state his case. Job has searched high and low, but in his heart, he knows that a just and righteous God must answer his queries and explain why he is suffering so much, even if his friends do not.

"God knows every step I take; if He tests me, he will find me pure. I follow faithfully the road He chooses, and never wander to either side. I always do what the Almighty commands; I follow His will, not my own desires" (23:10-12 NIV).

In chapter 24, Job lists the evils of wicked men: moving boundary stones to get more land, stealing sheep, forcing widows and orphans into debt, enslaving poor impoverished children, committing murder, adultery and theft.

In addition, the poor starve, freeze, huddle beside rocks for shelter without the basic necessities of life, while "In the cities the wounded and dying cry out, but God ignores their prayers" (24:12 NIV).

Zophar and Bildad continue their theme, merely reiterating old ideas, while Job swears that, whatever may be his lot, he will refuse to say evil, lie or agree that his companions are right. He will insist on his innocence. He declares the greatness of God's power, which his friends have seen for themselves (Chapter 27).

It almost seems that Job has condemned both wisdom and the Almighty. Job has shown that the wisdom of the ancients is worthless, for he sees it contradicted all round him, and he has also claimed that the Almighty is hidden and fails to answer the prayers of the righteous.

Both charges need to be dealt with.

Surprisingly, chapter 28 deals with the first by asking where wisdom can be found.

Many scholars believe the entire chapter to be irrelevant to the dialogue. It has been suggested that the words are Zophar's and that he has nothing new to say.

The chapter does not say who the speaker is, and the poetry is written in a totally different style from the rest of the book.

Perhaps a new student wished to add his view to the discourse.

Or the teacher-poet, himself, felt it essential to answer the charges made by Job.

If Job had challenged God and Wisdom, then, as the poet knew God was to defend Himself, the poet may have felt it necessary to deal with Wisdom first.

It seems logical, then, to suggest that the teacher of the group puts in the poem in praise of Wisdom. He shows how mining is like digging for Wisdom.

Silver and gold may be mined, but the precious metal itself needs refining. Men may work alone, hanging on ropes in the darkness, to dig for stones and dust. Only later, may they discover the gold or sapphires and other precious stones.

Birds and fierce animals may survive above ground, but precious metals and gems evade them. Only men know of their existence. But even so, jewels are found only in the process of refining.

Where may Wisdom be found? Does that need to be refined also? Or is it forever beyond human grasp?

Interestingly, this poem is divided into three sections. The first part deals with mining and its relation to Wisdom, and is a most extraordinary picture of humanity searching for an elusive truth.

It is almost as though the breaking and smashing of rocks and earth bring new insights into the treasures that lie hidden. In the same way, the poet is suggesting that blowing away tradition brings new insights into Wisdom's treasures.

The second section (verses 13-22) then reveals that men can never find Wisdom. It is not in the mines, nor in the depths of the ocean.

Silver, gold and precious stones cannot buy it. Its value is above coral, crystal or rubies, and finest topaz. Even in death, Wisdom is only a rumour.

Section three (verses 23-28) forms the finale of the poem. Only God knows the way. He sees to the ends of the Universe. He has given everything its power – the wind, the rain, and the thunderclouds.

Only the Almighty has Wisdom. That is why the poem ends, "the fear of the Lord, that is wisdom; and to shun evil is understanding."

(The word, Lord **Adonai**, is the only time another word for "God" is used in the dialogue).

Finally, Job comes back to summarise his case. In chapter 29, he gives a long personal testimony, the first picture of his life since the prologue.

There is no other man depicted in the **Old Testament** like Job. He walked before Almighty God, people respected him, the leaders of the clans became quiet in his presence, and people watched what they said.

He helped the poor and orphans. Widows and men wounded with misery sought his aid, which was freely given. He always acted justly and fairly, led the blind, walked for the lame, became a father to the poor, helped strangers in trouble, destroyed the power of cruel men and rescued their victims.

Job expected to live a long life and die in the comfort of his own home. He made decisions, encouraged the downcast, led them as a king leads his troops and seemed to be the epitome of perfection.

Now, however, these very people whom Job helped have turned on him, children and youths make fun of him, and he is despised, even by tramps and vagabonds. He is even attacked by a violent mob.

Again, he calls to God but receives no answer and states, "I know you will bring me down to death...Surely no-one lays a hand on a broken man when he cries for help in his distress." (30:23-24 NIV).

Job swears that he will not sin, and calls on God in order to recite his goodness before the Almighty. He tells God that he has never trusted in wealth, worshipped the sun or moon, or led others astray. He has never even been pleased to see his enemies suffer and has not even prayed for their disaster. In desperation he calls out: "Oh that I had someone to hear me! I sign my own defence—let the Almighty answer me; let my accuser put his indictment in writing." (30:35 NIV). With one final challenge to God, "The words of Job are ended."

* * * * *

At this point in the dialogue a strange intrusion takes place.

A new speaker enters the arena. "But Elihu son of Barakel the Buzite, of the family of Ram, became very angry with Job for justifying himself rather than God." (32:2 NIV).

In fact, he is also very angry with the three companions of Job because they were unable to properly refute him.

It is most puzzling that Elihu has not been mentioned previously, neither in the prologue nor in the dialogue.

The Almighty God refers to Jobs three friends in the epilogue, but not to Elihu. His interference with its three-fold pattern seems out of place.

Now is the time for the Almighty God to appear in order to justify His ways with men.

Perhaps this special poem of Elihu was added later and inserted between the ending of Job's cry to the Almighty and the appearance of the Almighty to meet Job's need.

However, Elihu is not one of the elderly wise; he is a young student who appears to have waited patiently for seven days, and eighteen speeches before adding his own small contribution to wisdom.

Elihu is of the opinion that Job's suffering is remedial and disciplinary. He believes himself to have the most important contribution to the discussion and even claims to be speaking under divine constraint (32:8 and 36:1).

So sure, is he of his message he wastes a great deal of time in telling the friends and Job to take heed to the wonderful words he is going to proclaim.

Almighty God has a purpose in allowing Job's suffering. It is to "listen to his warning to turn away from evil," (Job 36:10 GNB) that Job may learn to obey and serve God. If he fails, then he will be utterly destroyed, but if he learns to do so then honour and prosperity will come his way.

He speaks of God's majestic glory in the storm that God has caused "for punishment …or mercy". He looks at the sky and indicates that the dazzling light is the glory of God, which fills men with awe. God's power is so great that none can come near him.

There is nothing new in Elihu's discourse. It is the impassioned shouting of a pupil who is angry at the questioning and challenging of perceived wisdom.

Then something quite dramatic happens. For the first time, an answer to the problem of suffering and pain peeps over the parapet of comprehension.

Chapter 10

The Daring Insight into Human Suffering (Part 2)

"WHEN THE LORD ANSWERED JOB OUT OF THE STORM" (38:1 NIV).

The very thing Elihu claims cannot happen does. The Almighty is ready to state His case. As the top academic minds of the postgraduate school in Babylon are debating their cases, the teacher takes the place of *El Shadai*, himself.

This is a daring and innovative move in which the teacher attempts to explain the ways of the Almighty to his questioning class.

The insights he brings are new and challenging; and the beautiful poetic style, vocabulary and imagery are among the best in ancient literature.

The voice of Almighty God comes from the whirlwind, "Brace yourself like a man; I will question you, and you shall answer me" (38:3 NIV).

Job has repeatedly pleaded to meet the Almighty to plead his case, but instead of doing so, Job is speechless. He listens to an amazing account of creation and the wonders of the world of nature.

The inspired teacher, arguing from the viewpoint of the Almighty, offers no solution to the problem of Job's suffering. He does not tell Job of the work of the Accuser in the prologue.

Instead, he shows that mortal man can never understand the mind of God, for He is the only Wisdom. God is unsearchable – His wisdom is beyond human logic.

Job is called to exercise faith in the wisdom, strength and power of the Almighty who reveals Himself to his human interrogator as the Divine Interrogator who is true Wisdom and Power.

"Where were you when I laid the earth's foundations? Tell me, if you understand," thunders the voice from the storm.

Then, with a barrage of sarcasm, the Almighty *El Shadai* asks Job a series of questions about the time, seasons, seas, light, and death.

He reminds Job that only God has power to produce snow and frost. Can Job know the secrets of the wild goats, hinds, asses, unicorns, peacocks, and many other creatures that God cares for daily?

A further graphic description of stars, clouds and animals follows, so that Job is completely overwhelmed.

The whole dialogue is among the most vivid and descriptive of all ancient writing, as God seeks an answer from His servant Job.

Do you know when the mountain goats give birth? Do you give the horse his strength? Does the hawk take flight by your wisdom? Does the Eagle soar at your command? These are some of the questions asked by the Almighty. (Chapter 39)

Then God challenges Job, "Will the one who contends with the Almighty correct him? Let him who accuses God answer him!"(40:1-2 NIV).

Job is speechless. He can only blurt out, "I am unworthy-how can I reply to you? I put my hand over my mouth." Full of shame and remorse for daring to doubt God's goodness, Job remains quiet.

But the Almighty *El Shadai* has not finished. Again, he orders Job to brace himself, while God further questions him.

"Would you discredit my justice, would you condemn me to justify yourself?" (40:8 NIV).

Once more the Almighty bombards Job with unanswerable questions concerning "behemoth" (a large animal, possibly a hippopotamus or elephant) and "leviathan" (a seven-headed monster in Canaanite mythology, although some scholars believe it may refer to a crocodile in this passage). Can Job tame such beasts, keep them as pets, or kill them with the sword?

If not, does he claim to be able to constrain the Almighty, the creator of all living creatures? How can a man stand up against God when he is afraid of a simple crocodile or against one of God's lesser creations?

At this point, Job is overwhelmed and asks for forgiveness. Ironically, Job's friends insist that he repents for secret sin for which he is being punished.

Job does not do that; instead, he repents for having questioned God's sovereign power and perfect justice in the first place.

Job acknowledges the omnipotence of the Almighty:

> "I know that you can do all things;
> no plan of yours can be thwarted.
> You asked, "Who is this that obscures
> my counsel without knowledge?"
> Surely, I spoke of things I did not understand,
> Things too wonderful for me to know…
> My ears had heard of you
> But now my eyes have seen you.
> Therefore, I despise myself and repent
> in dust and ashes." (42:1-6 NIV)

* * * * *

Here the dialogue ends. The reader knows what Job never discovers – that his suffering is only because he is good and morally upright. The prologue has informed the reader of that. Such revolutionary thought was far in advance of the Hebrew wisdom of the author's day. God had revealed to him an inspired, new, vital and stimulating truth.

The Accuser is proved wrong. Human beings can love and serve God, despite the suffering that almost destroys them. Job goes further in the epilogue by sacrificing for and praying for his friends.

Once again, Job prospers so that all his previous wealth is returned with two hundred percent interest.

His terrible disease is cured. His family holds a feast in Job's house, they comfort and console him, and then each give him a gold ring and a Kesitah (a silver coin) to restore his lost wealth.

A further seven sons and three daughters were borne by Job's wife; and Job included his daughters in his inheritance as well as his sons.

The Drama of **The Book of Job** reveals an omnipotent God who has created mankind and provided him with the whole of the earth.

Even more so, that God is shown as willing to communicate with human beings as one wise being with another.

Job learns that the universe is not run according to human conduct, but it is God, the Almighty, who controls everything.

There is no room for evil powers. The Accuser needs permission before he can operate.

The Book of Job is not about a contest between God and Satan; it is about a battle of faith in which Job is the champion, acting on behalf of God.

Suffering is something over which human beings can rise victorious. The attitude of Job when he meets the Almighty One reveals a sense of awe and wonder. Job learns to subordinate his suffering to the privilege of living in the Universe itself.

There is no doubt that the poet-teacher understands the creative acts of the Almighty in ordering the heavens and establishing life on earth as positive and desirable, and contributing to human well-being.

God is far greater than the sages of Israel give Him credit. The Hebrew God, *Yahweh*, is just too small. He is not the resident policeman and judge of all. He is much more – He is Wisdom itself.

Job also realizes that his own tragedy is relatively minor as he contemplates the greatness of his creator. Suffering and evil are not the supreme problems in God's universe.

As Job examines himself before the Almighty, he realizes the relationship he has with God. It is not only spiritual and moral, but also physical.

When Job meets the Almighty his arguments and questions give way to humility and wonder. Job understands that God acts as a free agent, but also gives responsibility to humankind.

Margaret Crook suggests that the ultimate cruelty in Job is the stripping of all human relationships.

Job loses his children, his wife, his brothers and sisters, his friends, his colleagues and his hired hands. In the midst of suffering, we each need the sympathy and understanding of our friends and associates.

In addition, the epilogue shows true kindness.

Job prays for his friends to be delivered from the anger of the Almighty. The remainder of the epilogue is full of kindness, friendliness, and rejoicing over Job's recovery.

Not only does Job provide for his sons, but unusual for the ancient world, he provides also for his daughters.

The story has brought about the wonder of relationships, forgiveness, prayer, love for others, and care for lesser individuals, and above all – the possibility of a relationship with God.

Although the book is ultimately about faith, and of Job's reaction to his trial of faith, there is much to learn about the meaning of suffering.

For the first time I began to see some meaning, and the beginning of the answers to my questions. The answers were still unclear, and imprecise, but they provided the embryo for the future insights I was to gain in my quest for answers.

From my study of **The Book of Job**, I began to change my mind. The ancient patriarchal story was not to be taken literally. The universe does not run on Cosmic Wagers. There is no literal "betting", "throwing the dice" or "playing games" – those are the concepts of myth and legend.

The poet-teacher has been inspired to take an existing ancient story and break it asunder. The early story is the subject only of the prologue and the epilogue – the real argument, the inspiration and the insights come between.

Yet there is a sense in which the prologue is important. It shows that human beings are free individuals who are not conditioned to trust God and be religious just because of their wealth and health.

Job's trials show that faith and trust in God are independent of circumstances. Human beings are not robotic, but creatures of true freedom.

Although my understanding of the problems posed was only beginning to surface, it might be useful at this point to summarize some of the germinating thoughts as I completed my study of Job's story.

It seems that suffering and pain may have logical reasons for their existence. The story of Job suggests these ideas about suffering:

1. It may sometimes be a test of one's piety and goodness (Prologue).
2. It may come as punishment for wrongdoing (Job's three companions).
3. It may be necessary to discipline or correct (Elihu).
4. It is certainly not so great a problem as God's apparent unconcern.
5. It may sometimes be God's way of moulding the spiritual and moral personalities and saintly characters of His children.
6. We may be content to trust God without understanding our suffering.
7. Job's trial showed that forces outside themselves do not control human beings. Each person can make his or her own response to the setting in which we are placed.

8. Human beings are shown to be free and responsible for their own actions and attitudes. Job's triumph is a victory for all mankind.

9. There is no dualism in our universe. God is in control at all times. There is no spiritual schizophrenia between God and the Devil. Satan has no power to destroy God.

10. Faith in God is not dependent on happiness, wealth or other circumstances.

11. Job's original faith was based on hearsay – at last he met with his Creator.

12. Although God does not answer Job's questions, the Almighty does respond to Job's faith by showing His divine power and wisdom.

God's ways are above and beyond human reasoning. His will is freely transferred into action, although He doesn't always act in the way we expect. Job's suffering made no sense because wise people believed that good people would always be healthy and rich. In Job's meeting with the Almighty, God's omnipotence and wisdom were revealed in new and exciting ways.

At a time when little was known about life after death – no clear understanding of a resurrection was known to the Hebrews – it was inevitable that pious people believed that faith would be rewarded during this present lifetime. Concepts such as "Heaven" were to be developed later.

I now began to understand something of the value and purpose of suffering from my study of the Book of Job. It still did not answer the majority of my questions, but it was a start. There was to be much more for me to discover in my search for meaning in suffering and pain.

The insights or inspiration given to the poet-teacher who wrote the astoundingly dramatic poem that challenged the wisdom of his contemporaries, were as far as one could go with the information and observations at his disposal.

Future revelations of **New Testament** faith, and much later understanding of the categorizing of new observations which were to form much of modern science, bringing a new understanding of both the physical universe and the psychological world, were to change my views on the problem of suffering.

Chapter 11

Answers from the Prophets

Having looked at the Wisdom writers, I decided to examine those writers known as Prophets to see if they had any answers to the problem of pain and suffering.

While they had a great deal to say, I found their answers rather too similar to the Wise ones – they each stressed the judgement of Yahweh on wicked unjust nations, rather than on individuals and linked this suffering to a coming "Day of the Lord" that was to annihilate the evil world with only the righteous saved.

Perhaps this was because all the Hebrew prophets wrote during times of crisis and violent upheaval. I found it impossible to understand the predictions of the prophets, without an understanding of the history of the period during which the prophecies were written. Therefore, I had to delve into the history of the Hebrews before getting to grips with the prophetic messages.

During the kingship of Solomon, the son of King David, the twelve tribes of Israel prospered as the Kingdom of Israel. During a time of extended commerce and peace Israel extended her borders to the north and south. The Hebrews believed they would see "The Throne of David" last forever.

Following Solomon's death, the kingdom broke up. Judah remained loyal to the descendants of David and Solomon, together with the tribe of Benjamin. They were the two southernmost tribes whose capital city was Jerusalem, where Solomon's Temple was based.

The ten remaining tribes, named Israel, built a new temple near Samaria, which became their capital. Samaria was north of Jerusalem. Israel had its own kings who were quite separate from those of Judah.

Both countries continued to prosper, and their wealthy merchants, middle class farmers, professional people and leaders enjoyed lives of luxuriant opulence. They became idol worshippers, indulged in sexual prostitution and even murdered their own children to appease gods such as Molech, a local Canaanite deity.

Injustice, poverty, slavery and theft left the remaining inhabitants suffering at the hands of the rich.

Israel and Judah were sandwiched between two vast trading and warring nations whom they sought to appease. Egypt lay to the south, both alongside the Nile and throughout the Sinai Peninsula. To the North lay the vast Empire of Assyria, stretching from modern day Syria to much of Iraq. Its capital, Nineveh, was a huge fifteen-mile square city built on the banks of the Tigris River.

Assyria threatened the area for almost two hundred years, and a few prophets foretold coming invasions from Assyria and of its eventual defeat. Rising to power just after 900 BC, it flourished in war and constantly attacked and destroyed villages and townships in both Israel and Judah.

Eventually, Samaria was captured in 722 --721 BC and all its citizens transported to Assyria. Soldiers settling in the area married local women whose descendants were known as "Samaritans". They remained permanent enemies of Judah.

Judah was ravaged by the Assyrian troops, and often sought help from Egyptian allies. Jerusalem held out against its invaders for almost 140 years after the fall of Israel, until the Judeans believed they were unassailable as God's "chosen" people. Many prophets predicted the destruction of Jerusalem when the day of judgement, "The Day of the Lord", arrived.

The eventual collapse of Assyria came in the seventh century BC. Nineveh. The capital, was defeated in 612 BC, through the genius of Nebuchadrezzar II (sometimes known as Nebuchadnezzar).

Nebuchadrezzar commanded a superior army from Babylon, a huge fortified city noted for its hanging gardens. Situated on the Euphrates River, and surrounded by a moat, Babylon was considered impregnable. The Babylonian army attempted to capture Jerusalem. All Judah had fallen before the enemy onslaught, but Jerusalem held out for almost 30 more years

In 597 BC, King Jehoiachin surrendered Jerusalem to Nebuchadrezzar who removed all the temple treasure, took 10,000 prisoners (including the prophet, Ezekiel, together with all the skilled workmen and courtiers) back to Babylon and ordered Jerusalem to pay a city tax. The Babylonians left Zedekiah as the king of Jerusalem, but he rebelled and the Babylonian army besieged Jerusalem for over a year.

Eventually, Jerusalem was destroyed in 586 BC. Nebuchadrezzar's troops blinded the Judean King, razed the temple to the ground, set fire to the city and transported all males to Babylonia in chains.

Now began the second Exile. The Israelites had been exiled to Assyria and now Judeans to Babylon. No trace of the ten tribes of Israel has been found since their exile.

War with the great powers had occupied almost three hundred years of constant horror. The Assyrian armies were noted for their cruelty, enslavement and total ethnic cleansing. Conquered peoples starved to death or turned to cannibalism.

After fifty years in Babylonian Exile a new power under Cyrus, King of Media and Persia, captured Babylon in 539 BC, by damming the Euphrates and allowing soldiers to enter under the city via the water supply.

Cyrus ordered the release of prisoners, and an Edict allowed the Jews (as the Judeans were now called) to leave their Exile and rebuild Jerusalem and its temple some years later. The prophets constantly refer to one or other of these great powers in their predictions concerning the judgement of their God, Yahweh. Not only is judgement to come on God's own "wicked" people, but also on all the surrounding smaller tribes and countries such as Edom, Moab, Philistia, Syria and numerous others.

Chapter 12

The Answers of the Minor Prophets

*H*aving studied the background history, I now recommenced my study of suffering and pain in the writings of the Minor Prophets. The prophets generally predict coming destruction and judgement on various nations.

Two minor prophets, Jonah and Nahum, target their prophecies at Nineveh, the Assyrian capital.

JONAH

Jonah calls on Nineveh to repent of its evil deeds and turn to Yahweh, Israel's God. For a time, the Ninevites appear to accept Jonah's message, before destroying the whole of Israel and deporting the entire population.

The Book of Jonah differs considerably from other prophecies by being primarily a narrative account of a single prophetic mission. Some interpret it as a fictional short story (with Jonah being swallowed by a great fish), whilst others see it as a tract for the times, an allegory or parable of Yahweh's concern for all people.

NAHUM

Nahum predicts the fall of Nineveh. Assyria had already destroyed Samaria in 712 BC, taken all the inhabitants of Israel into slavery, and currently threatened Judah.

The brutality and ferocity of total ethnic cleansing, together with torture and mutilation of those captured, demands punishment. Nahum's vision is that God, who moves in the clouds, whirlwinds and storms, will destroy Nineveh.

He reveals *Yahweh's* indignation and fierce anger (1:6). God will tolerate no rivals for He is a "jealous and avenging God" (1:2 NIV). *Yahweh*, as the tribal God of the Hebrews will not allow rivalry or unfaithfulness.

He has a covenant relationship, which is like that of a marriage to Israel, so that God claims exclusive rights to possess Israel and own her love and allegiance.

ZEPHANIAH

Zephaniah, also writing at the height of Assyrian power, has a particularly gloomy message.

""I will sweep everything from the face of the earth," declares the Lord. "I will sweep away both men and animals.

I will sweep away the birds of the air and the fish in the sea. The wicked will have only heaps of rubble when I cut off man from the face of the earth," declares the Lord" (1:2-3 NIV). Zephaniah predicts the stark horror of the approaching "Day of the Lord". He refers to "that day" fourteen times and to "the Day of the Lord" a further five.

"Judgement and annihilation are to come, and no hope is given. The great day of the LORD is near – near and coming quickly. Listen! The cry on the day of the LORD will be bitter… That day will be a day of wrath, a day of distress and anguish, a day of trouble and ruin, a day of darkness and gloom…" (1:14-15 NIV).

This fate is to befall Assyria, Gaza and Jerusalem, and also many localized tribes such as Ammon and Moab. Even judgment on Sudan is predicted.

Yet, despite the horrors of the coming "Day", A minority will survive to repopulate a new and prosperous world with God's own presence, new life and love. The prophecy breaks into a song of joy as the scattered remnant returns home.

AMOS AND HOSEA

As the Assyrians begin to attack the Northern Kingdom of Israel, Hosea and Amos commence their prophecies. Both Israel and Judah were prosperous, overflowing with opulence, while injustice and moral corruption flourished. The poor were being cheated and exploited by rich landowners and merchants.

Amos, a stranger from Judah, vigorously condemns Israel's neighbours. He proclaims that "God roars from Mount Zion (Jerusalem)" to accuse Syria of cruelty, Gaza of enslavement, Tyre of broken treaties and the subjugation of whole nations, Edom of revenge and hatred, and Ammon of brutality.

Further, God reveals Moabite evil because of the desecration of the bones of dead kings, and Judah as godless.

Amos announces that God's judgment will fall especially upon Israel for its immorality, drunkenness, injustice, intimidation, slavery and idolatry.

In a series of visions Amos reveals the longsuffering of God. He sees a locust plague, a consuming fire, and a vision of a plumb line to measure the crookedness of the Israelites, and a basket of rotten fruit, each vision relating to Israel's relationship with Yahweh.

Amos is apparently the first prophet to use the phrase, "The Day of the Lord" in reference to the Day of *Yahweh's* judgment. He also anticipates the restoration of God's people, should any be left alive after that Day.

Amos's predictions were fulfilled. Of the five kings who took the throne during the next thirteen years, four were assassinated by their successors (Zechariah, Shallum, Pekakiah and Pekah) and one (Hoshea) was captured in battle. Assyria destroyed Israel's army, sacked its villages and totally destroyed Samaria in 722-21 BC, deporting the survivors to Assyria as slaves.

Hosea, contemporary with Amos, prophesied for almost forty years. His life seems to symbolize God's message.

Gomer, Hosea's wife, was a prostitute who left her husband with three children and was sold back to Hosea from the slave market. The message of Hosea is that Israel is "playing the whore" and is enslaved by idolatry and sin, when she is in reality married to Yahweh.

Unlike the other Minor Prophets, Hosea proclaims *Yahweh's* love for his people. In the early chapters "love" and "loved" are mentioned twelve times, and the keyword "return" sixteen times.

God calls on His estranged wife, Israel, to return and be restored, as God's own, just as Hosea restores his own wife to a new family relationship. The Israelites are to be called "My People" and "My loved one" (2:1 NIV), and Hosea is told to seek out his erring wife. "Love her as the Lord loves the Israelites, though they turn to other gods…" commands Yahweh (3:1).

But Israel does not return to Yahweh. The remainder of **Hosea** condemns Israel for its pagan worship. Sins such as sexual relationships between God's chosen people and temple prostitutes, lying, murder and theft lead to Yahweh's judgement.

Once more, the Day of the Lord will come. Israel and Judah will be at war, and Israel is seeking help first from Egypt and then from Assyria. Both Judah and Israel are doomed and will be totally destroyed.

Intermingled with coming catastrophe are poems of love. Chapter 11 recounts the loving mother, Yahweh, calling her son out of Egypt. The son has turned to Baal worship but the mother's love continues.

"It was I who taught Israel to walk, taking them by the arms," says the Lord. "I led them with cords of human kindness, with ties of love." (3 and 4 NIV)

Yet the Israelites have rejected their relationship with God, and will return to captivity in Assyria. "Plague, death and destruction will surely come" is the message that was fulfilled by 722BC, as Samaria fell and the Israelites entered their Exile.

HABAKKUK

With the complete annihilation of Israel, the prophets now vent their wrath on Judah in the South. Slowly the villages and towns are overrun, until only Jerusalem is left. Babylon will also take Judah into exile when the "Day of the Lord" comes.

The prophecy of **Habakkuk** is one of the most questioning of the Minor Prophets. Habakkuk cannot understand why God is silent while wicked nations succeed with their ethnic cleansing. Neither can he appreciate why God fails to answer his prayers.

He cries, "How long, O Lord, must I call for help, but you do not listen?" (1:2 NIV) In addition, he is horrified by the thought that God is using evil Babylon to punish Judah. The Babylonian army catches people with hooks, drags them away in nets and leaves no men alive, he says. Nowhere is the dilemma more clearly expressed than in Habakkuk's opening prayer:

> "O Lord, are you not from everlasting….? O LORD
> you have ordained them (the Babylonians) to punish"
> (1:12NIV).

He cannot understand why God can stand these treacherous evil men? His eyes are too pure to look at evil, and God cannot stand the sight of people doing wrong. So why is He silent while they destroy people who are more righteous than they are?

Yahweh does answer. He explains that evil people will be destroyed but that the righteous will live if they are faithful to God (2:4).

Most of the remainder of the book is a prophecy of doom, which God tells Habakkuk to write on clay tablets. However, Habakkuk concludes with a prayer.

The prophet is filled with awe and explains that *Yahweh* will come with lightning, send disease and command death to follow him. He also causes the earth to quake, mountains to shatter and rivers to flood. Trees are destroyed and fields produce no crops.

Yet "though the sheep all die and the cattle stalls are empty," Habakkuk says he "will rejoice in the LORD, I will be joyful in God my Saviour." (3:17-18 NIV) He gives no reason for his faith, but seems to cling to it in the same manner as Job.

MICAH

The prophecy of Micah predicts the fall of Samaria, alternating between doom and hope. Micah's theme is God's judgment and deliverance. The very sins of idolatry, child sacrifice and witchcraft for which Israel was punished are now entering Judah. Judah will sing a dirge of despair, "We are completely ruined!" (2:4 GNB). Yet Micah is clear about God's requirements - "to act justly, and to love mercy and to walk humbly with your God" (6:8 NIV)

OBADIAH

It is difficult to accurately date **Obadiah**, the shortest book in the Hebrew Scriptures. Obadiah proclaims Yahweh's vengeance on the Edomites who are hostile to Judah. They appear to gloat over the fall of Jerusalem and Judean misfortune. God will judge the nations, but Edom will "vanish away" as the people of Jacob (Judah) will possess the land that is theirs by right. (verse 17).

The great Babylonian Empire eventually became a threat to Assyria. When Assyria finally falls in 612 BC with the sacking of Nineveh, Assyria disappears and the ten tribes of northern Israel appear lost forever.

Within twenty-five years, Babylon is to totally destroy Jerusalem, the only Judean city remaining. Nebuchadrezzar II eventually sacks the city, destroys the temple, and transports the remaining population into exile in Babylon itself.

Ethnic cleansing is described in minute detail in the contemporary prophetic writings. Pogroms and mass murder are not the prerogative of the twentieth and twenty-first centuries. Ancient history is full of such horrors.

LAMENTATIONS

An unknown author in a state of dazed grief writes five dirges-funeral songs. In four acrostic poems, **Lamentations** reveals the full horror of the destruction of Jerusalem. Each verse begins with a new letter of the Hebrew alphabet.

Poems 1, 2 and 4 have twenty-two verses with three lines each; poem 3 has three verses to each letter, making sixty-six verses; whilst poem 5 has twenty-two non-acrostic verses. It is possibly that this highly structured system of writing enabled the writer to deal with horrifying topics without breaking down emotionally.

He states that his eyes are worn out with weeping; his soul is in anguish. He is exhausted with grief at the destruction of his people, while children and babies are fainting in the streets of the city (2:11).

Because Jeremiah is described as a "weeping prophet", tradition suggests that he may have been the author of **Lamentations**, but the style of writing is quite different from that of the prophet Jeremiah.

Today, the **Lamentations** are often read by Orthodox Jews at the Western Wall (also called the "Wailing Wall") in Jerusalem. Jews also read the five dirges during festivals to commemorate the fall of both Solomon's temple in 586 BC, and the fall of Herod's Temple in AD 70.

Furthermore, the **Lamentations** form part of the liturgy, read during the last three days of Holy Week by the Roman Catholic Church.

The key words in the dirges are "desolate", "desolation", "tears", "weep" and "weeps" - each word occurring seven times in the KJV.

The first dirge describes the emptiness of Jerusalem: helpless slaves forced away from home, children captured and taken. As the poet describes the lonely ruins, the plundered treasures and the starving masses, he cries out, "Is any suffering like my suffering?" (1:12 NIV).

There is no comfort in sorrow. Priests and leaders have died in the city streets looking for food; others have been murdered.

But the horror is that God, Himself, has brought the pain and destruction: "Is any suffering like my suffering that was inflicted on me, that the LORD brought on me in the day of his fierce anger" (1:12 NIV).

Finally, the poet calls to God, "May you bring the day you have announced so that (my enemies) may (suffer) like me" (21).

Worse is to come in the second lament. Every village in Judah has been destroyed, the city gates reduced to rubble, there are no prophets left to tell of God's will, and the temple is a dark ruin.

Children and babies are hungry and thirsty...cry to their mothers, they fall in the streets as though they were wounded, and "their lives ebb away in their mothers' arms" (2:12 NIV).

Even more horrifying is the question to God, "Whom have you ever treated like this? Should women eat their offspring, the children they have cared for?" (2:20), which is reiterated in the fourth poem where "compassionate women have cooked their own children, who became their food" (4:10 NIV).

Cannibalism is rife among the starving peoples. Even more horrifying acts of cannibalism and eating from the stomachs of the dead are recorded in the writings of Josephus.

The third poem is personal. The writer claims that God has driven him "deeper into darkness" (3:2 GNB) and beaten him "with merciless blows" (3:3 GNB). God "has left my flesh open and raw, and has broken my bones. He has shut me in a prison of misery and anguish...I cry aloud for help, but God refuses to listen." (3:4 GNB)

The imploring cry of the crushed individual expresses the agony of the whole Hebrew nation. God does not answer their prayers. He has completely deserted his people. The anguish and pain of all deserted people are echoed in the words of one man whose trust in God has gone: "My splendour is gone and all I had hoped from the LORD." (3:18 NIV).

Then a transformation takes place in his soul. At this point where faith is almost lost the poet produces a beautiful picture of assurance in Yahweh's final deliverance. "Because of the LORD's great love, we are not consumed, for his compassions never fail. They are new every morning: great is your faithfulness." (3:22-23 NIV).

When the writer is lost and at his lowest ebb, God is still there, ready to pick him up. A crescendo of praise takes over. "The Lord is good" (3:25 GNB), he is "merciful" (3:31 GNB), "he will show compassion, so great is his unfailing love" (3:32 NIV), and in the past "you took up my case: you redeemed my life." (3:58 NIV).

Meditating on his newfound assurance, the poet declares that "we must examine our ways", turn back to God, open our hearts to God "until the Lord looks down from heaven and sees us" (3:50 NIV).

His prayer continues as he pleads for God to destroy, curse and fill his enemies with despair. The last stanza calls on Yahweh to, "pursue them in anger and destroy them." He wants God to hunt them down and wipe them off the face of the earth!

There is to be no forgiveness of those who have brought total ruin to Israel and Judah.

The fourth dirge praises suckling wolves that care for their cubs. By contrast, Judean mothers allow their children to die of famine and thirst, and even boil them in the cooking pots to eat. Previously wealthy people "who once ate delicacies" are pawing through refuse for food. (4:5 NIV).

The author acknowledges that those who died in the war were better off than those who died later, who starved slowly to death, with no food to keep them alive." (9). The author describes black, wizened faces, dried skin shrivelled on the bone, and the wounded so bloodstained that others reject them.

The ultimate disgrace comes from the gloating Edomites and people from Uz (the land of Job), for whom the writer can only proclaim approaching disaster as God sends his own day of reckoning.

Finally comes the fifth poem. This is really a prayer culminating in the cry that God has "utterly rejected us; thou art very wroth against us" (5:22 AV).

(There is a similar, sombre ending also in **Isaiah** and **Malachi**).

In his prayer, the poet reminds God of defeat, loss of freedom, rape, murder, slavery, and of the excessive costs of food, firewood and even water. He pleads for restoration to God: "You, O LORD reign for ever: your throne endures from generation to generation."(5:19 NIV).

I found **Lamentations** quite different from the Minor Prophets, as it addresses itself exclusively to Yahweh. The poems are each separate prayers or elegies to God. There is no call for national repentance, no message of doom or hope to others.

Instead, it is an intensely personal series of structured prayers offered by the poet in his agony of mind and soul. No answers are given – only the numbing truth poured from experience of the horror and madness of war, ethnic cleansing and total destruction, when hope seems so elusive. But I had not quite finished my study of the Minor Prophets. Three more follow the destruction of Jerusalem:

Haggai, Zechariah and **Malachi**. And there was still Joel, a prophet whose date no one knows.

The Hebrew people were exiled in Babylon for over fifty years before Babylon was captured in a single night by Median and Persian troops secretly entering the city by its underground waterway and coming up through the city drains. Cyrus, the Persian, took control and released the prisoners, allowing them to return to their own countries.

About 50,000 Jews returned to Jerusalem to rebuild their temple but found almost insurmountable problems. (The people from Judah were now called Jews).

Local soldiers from earlier Assyrian and Babylonian settlements had intermarried with the remaining Israelite women and worshipped in Samaria, the old capital. The local inhabitants, who were known as Samaritans, resisted and taunted the returning Jews. They opposed the rebuilding of the temple for almost sixteen years until Darius the Great became the new Persian king in 522 BC.

HAGGAI AND ZECHARIAH

Haggai and Zechariah both encourage the returned exiles to rebuild their temple and assure them that "The Lord of Hosts" is with them. Zechariah, in the six last chapters of his prediction, deals with new puzzling references to judgment, destruction, and the fall of tyrants, terrible suffering and new attacks on Jerusalem which form part of a new type of "apocalyptic" literature that will be discussed later.

MALACHI

Malachi, the last known prophet of Judah, appears eighty years later, to spur the people on to rebuild their temple. He calls the priests and people to renew their covenant with God, and tells of a messenger to be sent to prepare for the forthcoming judgement. The last book in the **Old Testament** ends with the promise that Elijah will come "before that great and terrible Day of the Lord."

One minor prophet, **Joel**, is different from all the others. No one knows where and when he lived. He predicts three events: a plague of locusts, a promise of restoration and the coming "Day of the lord".

His description of locusts reminds me of a Shell Petroleum film on locust devastation, which I saw in the middle 1960s. The plague was twenty miles wide, many miles long and hundreds of feet high. An aeroplane was spraying the swarm, but even after a day of spraying, with locusts lying dead in piles up to three or four feet deep over a 200 square mile area, the plague continued almost undiminished. On its return, the aeroplane was red with the locust blood.

Joel describes how swarm after swarm of locusts settled on the crops; what one swarm left, the next swarm devoured. (1:4).

A description of the Great Plains' locust plague in Kansas in 1874 suggests that 120 billion locusts covered an area 100 miles wide, 300 miles long and up to a mile high (**Great Disasters**: Reader's Digest).

The army of locusts destroys grape vines, fig trees, corn and olives, causing distress among the sheep and cattle (**Joel** 1). The devastating famine and drought that follow are a warning that "the Day of the Lord is near." (1:15 NIV) The insects pour in like darkness spreading over the mountains.

Before them the land is like the Garden of Eden but behind it is a barren desert.

Joel has seen nothing like this plague. He describes the "attack like warriors" (2:7 GNB), the sound of crackling "like dried grass on fire". The earth shakes at their advance and the sky "trembles". They are the troops of God – "The day of the LORD is great: It is dreadful. Who can endure it?" (2:11 NIV).

The promise of restoration comes as Joel appeals for the people to repent and seek God's love. "He is gracious and compassionate, slow to anger and abounding in love." (2:13 NIV).

God promises to bless the faithful with new crops so that starvation will be a thing of the past.

Before the Day of the Lord arrives, the prophet foretells that God will pour out his spirit on all flesh, sons and daughters will preach God's message, old men will have dreams and young men will have visions. There will be cosmic upheaval as the sun is darkened and the moon turns to blood "before the coming of the great and dreadful day of the LORD." (2:28-32 NIV).

Finally, God will judge the nations and give them to Judah. He will order his people to "beat your ploughshares into swords and your pruning hooks into spears." (3:9-10 NIV).

God's people will be defended and will know the power of their deliverer. "Then, Israel, you will know that I am the Lord your God" (3:17 GNB). God will live on Zion, and Jerusalem will be a sacred city never to be reconquered.

The prophecy ends with "Judah will be Inhabited forever, and Jerusalem through all generations."

SUMMARY

Twelve Minor Prophets with much to say about suffering, but I found that none of them made sense in the twenty-first century.

They all seemed to be preaching a similar message of forthcoming judgement, destruction, death, famine, murder, enslavement, and ethnic cleansing, as part of "the Day of the Lord".

Suffering was seen here as God's judgement. The Day of the Lord had come to Israel, to Judah, and the surrounding nations, but the postexilic prophets were still predicting it.

It is amazing, however, that the same "destruction, death, famine, murder, enslavement and ethnic cleansing still take place well over 2000 years later in the 21st Century.

Central Africa, Yemen, Syria, Iraq, Afghanistan, Israel, Gaza and Ukraine plus other areas, are no different in their pain and suffering from those discussed in the minor prophets. Almost all the prophets reveal the restoration and blessing of the faithful Jews. Yet each warns of a new approaching "Day". The Day of the Lord had come many times, but was still to come.

The Day of the Lord, "that day", also called "the last days" or "the latter days", seems to occupy the thinking of almost a third of the writers of the **Old Testament**. I was to come across the idea again in the **Major Prophets**, and in the apocalyptic literature of **Daniel,** and later in **The New Testament**, especially in **The Apocalypse**.

What did the "Day" mean to the prophets? Was it the end of the world, Judgement Day, the end of the present order, or the "hereafter"?

I found that the concept of God judging the world was not limited to the prophets. The psalmists often spoke of One who would judge the world in righteousness (e.g. **Psalm** 59:8, 96:13 and 98:7).

It clearly did not refer to any one event, but rather a kind of pattern in time. Divine judgement was followed by redemption and restoration just as later, death would be followed by resurrection.

The Day of the Lord, as first mentioned by Amos, referred to God's judgement on unrighteous behaviour, especially among His own people. But that "Day" appears to refer to any coming punishment, whether by invasion, locust swarms, or the coming of God to judge nations.

It also meant the day when Yahweh would intervene in world affairs to place Israel as the head of all nations, and the day when God would bring retribution on all Israel's enemies.

A number of disturbing thoughts came to mind as I read the predictions of the **Minor Prophets**. Many have been literally fulfilled, as Christian books on prophecy are keen to point out. I could not help wondering if some of these prophecies were written after the events they describe (e.g. "the fall of Samaria or Jerusalem") or even if some prophecies (especially those that claim to be related to Jesus) were deliberately taken over by later writers.

Some prophecies were clearly not fulfilled literately (e.g. "the moon shall be turned to blood", and "Jerusalem shall not be destroyed again"- it was totally destroyed in AD 70 under Titus).

I wondered at the vagueness of some predictions and whether prophecy was easy to misinterpret. But these questions would have to wait until I had reread the remaining Major prophecies, when I could evaluate all of them together.

Chapter 13

The Covenant Relationship, A Partial Answer

*H*ebrew history starts with Abraham, a merchant Bedouin from Ur of the Chaldees. With his thousands of sheep and goats he travelled to Haran in the northern Euphrates valley where God told him that he would become the father of a great nation in whom the entire world would be "blessed". God promised to make a "covenant" with Abraham, perhaps as long ago as 2000 B.C.

Stan Telchin, a Messianic (Christian) Jew, in his book **"Betrayed!"** (Marshall, Morgan and Scott) explains the Jewish concept of covenant cutting, the highest form of agreement in the ancient world. Tribal chiefs wishing for peace between their people, would "cut a covenant" at a formal ceremony where the partners would exchange weapons, clothing and names.

They would recite blessings for keeping the covenant, and curses if either of them broke it. They would pledge their strength, substance and identity to each other.

In the actual "cutting of the covenant", blood was always shed.

Sometimes face or arms were cut and the two partners in the covenant would become "blood brothers". On other occasions their blood might be mixed in a bowl and drunk.

Ashes might be rubbed into the wounds so the scars became a permanent reminder of the covenant promise.

Such actions "sealed" the covenant. Afterwards, the partners would sit together for a "covenant meal", where family, friends and tribal members would share in the joy of the newly cut covenant.

It is not clear whether the Hebrew word for covenant actually means "fettered," "bound," or "obligated" from bara ("to bind"); or if it means "a meal" or "food" as the verb bara may also mean "to eat" (**Baker's Dictionary of Theology:** Pickering and Inglis). It doesn't really matter which – the covenant was an unalterable and permanently binding obligation, ratified by the shedding of blood and enhanced by the sacrificial covenant meal.

Later the covenant given to Abraham was extended to members of his family, Isaac and Jacob; and later to Moses and the twelve Hebrew tribes, but only if they manifested the faith and obedience of Abraham.

"Now, if you obey me fully and keep my covenant, then out of all nations you will be my treasured possession.

Although the whole earth is mine, you will be for me a kingdom of priests and a holy nation," are the words of God as given by Moses at Mount Sinai (**Exodus** 19:5-6 NIV).

I had come across the idea of this covenant three times in the Minor Prophets – **Hosea** tells of Israel's whoring after false "lovers" (i.e. "fertility gods") and states that "they have broken the covenant" (6:7 NIV).

God's part of the covenant, however, is portrayed in the promised restoration of Israel given to the returning exiles by **Zechariah**:

"Because of the blood of my covenant with you, I will free your prisoners," or "that was sealed by the blood of sacrifices, I will set your people free." (9:11 NIV).

Malachi refers five times to the broken covenant in his second chapter, and also mentions the messenger who will prepare for God's return to the temple who "will come and proclaim (God's) covenant" (3:1 NIV).

These few references had not really registered with me as part of the answer to suffering in Jewish history until I began to explore the Major Prophets. Then they added a new dimension to the oft-repeated message of the Minor Prophets – "The Covenant has been broken", "The day of the Lord" brings justice, and *Yahweh* restores his faithful people. The three Major Prophets were not just "major" in length or quantity, but because of their great insights into the "mind" of Yahweh (to use an anthropomorphism) and His plans for the whole of humanity.

Chapter 14

Neurotic Jeremiah's Uncut Covenant

eremiah was an unhappy, insecure, depressed, empty and miserable prophet. There is no beautiful poetry as found in Lamentations, but the expression of feeling, which Jeremiah reveals, gives a disturbing glimpse into the mind of one suffering from reactive depression.

From the call of Jeremiah when he answers, "Sovereign Lord, I do not know how to speak: I am only a child" (1:6 NIV), until the end of his prophecies some forty years later, we see the prophet's sensitivity and fear.

Jeremiah was a priest from Anathoth in Judah, who served five kings from 626 BC until after the Babylonian exile in 586 BC. King Josiah, whom Jeremiah served first, was killed near Megiddo by Egyptian forces attempting to assist Assyria's Capital, Nineveh, from capture by the Babylonians.

His visions were of ordinary items and trivial incidents from which he proclaims God's message. First, he visualises an almond tree, followed by a boiling pot. Hebrew for "almond" is "*shaqed*" but, by playing on words, Jeremiah calls it "*shoqed*" or "watching".

While Jeremiah sees an almond tree, the Lord says, "I am watching to see that my word is fulfilled" (1:11-12 NIV). The pun suggests that the almond tree shows God watching, while the boiling pot indicated that "destruction will be poured out on all who live in the land (1:14 NIV).

In further visions of water-pots, cracked water cisterns, rotting vines, strong soap that cannot remove stains and wild camels on heat, Jeremiah proclaims that the people have broken their covenant with Yahweh and followed other gods. God has offered fresh water, the Hebrews have built broken cisterns and cracked water pots, stained themselves with sin, while the sexual activities of an idolatrous people are like "a swift she-camel, running here and there, a wild donkey accustomed to the desert, sniffing the wind in her craving." (2:23-25 NIV).

The Hebrews stand accused of breaking their covenant. Coming destruction, barren earth, darkened sky and shaking mountains, will follow the northern invasions predicted by contemporary Minor Prophets.

Yahweh speaks to Jeremiah saying, "Listen to the terms of the covenant. Tell the people of Judah and of Jerusalem that I, the Lord God of Israel, have placed a curse on everyone who does not obey the terms of this covenant... tell the people to listen to the terms of the covenant and to obey them. When I brought their ancestors out of Egypt,

I solemnly warned them to obey me, and I have kept on warning the people until this day" (11:1-8 GNB).

In his commentary, David Day, "Jeremiah: Speaking for God in a Time of Crisis" (**Bible Biographies:** Inter-varsity Press), explains that sin was and is a kind of adultery. He says that: "Sin is about betraying the divine lover. It arises out of a personal relationship. It is about spurning the love God has for us. It is about unfaithfulness. It is about a desperate, irrational, self- destructive, unnatural, hell-bent determination to go it alone and play God for ourselves" (p.33).

The evils of the Hebrew covenant breakers include putting idols of Baal in the Temple and building altars in The Valley of Hinnom, "so they can sacrifice their sons and daughters in the fires". Hinnom becomes "the Valley of Slaughter" (By the time of Jesus, "Hinnom" will have become the word translated as "Hell" in the **English Bible**). There, the "corpses will be food for birds and wild animals" (7:29-34 GNB).

Constantly, Jeremiah condemns the sins of betraying the husband (God), playing fast-and-loose with Canaanite fertility gods, sacrificing children in the fires of Molech, playing power politics with Assyria and Egypt, and breaking not only the covenant sealed with blood, but also being completely unjust towards their fellow covenant-making "brothers".

A "scorching wind from the desert", "a boiling caldron from the north" and "a roaring lion" will destroy the people.

Slowly it becomes clear that this is to be Nebuchadrezzar II from Babylon. Jeremiah's visions include a pair of ruined linen shorts symbolising the ruin of Jerusalem, and full wine-jars that are smashed together showing "no pity, compassion, or mercy" as the Hebrews are destroyed. He uses the phrase "sword, famine and plague" on fifteen separate occasions (e.g. 14:12, 21:7-9, 29:17-18 NIV).

God orders him not to marry or have children for "they will die of terrible diseases…will be killed in war or die of starvation" (16:4 GNB). Jeremiah also enacts his own parables such as wearing a yoke of leather straps and wooden crossbars on his neck (27:2) as he urges King Zedekiah of Judah to submit to the yoke of Babylon.

It is no wonder the king, courtiers and people regard Jeremiah as a traitor (chapter 27 to 29), and that other prophets reject him and seek his death.

Later, Jeremiah writes his predictions on a scroll, which when read to the king's court cause such offence that the king cuts the scroll into pieces with his pen knife and throws them into the fire before ordering Jeremiah's arrest.

Jeremiah rewrites his prophecies whilst in hiding, adding that Zedekiah's descendants will never succeed to the throne, a prediction that is to prove true like the others (36-37)

Jeremiah was condemned to death. He was thrown into a dried up well, where he sank into the mud at the bottom. Fortunately, a Sudanese eunuch accompanied by three men from the palace rescued Jeremiah. But the palace was to be his prison until the day Jerusalem was captured (38).

The resulting fall of Jerusalem is described in detail. Zedekiah saw his sons executed, then his own eyes were put out, the palace was burnt and the king taken in chains to Babylon (39).

Meanwhile, Nebuzaradan the officer in charge, releases Jeremiah from his chains in acknowledgement of his pro-Babylonian prophecies, and provides him with food in a starving city! (40).

Jeremiah stays in Jerusalem and pleads with the people to honour Yahweh.

Promising that God will restore his people if they return to the true God, Jeremiah still finds his message rejected. Instead, the remaining population migrate to Egypt, forcing Jeremiah with them, and place themselves under the protection of King Neco.

While in Egypt, the whole Judean population continues to offer sacrifices to the goddesses of Canaan.

Jeremiah predicts that the Egyptian army will be destroyed by the Babylonians, and places three boulders under the sand in full view of the Judean exiles. He swears that Nebuchadrezzar will place his throne on these stones (42-45) as Egypt falls.

The entire Egyptian army is defeated at Carchemish, near the Euphrates, and Nebuchadrezzar captures "Egypt... like a splendid cow attacked by the stinging fly from the north" (46:20 GNB). Jeremiah calls Neco, "Noisy-Braggart-Who-Missed-His-Chance" (46:17 GNB).

As the Babylonian army moves swiftly to attack, Jeremiah also preaches doom (chapters 47 to 49) on Philistia, Moab, Ammon, Damascus, Kedar and Elam.

Finally, in the last three chapters, the destruction of Babylon and Israel's return to Jerusalem is predicted.

SUMMARY

Suffering now becomes the punishment for violating the covenant. Such was the legally binding nature of a cut covenant with blood-shedding that any break-down called for the curses that had been recited at the original covenant undertaking.

Blessings were promised for keeping the covenant and curses laid down. Promises of national growth, abundant crops, cattle and sheep, and freedom from attack followed the keeping of the covenant.

Towns, villages and families would be cursed, and disaster and destruction ensue should the covenant be violated (**Deuteronomy** 28).

It is impossible to read the indictment of the prophets without realizing how human action reaps its own just deserts. Israel and Judah grew prosperous under Solomon, resulting in extravagant indulgence in luxurious living by the rich at the expense of the poor who became enslaved by dishonest merchants, court bribery, and privileges bought from the court.

Injustice, oppression and self-satisfaction made the two countries sneer at their neighbours. The wealthy felt politically secure. They were Yahweh's covenant people, and were being blessed by their wealth for burning animal offerings in Samaria and Jerusalem.

Yet their very prosperity only increased Israel's and Judah's religious and moral corruption. The prophets repeatedly warned the people against unfaithfulness, disobedience to the Mosaic Law, and covenant breaking.

Their idolatry led them to indulge increasingly in fertility prostitution, group sexual licentiousness and, eventually to child-sacrificial murder, all condemned by successive prophets.

The coming Day of the Lord, "Judgement Day", could not arrive soon enough. A politically and morally unjust state was ripe for outside intervention. The prophets of ancient Israel were clearly politicians concerned with the international stage of world events.

They saw how ethical behaviour was tied in with the covenant. Israel was betrothed – married – to Yahweh. God had chosen Israel as his bride. He declared Himself "a jealous God" (**Exodus** 20:5; 34:14; **Deuteronomy** 4:24; 5:9; 6:15 KJV).

Yahweh's love is always inclusive, and the commandments or laws laid down under Moses required undivided obedience and love of the nation.

It was because God specially chose the Hebrews, as Abraham was initially chosen, that the prophets are so fierce in their portrayal of judgement for breaking the covenant.

The one belief that all Jews shared was the knowledge that they were a chosen people. They knew that in some way they belonged life and soul to God. As God's chosen ones, they knew that they had to keep the law.

They had a horrifying sense of responsibility; but the abandonment of their responsibilities both towards God and to their fellow human beings brought greater prophetic condemnation.

As God's chosen ones, they were obliged to obey the law and set themselves apart from their neighbours. Jews were to be different in their dietary regulations, abstaining from certain foods, killing animals in a particular way so that no blood was left in the meat, and observing rituals that amounted to 613 different rules and regulations.

They were to be holy, like Yahweh himself. "Holy" simply means "different" or "separate" from others. Jews were to be unique, set apart from the peoples around them. There could be no intermarriage, no covenants with other nations, and apostate Jews were to be discarded or exiled from the faithful.

Thus, the Day of the Lord was to be the time of God's punishment of the unfaithful. They were said to have brought judgment upon themselves. The proud were humbled by their fall; the "wild oats sown" had brought their own harvest.

Those who had spurned God's love, who betrayed their divine lover, could not expect his help when new and powerful political forces attacked their little states of Israel or Judah.

REACTIVE DEPRESSION

Reactive depression is a clinical term used to define those individuals who feel let down, lose their self-respect and confidence, and indulge in self- pity. Jeremiah certainly reveals the inferiority of the prophet. He wishes he were dead, yet fears death. He is constantly ridiculed by his own countrymen and has very few friends.

He constantly reveals his feelings. "The pain! I can't bear the pain! My heart! My heart is beating wildly!" (4:19 GNB). Often, he complains to God, "What an unhappy man I am! Why did my mother bring me into the world?" (15:10 GNB) He pleads with God to "Let me have revenge on those who persecute me" (15:15 GNB), and asks God not to terrify him (17:18 GNB).

The very openness of his prayers reveals his hatred on those who bring false charges against him: "O Lord, let their children starve to death; let them be killed in war. Let the women lose their husbands and children; let the men die of disease…send a mob to plunder their homes without warning; make them cry out in terror" (18:21-22 GNB).

He wishes his "head were a well of water, and (his) eyes a fountain of tears" (9:1 GNB) and explains his emotions as, "My heart is crushed, and I am trembling" (23:9 GNB). It is obvious why some believe this weeping prophet is also the author of the five Lamentations.

Here is suffering in a different context – the suffering of an individual who proclaims a message that he believes to be from *Yahweh*, yet who is constantly snubbed and ridiculed until he loses all self-confidence. His countrymen never accept his preaching, even though his predictions cover more than forty years.

Yet, the prophet never doubts God. He fearlessly proclaims the coming destructive enemy forces, and remains true to his calling as prophet, despite his timid nature. He remains dependent on Yahweh and prays openly and fearlessly to him. Never does Jeremiah refuse to give his doleful message.

THE CUTTING OF A NEW COVENANT

Despite the gloom and doom, and the intense depression of Jeremiah, hope breaks through Judah's suffering and pain. Jeremiah is ordered to "write down in a book everything" that God has told him "because the time is coming when I will restore my people" (30:1-3 GNB). Yahweh will free his people and cause Jerusalem to be rebuilt. He has "always loved" Israel, and will "continue to show you my constant love" (31:3 GNB).

As the people lament their suffering, Jeremiah introduces a beautiful metaphor of a mother weeping over her child, her tribe, and her children. The sorrowful departure of slaves into Babylon reminds him of Rachel, the mother of Benjamin, who was buried in Ramah, near Bethlehem. "A sound is heard in Ramah, the sound of bitter weeping. Rachel is crying for her children; they are gone, and she refuses to be comforted" (31:15 GNB).

Later, Matthew, when writing of the death of young boys in Bethlehem, uses the same picture as he suggests that the nearby mother, Rachel, fulfilled the sorrow of Bethlehem's mothers during Herod's massacre.

Mothers are to cease their crying, for their children "will return from the enemy's land. There is hope for your future; your children will come back home" (31:16-18 GNB).

God feels deeply loving, and his heart is breaking over the failure of his beloved people. Full restoration is predicted. The Lord God will "make a new covenant with the people of Israel and of Judah." It will be totally different from the old covenant of the law. Although God was a husband to his people, they never kept the covenant", states God.

The new covenant will be unique: "I will put my law within them and write it on their hearts. I will be their God, and they will be my people ... I will forgive their sins and no longer remember their wrongs" (31:33-34 GNB).

God promises the new covenant will be eternal. God will never stop doing good things. The Jews will return and claim the land of Israel and Judah for themselves. God will be their leader, and a "descendant of David" will be enthroned as their king (30:9).

One thing, however, was missing from this new covenant – there was no blood shedding. How could a covenant be meaningful without blood? When Moses had declared the covenant, he had mixed half the blood from sacrificial cattle and put it in bowls, which was thrown on all the people.

Moses had said, "This is the blood that seals the covenant which the Lord made with you when he gave all these commandments" (Exodus 24:8 GNB). The other half of the blood was thrown against the altar.

Jeremiah mentions no blood! Although it would be almost six hundred years before light would be shed on this new covenant, the prophecy of **Isaiah** was to begin that process.

Chapter 15

God has Saved Us!

Isaiah simply means, "Yahweh has saved" or "Salvation is of the Lord". Unlike the other prophecies, the first part of **Isaiah** (chapters 1-39) is quite different from the rest of the book.

The first 39 chapters, set in Israel during the reigns of Kings Uzziah, Jotham, Ahaz and Hezekiah, deal with the Assyrian threat between 730 – 680 BC, almost a hundred years before Jeremiah. Isaiah, the temple, priests, and kings are mentioned, and historical narrative is intertwined with prophecies.

Deutero ('second') **Isaiah** (Chapters 40 to 55) mentions no kings, and is set over a hundred years later while the Jews are in captivity in Babylon. There is no priesthood or temple. Isaiah is not mentioned, neither is any historical material, but the events predicted were to occur between 580 and 530 BC. The last ten chapters, (often named **Trito** ('third') **Isaiah**) may be set even later, or may be a restatement of the second section. No one is sure, but they deal with the return of the Jews to Jerusalem over 200 years after Isaiah began his ministry.

Some scholars believe a different author wrote each section. In the Hebrew texts and the Dead Sea Scrolls, however, the three parts are combined as one book, and there is a clear unity throughout. Phrases like "Lord, the Almighty God" (occurring 65 times), words denoting salvation (e.g. save, saviour, saved) (53 times), righteousness or righteous (42 times), Zion for Jerusalem (37 times), and "Thus says the Lord" (40 times) suggest a single author writing from three different viewpoints.

Perhaps Isaiah wrote his three prophecies at different periods in his life.

Or there may indeed be three different authors with virtually identical vocabularies and style! It does not really matter.

An important theme of **Deutero Isaiah** is that God is in control of history, and His plan includes all nations of the world. It is possible, therefore, that Isaiah wrote predictions hundreds of years beforehand under some kind of divine inspiration. Clearly the references to the Messiah were written long before Messianic figures appeared during Roman times.

Isaiah, a Jerusalem priest, received his call in the Temple in 740 BC, the year of King Uzziah's death. His vision of God, "the King, the Lord Almighty" seated on a throne surrounded by flaming creatures, filled him with fear.

In his vision, a creature with six wings touches Isaiah's lips with burning coal from the altar of sacrifice, indicating that Isaiah's sin is forgiven (6:1-6). Volunteering to become Yahweh's messenger, Isaiah is told that no one will understand, for judgement and desolation are coming, all will be destroyed except "the stump of an oak tree that has been cut down. The stump represents a new beginning for God's people" (6:13 GNB).

Although Isaiah predicts the coming day of the Lord, he condemns the people for covenant breaking and behaving like "whores" before fertility gods, and prophesies the coming invasions of Assyrian and Babylonian armies.

It was something quite different that caught my eye. It was the "stump of the oak tree"!

The first section of **Isaiah** (First Isaiah) constantly refers to a "remnant", "a stump", "a booth in a garden of cucumbers", "a watchman's hut in a vineyard", and linking such metaphors to survival: "If the Lord Almighty had not let some of the people survive, Jerusalem would have been totally destroyed" (1:9 GNB).

This saving of a small remnant is one of the major features of Isaiah, linked to predictions of the coming "Messiah".

The future is constantly balanced between accounts of the coming day of judgement and the day of restoration, when God comes to Zion, ruling through a new and righteous King. **Isaiah** begins by referring to rich people and priests covered with blood through their useless animal sacrifices.

If they repent, God will wash them "White as wool" –as clean as the very sheep they are killing.

Like Amos, **Isaiah** urges people to stop evil and "learn to do right. See that justice is done – help those who are oppressed, give orphans their rights, and defend widows" (1:17 GNB).

Seven times Isaiah states, "You are doomed" (chapters 5-6 (GNB). He uses the phrase to condemn covetousness, drunkenness, blasphemy, falsity, vanity, bribery and injustice, and also to acknowledge his own sinfulness before the throne of God in the Temple

The remnant that survives the Day of Judgment becomes a major theme. From the loneliness and isolation of the "shed in a cucumber field" (1:8 GNB) to the "stump of the oak tree" (6:13 GNB), the small number of survivors of the divine holocaust will form the new Israel of God, gradually increasing until Gentiles from the whole world become part of The Lord God Almighty's new kingdom.

Interspersed with the salvation of a remnant, I discovered a new concept of a "saviour king."

Ahaz, alarmed by the threat of invasion from Syria and Israel, seeks help from Assyria. Isaiah tells him to ask for a sign from God, but when Ahaz refuses, Isaiah predicts that God will give the sign of a pregnant woman who will have a son called "Emmanuel" (7:14 GNB).

By the time he is "old enough to make his own decisions" the kings of Israel and Syria will have been defeated.

The importance of this prediction is that it is given to "the descendant of King David". How it was to be fulfilled is an unresolved matter.

The child may have been Isaiah's own, for he states that his wife became pregnant, and that Damascus and Samaria were defeated by Assyria before his son could speak (8:3-4).

However, Isaiah's son was named Mahershalel Hashbaz (meaning "Quick-Loot-Fast-Plunder") rather than Emmanuel. Perhaps other women had children whom they named Emmanuel. Or the prediction may have been messianic.

Much has been made of this prophecy. In Hebrew the word used for pregnant woman is simply that – a young woman of childbearing age, *"Almah"*. But in the second century BC Greek **Septuagint** of the text of **Isaiah**, the word is translated as "virgin" ("Behold, a virgin shall conceive and bear a child") and **Matthew**, writing later, quotes the Greek version with reference to the birth of Jesus.

Isaiah foretells the Assyrian attacks on Judah, declaring, "Here I am with the children the Lord has given me. The Lord Almighty, whose throne is on Mount Zion, has sent us as living messages to the people of Israel" (8:18).

Then he describes in beautiful poetry the coming of a future king:

> "The people who walked in darkness have seen
> a great light…
> Unto us a child is born!
> Unto us a son is given!
> And he will be our ruler.
> He will be called, "Wonderful Counsellor,"
> "Mighty God," "Eternal Father,"
> "Prince of peace."
> His royal power will continue to grow;
> his kingdom will always be at peace.

He will rule as King David's successor,

basing his power on right and justice,

from now until the end of time.

The Lord Almighty is determined to do all this"

(9:6-7 GNB).

The Messiah is revealed not only in human terms as the "child born", "son" "our ruler", "counsellor", "father" and "prince of peace", but also in divine terms as "wonderful", "Mighty God" and "Eternal". The phrase "a son is given" may imply his divine paternity.

It seems to me that the prophecy of the "young woman" giving birth to a child "Emmanuel – God with us" and the passage above both relate to the coming Messiah.

"Messiah" was the name given to one who was "anointed with oil". In Hebrew times "anointed ones" included prophets, priests and kings - all anointed into their respective offices.

As I read of this coming "anointed one", I became aware that he was to be a mixture of all three - a prophet, priest and king.

In one of his most picturesque visions of Yahweh's coming kingdom, Isaiah sees global peace. "The royal line of David is like a tree that has been cut down; but just as new branches sprout from a stump, so a new king will arise from David's descendants" (11:1 GNB).

I began to understand the link with the "stump of the oak". This new king from David's line would be given wisdom, knowledge and skill through the "spirit of the Lord" to rule justly.

There would be a complete absence of fear, symbolised by the pictures of wolves and sheep dwelling together, leopards with young goats, calves and lion cubs, cows and bears, lions eating cattle straw, and even babies playing with poisonous snakes without harm.

"On God's sacred hill, there will be nothing harmful or evil. The land will be full of the knowledge of the Lord as the waters cover the sea (11.10 GNB)."

A day is coming when the new king from the royal line of David will be a symbol of the nations. This idea of a new king, the stump of the oak, was to develop not only into a promised Messiah, but also into the coming of God himself.

A hymn of praise is offered, as the Day of the Lord becomes not the day of judgement but the time of salvation. "God is my saviour...Let the whole world hear the news... Israel's holy God is great, and he lives among his people" (12:1-6 GNB).

Twelve chapters of prophetic insight into the fall of Babylon and the return from exile a hundred years later, together with predictions of the destruction of surrounding nations and general world judgement, are followed by a further messianic hymn of praise for the Almighty God who has carried out his earthly plans (chapter 25).

The Lord Almighty is to present a banquet for all the world's nations on Mount Zion. Death will be destroyed.

"The Sovereign Lord will wipe away the tears from everyone's eyes and take away the disgrace his people have suffered throughout the world" (6-9 GNB). Victory and "perfect peace" are offered to those who trust God, while in a rare statement of resurrection, the prophet proclaims:

> "Those of our people who have died will live again!
> Their bodies will come back to life.
> All those sleeping in their graves will wake up and
> sing for joy.
> As the sparkling dew refreshes the earth.
> So, the Lord will revive those who have long been
> dead" (26:19 GNB).

Much of the poetry of Isaiah is repeated in **The New Testament**, especially in **The Apocalypse, The Book of Revelation**.

Zion becomes a symbol for God's presence in Jerusalem, where a "strong and firm foundation" is to be laid. On it will be a solid cornerstone recording the words, "Faith that is firm is also patient" (28:16).

Justice and honesty are at the core of the foundation. When God comes to his city, the prophet exclaims that all weapons will vanish like a dream (29:7).

The Day of the Lord is to reveal God's mercy and compassion. "The Lord will make you go through hard times, but he himself will be there to teach you" (30:20 GNB).

God "bandages and heals the wounds" and will protect his own "just as a bird hovers over its nest to protect its young" (31:5 GNB).

He promises again that a king will rule with integrity as God once more sends his spirit (Chapter 32). This king is mentioned in the future when the Lord will show his glory. "You will see a king ruling in splendour" (33:17 GNB) and, later, "The Lord himself will be our king; he will rule over us and protect us. No one… will ever again complain of being ill, and all sins will be forgiven" (33:23-24 GNB).

God as the new king is the theme reverberating through the song of Chapter 35: "The desert will rejoice and blossom", "God is coming", "the blind will see", "the deaf will hear", "the lame will leap and dance", "the dumb will shout for joy". Visions of desert springs, highways leading to God, gladness and singing "ever free from sorrow and grief" complete the picture.

Messiah, the king, is to come. He is none other than God himself. That great and terrible day of judgement and destruction, explains the prophet, is also a day of joy when right and truth will prevail.

As I traced the theme of the oak stump, through the coming child – the "son given" - and saw the development of the coming king from the stump of David, who turned out to be a new Messiah and then none other than God himself, I began to understand something of the transitory nature of suffering. There was something beyond the here and now. But what that was, I still did not know.

Chapter 16

The Suffering Servant

eutero Isaiah makes no mention of Israel's kings, Assyria or Egypt. Neither is Isaiah referred to. We are well over a hundred years into the future. Jerusalem has fallen. The day of judgement has come. Jeremiah's predictions have come true, and the new Isaiah foretells the future entirely from the viewpoint of the Lord God Almighty, himself.

There are strong similarities with the Almighty in **Job,** especially as **Isaiah** shows the Lord God Almighty as the creator and controller of the whole world.

"Comfort my people," says God (40:1 GNB), and a voice cries in the wilderness to prepare a way for the Lord.

Hills are to be brought low and valleys filled to reveal God's glory. "The Sovereign Lord is coming to rule in power, bringing with him the people he has rescued." He is the shepherd who will "gather the lambs together and carry them in his arms" (40:10-11 GNB).

Good News, "the Gospel", is to be shouted throughout Zion - "God is coming". The God of creation knows of human suffering and will give strength to the weak: "They will rise on wings like eagles; they will run and not get weary; they will walk and not grow weak" (40:31GNB).

God reminds the people that he is the controller of history. He brought the Babylonian army to power and gave victory to the enemy. And now he will reveal the future progress of his people, "Israel my servant".

Israel is Yahweh's servant, whom Yahweh chose through the covenant. On many occasions, God calls Israel "my servant", and himself "The Lord, the king of Israel".

He asks if idols can control history by foretelling the future. Can they rule the world? To prove that only He is in control of the future, God promises to raise a man who lives in the east to attack Babylon, Cyrus the Persian (45:1).

Cyrus will release the exiles and the message to Jerusalem is, "Your people are coming! They are coming home!" (41:27 GNB).

The "servant" is reintroduced in Chapter 42. There he is "my chosen one, with whom I am well pleased", "filled with my spirit", words reminiscent of those spoken at Jesus' baptism by John the Baptist 500 years later.

A covenant is made with the whole world in which the "light to the nations" will "open the eyes of the blind". As God prepares for battle, to free his people, the whole world sings his praise.

God again pledges to save his people: "When you pass through deep waters, I will be with you; and your troubles will not overwhelm you" (43:2 GNB)."

Again, God challenges the idols of surrounding nations to predict the future. He will provide a "shepherd king" to lead the Jews home. This shepherd is named as Cyrus who will order Jerusalem to be rebuilt and the temple foundations to be laid (44:28).

So, there can be no mistake - the Lord anoints Cyrus as his Messiah: "The Lord has chosen Cyrus to be king!" (45:1 GNB). Again, God announces that he controls history.

He has "stirred Cyrus to action" (45:13 GNB) and ordered him to rebuild Jerusalem and set the people free (the Edict for Jewish Release was issued in 535 BC, two hundred years after Isaiah began his ministry.) God claims to be with his people in their release – "The God of Israel, who saves his people, is a God who conceals himself" (45:15 GNB).

The Creator of the Universe calls on his covenant people to trust Him for salvation. He informs the Israelites that the Babylonian gods, "Bel" and "Nebo," have been destroyed (46:1). Gods made of wood or gold are dead and lifeless, but Yahweh is the Lord of all creation who predicts the future course of world events. "Long ago I predicted what would take place; then suddenly I made it happen," says the Lord (48:3 GNB).

Then, as God foretells the destruction of Babylon, He warns His people to avoid witchcraft, fortune telling, "magic spells and charms" and astrology.

No one knows the future except the Lord Almighty, for all others "will leave you and go their own way, and none will be left to save you" (47:15 GNB).

God is determined to drive home His message: "Listen to me...I am God, the first, the last, the only God!" (48:12 GNB). He explains again that He is creator of the universe and will predict the coming of his chosen ("anointed") man, Cyrus, to attack Babylon. The people are to know that "The Lord has saved his servant, Israel" (48:20 GNB).

Israel is portrayed as a child born to be God's servant. Israel is to serve the nations (Chapter 49). But the idea of an individual servant is developed beyond Cyrus.

Another servant will come, with great honour, not only in saving Israel's survivors, but also by being "a light to the nations – so that all the world may be saved" (48:6 GNB).

Once more there will be a universal covenant (49:8). The heavens are to shout for joy, the earth and mountains will burst into song; and God will show pity on his suffering people.

The second half of Chapter 49 presents a question-and-answer session between God and the people. They claim that God has abandoned them, but God asks whether a woman can forget her own baby and not love her own child. God loves his children and has written all their names on his palms (49:14-16 GNB).

The people also doubt God's power: "Can you take away a soldier's loot?" Can you rescue the prisoners of a tyrant?" God replies that that is just what will happen – prisoners will be released, the tyrant's loot will be seized, Israel will be free and all mankind will know that the Lord is Israel's powerful God.

For the first time the servant speaks (50: 4-11 GNB). He serves the Sovereign Lord who has strengthened him through suffering. He says that he has "bared his back to those who beat" him. He has been insulted, his beard has been pulled out, and he has been spat on. Yet he is innocent of any crime, and God is near to prove his innocence.

Those who honour God and obey the servant will find that, "the path you walk may be very dark indeed, but trust in the Lord, rely on your God" (50:10 GNB).

It becomes clear that the true followers of the Lord Almighty will suffer as and with the servant.

I wondered who this servant was meant to be. Seven or eight times he is clearly Israel, yet he is also an individual, named as Cyrus the Persian. Most commentators seem to suggest that the servant is Israel, shown sometimes as the whole nation, sometimes as the remnant returning from Babylon, and sometimes as a perfect representation of Israel as an individual.

In the Jewish **Targum** (a translation of the Hebrew Scriptures into Aramaic) the servant of Chapter 53 is translated as "my Servant the Messiah".

Does Yahweh choose the suffering of Israel, either as the whole nation or as a faithful and godly remnant within the nation, for Israel's salvation? Or is the servant an individual such as Cyrus (or even Isaiah, himself)? Cyrus is clearly named "my servant" and did release the Jews from captivity. Or is he to be some ideal figure in the future – a "Messiah" or "Anointed One" – God's agent in redeeming and saving his people? Neither Isaiah nor any other author is mentioned in **Deutero Isaiah**, yet the author is faithful in proclaiming God's message to his people and is thus also a servant of Yahweh.

Even the Jews had different ideas about this "Servant figure". Greek- speaking (Hellenistic) Jews tended to believe in the servant in a collective way. They saw in the terrible Jewish purges under the Greeks and Romans, the "Suffering Servant" as Israel suffering in order to redeem the world.

The traditional Jewish position of the Pharisees of Jesus' day, and the Essenes who hid the Dead Sea Scrolls, was that the servant was an idealized figure in the future, the "Messiah" who would defeat their enemies on the Day of Judgement, that Day of the Lord, after which Israel would rule the world from Jerusalem.

Scandinavia scholars have suggested that the figure of the servant arises from a Babylonian myth of the death and resurrection of the god Tammuz. The "servant" is a quasi-mythological concept.

According to **Ezekiel** 8:14, there is mourning for the death of Tammuz, the god of lamentation, thought to die when vegetation burns up at the height of summer, and resurrected the following year. He is also called "Lord of healing" and "Lord of the pastures" (or "Shepherd") by the Babylonians.

However, I realized that Cyrus could not possibly stand for Israel. He was an outsider, who while redeeming the Jews would face his own defeat. His idolatry as a Babylonian would not be acceptable to monotheistic Jews.

Neither could I accept Isaiah the Prophet. He was not the "perfect, righteous one" who would save Israel. And I could find no other reference to Jews accepting Babylonian mythology into their belief system. Isaiah specifically condemns "foreign gods" on numerous occasions, so Tammuz seems a most unlikely candidate.

Already it seemed to me that the servant figure was a corporate personality in which both collective and individual portrayals are given.

In the **Old Testament**, an individual often embodied his people or tribe. Abraham stands for the Israelites, Moses stands for the Law, King David represents the Nation, and it seems logical to suppose that the servant is collectively both an individual and the personification of Israel. The servant as an individual with a mission to save Israel is at the same time the sum of all that Israel represents.

Returning to **Deutero Isaiah**, I read through Chapter 51 where God comforts Jerusalem. He reminds his listeners that he blessed Abraham and covenanted to produce a great nation; he recalls the Mosaic laws and how he released his people from Egypt, and then reminds them of both his creatorial powers and his punishment for their covenant breaking.

But the fifty-second and fifty-third chapters held me spellbound! Chapter 52 calls on Jerusalem to "awake". A messenger runs across the mountains with the good news of victory and the cry, "Your God is King."

People cry with joy for they "can see with their own eyes the return of the Lord to Zion". God has come to rescue his people. There is a build-up of tension and excitement as God, Himself, returns to save, lead and protect his own. Twelve verses bring a hymn of rejoicing and anticipation of the coming King – God himself.

Then comes the great shock!

God points to his servant – "he will succeed in his task: he will be highly honoured" – and the people "were shocked when they saw him; he was so disfigured that he hardly looked human" (52:14 GNB).

Rejoicing Israel, fully expecting God to appear, get a servant instead.

"Nations marvel", "Kings are speechless with amazement", "they will see and understand something they had never known before."

"The people reply, "Who would have believed our report? Who could have seen the lord's hand in this?"

Stunned, Israel sees the servant growing like a plant out of dry ground, like the stump of David or the stump of the oak. He has no dignity or beauty – there appears a degree of disfigurement. "There was nothing attractive about him". Instead, he is despised and rejected in his suffering and pain, ignored as if he were nothing.

Yet he endures suffering and pain "that we should have borne". The people think his suffering is God's punishment, but he is declared innocent.

It is because of "our sins" that he is wounded and beaten. "We are healed by his punishment" and blows. "We are all like sheep that are lost, but God punishes his servant for all that his people deserve" (53:6 GNB).

The servant says nothing as he led like a lamb to the slaughterhouse. He is arrested and killed, put in the grave of evil men, buried with the rich, even though he is completely innocent and guileless.

God explains: "It was my will that he should suffer; his death was a sacrifice to bring forgiveness." Yet he is to be raised "so he would see his descendants" (53:10 GNB).

The servant would live long and cause God's divine purpose to succeed. After a life of suffering, the suffering servant "will again have joy; he will know that he did not suffer in vain. My devoted servant, with whom I am pleased, will bear the punishment of many, and for his sake I will forgive them" (53:11 GNB).

Finally, the servant will have a place of honour with the great and powerful. He willingly dies for evil people, takes the place of sinners and prays for their forgiveness.

After the shock of the servant's appearance, Zion can sing and rejoice (54:10). The Lord Almighty, creator and ruler of the world, will be a husband to Israel, his "young wife" in her "desperate loneliness as a widow" (54:4-6). God seeks to show his deep and endless love, promising a new and lasting covenant (55:3).

"My thoughts are not like yours, and my ways are different from yours. As high as the heavens are above the earth, so high are my ways and thoughts above yours," declares *Yahweh*. He is merciful and quick to forgive. God's mercy and eternal love are the theme of this final chapter.

The clear note of **Deutero Isaiah** is salvation and universal dominion. I could not help but link all the earlier reference to the remnant and the messianic prophesies recorded in the first section with the predicted "servant".

A child was to come - "a young woman shall bear a son", "a child born", "a son given". He was to be descended from David, but was to be "Emmanuel – God with us", "Wonderful Counsellor", "Everlasting Father", "Prince of Peace".

"The royal line of David is like a tree that has been cut down", "a new king will arise from among David's descendants", and "The spirit of the Lord will give him wisdom".

Furthermore, "God will lay a precious corner stone in Zion", "God, himself, will be your king", "God is coming to Zion", and then the surprising announcement, "Behold my servant!"

Looking at these references, it seemed clear to me that here was direct prophecy that could find its fulfillment only in the Messiah.

Micah had foretold of one born in Bethlehem who was from "everlasting", and **Zechariah** had referred to the "king coming on a donkey," to betrayal for "thirty pieces of silver", and to the "smitten shepherd."

Even a number of **Psalms** seem "messianic": "Thou art my son, this day have I begotten you" (2:7); "they pierced my hands and my feet" (22:16); "they divided my garments amongst them and for my clothing cast lots" (22:18); "for my thirst they gave me vinegar to drink" (69:21). These or similar words are found in all Biblical versions.

It is easy to examine each individual text and make it apply to Cyrus, Israel, Babylon, Isaiah, or to the current situation every time a prediction of the Messiah or some such "messianic" truth is given. I had been doing just that.

But I began to realize the value in seeing the entire picture.

There seemed to be a pattern. As Professor Bernard Ramm commented about references anticipating the Messiah, "Critics too minutely questioning each individual text are accustomed to confuse the chemistry of paint with art" (**Protestant Christian Evidence,** Moody Press).

Could I be reading too much into these messianic statements? Or was the whole picture about to emerge?

It seemed that I was digressing from the theme of suffering and pain with which I started. But that was not so. What I had so far learnt from the prophets, and especially about the "suffering servant", made me want to examine the evidence thoroughly in order to understand the prophetic viewpoint on suffering.

I realized that the prophets saw suffering as the result of covenant breaking, of sin and evil in the presence of a holy God who came in judgement on the Day of the Lord; but I also realized that beneath the surface was smouldering a wisp of hope – that day was to bring not only judgement, but also hope, salvation and restoration.

How? I did not yet know. But **Deutero Isaiah** had shown the "servant messiah", the "servant king" who was God himself. And that was a vital piece of the puzzle.

Chapter 17

Coming Home at Last

The third section, **Trito Isaiah**, is concerned entirely with the homeland of Judah after the exile. Jerusalem is to welcome foreigners and outcastes. The New Jerusalem is for all people of faith.

Yet there are those who still "worship the fertility gods by having sex under sacred trees," and children are offered "as sacrifices in the rocky caves" (57:5 GNB). The new citizens are to be humble and repentant so God can heal and restore confidence and hope to all, and give comfort to those who mourn.

Those who return make no response, so God urges them to shout aloud, tell others how to live without oppressing the workers, share their food with the hungry and open their homes to the homeless.

The condemned people repent and confess their failings. As a result, God, the warrior, comes personally to deal with evil (59:16-21 GNB).

The "Suffering Servant" is also the "Warrior God" whose armour is justice and helmet is saving power. A new covenant is made and the children are to learn and teach their descendants to obey the Lord.

Jerusalem is filled with God's glory as the Jews return home. Camels cross the desert and ships fill the harbours. Foreigners help to build the walls, and salvation comes to all. Good news is offered to the people of Zion.

The servant speaks: "The Sovereign Lord has filled me with his spirit. He has chosen me and sent me to bring good news to the poor, to heal the broken-hearted, to announce release to captives and freedom to those in prison. He has sent me to proclaim that the time has come when the Lord will save his people" (61:1- 2 GNB).

Later, Jesus of Nazareth was to read these words in his home synagogue and declare that the prophet wrote of him, and that he, Jesus, was about to fulfill these very words (**Luke** 4:18-19).

Then the scene changes.

A horrifying picture emerges of the avenging God with bloodstained clothing. It is the ultimate paradox that the gracious Saviour is also the judge who tramples evil like a vinedresser treading grapes. God has trampled whole nations and poured their life-blood on the ground (63:2-6 GNB).

Israel proclaims God's unfailing love and mercy to those who repent, and recalls all God's goodness and faithfulness in the past. Then Israel calls on Him to acknowledge that He is their father, and asks if He will punish them further.

God answers their prayers in a striking manner. He will destroy all evil, which includes all wicked people. The faithful will receive a new name and enjoy peace in the New Jerusalem that is beyond comprehension. Such peace and joy will be like "a woman who suddenly gives birth to a child without ever going into labour" (66:7 GNB). God promises to be a nursing mother to his people, and that Israel will bless all nations.

The prophecy ends on a harsh note. God will come as a storm to annihilate evil. The new earth and the new heavens will endure, but the dead who reject God will have their bodies eaten by worms that never die and burnt by an eternal fire, so that "the sight of them will be disgusting to all mankind" (66:24). These themes of final judgement and full salvation do not recur until the end of the **New Testament**, when they are reviewed in the **Apocalypse.**

PROBLEMS WITH PROPHECY

A number of problems presented themselves to me concerning the message of the prophets. Could they really predict the future? Some predictions have not been literally fulfilled (e.g. "The moon shall be turned to blood").

Others seem rather vague. Could some have been written after the events referred to, rather than before? Are prophecies misinterpreted (e.g. "a young woman (virgin) shall have a son" or "Out of Egypt have I called my son"), both applied later to Jesus, seemingly out of context.

Or is prophecy self- fulfilling or deliberately taken over to appear as fulfilling earlier predictions?

Could a prophet predict the fall of Babylon when it had not yet risen to a position of domination? Would a prophet be understood if he really did predict release from Exile and the rebuilding of Jerusalem over two hundred years before Jerusalem had even fallen? How could he name Cyrus when such Persian names were not even known to the Hebrews?

Before I could make sense of the Prophets, I had to answer these questions. But before I did, there was one more prophet and one other book I wished to examine in the Hebrew writings (**Ezekiel** and **Daniel**). I would seek to answer my questions after I had studied their particular messages concerning suffering.

But I was already beginning to understand something of the way suffering and pain fitted into the twenty-first century.

The portrayal of the omnipotence of the Almighty portrayed by the writer of **Job**, and by the Lord God Almighty as revealed in **Isaiah**, however, reinforced the problem of how an almighty, omnipotent God could both love his creatures and still allow them to suffer.

Very slowly an idea was germinating. Things were beginning to make sense. But I had not yet solved the mystery. Something was missing. In fact, there were still a number of missing pieces to the puzzle.

Chapter 18

Space Ships and UFOs

*I*f any one book of the Bible has excited the interest of science fiction writers like Erich von Daniken, author of **Chariots of the Gods**, then it must be **Ezekiel**. His vividly gross and crude description of Yahweh makes me think of science fiction at its worst.

Four living creatures come out of a northern storm, appearing to be human with four faces, four wings, straight legs with bull's feet, their extended wings forming a square. They move without turning their bodies, shine like bronze and each have the face of a human in front, with a lion, eagle and bull on the other three sides. Blazing lights illuminate them as they dart about with "the speed of lightning" (1:14).

Ezekiel records: "As I was looking at the four creatures, I saw four wheels touching the ground, one beside each of them. All four wheels were alike; each one shone like a precious stone, and each had another wheel intersecting it at right angles, so the wheels could move in any of the four directions. The rim of the wheels were covered with eyes...Above the heads of the creatures there was something that looked like a dome made of dazzling crystal...Above the dome was something that looked like a throne made of sapphire, and sitting on the throne was a figure that looked like a man...shining like bronze in the middle of a fire.

It shone all over with a bright light that had in it all the colours of the rainbow. This was the dazzling light that shows the presence of the Lord" (1:4-28 GNB).

Whereas the visions of Isaiah were impressive and intelligible as he portrays the majesty of God, Ezekiel gives a fantastic spectacle that is totally incomprehensible to the modern mind.

Both **Isaiah** and **Ezekiel** reveal *Yahweh* as the King enthroned, attended by creatures declaring His glory – visions of absolute and total authority.

Isaiah sees *Yahweh* in the Temple; now *Yahweh* has been transported on His throne by the spontaneous energy of the "storm from the north" direct to Babylon!

Ezekiel had trained for the priesthood in Jerusalem, but as far as we know, he never took office. He had been taken to Babylon when Nebuchadrezzar captured Jerusalem and had been in Babylonian exile when Jerusalem had finally been destroyed.

Although he was in Jerusalem during the prophetic ministry of Jeremiah, neither prophet mentions the other.

He tells us that he had lived in Babylon five years before he was called as a prophet by this strange vision.

"There in Babylon beside the River Chebar, I heard the Lord speak to me and I felt his power" (1:3 GNB).

As an undergraduate I took a course in "Multimedia and Audiovisual Technology".

Ezekiel is full of visions and symbolic actions that represent a "Multimedia and Audio- visual" approach to the prophetic ministry. Wheels within wheels, a valley of dry bones, a gigantic temple with a river running from its centre in a New Jerusalem renamed, "The- Lord-is-There", are some of the images presented.

The opening vision emphasises the universality of God who can travel to all realms on a chariot that moves like lightning, and is itself full of life ("wheels full of eyes").

God is all seeing with eyes everywhere, while the living creatures are symbolic of power and dignity.

The immortal God calls Ezekiel "Mortal man" (or "Son of Man"), thus emphasising Ezekiel's human weakness and personal insignificance, perhaps similar to Isaiah's cry, "I am doomed".

God gives Ezekiel a scroll with writing on both sides – "cries of grief were written there, and wails and groans" (2:9 GNB). Ezekiel eats the scroll which tastes like honey in order to become as "stubborn and tough as [the exiles] are" (3:8), and is picked up by God and redeposited at Tel Abid with the exiled Hebrews.

Ezekiel returns home after seven days, is tied with rope and is paralysed in speech. He scratches lines to represent Jerusalem and, using iron pans for "walls", lies on his side for 390 day and then turns to face the vision for a further 40 days, regularly shaking his fist to remind the Jews of their years in exile.

He is ordered to eat only one meal a day – bread baked on human excrement. Pleading with God to spare him that, the Lord allows him to bake bread on cow dung.

At the same time, Ezekiel shaves off all his hair, burns a third, chops up a third with his sword and scatters the rest with the wind.

Such drastic actions symbolise the famine and death of the inhabitants of Jerusalem (Chapters 4 – 5).

A grotesque vision of God on fire below his waistline, stretching his hand to pick Ezekiel by his hair and carting him off to Jerusalem's temple comes next (chapter 8).

There, through a hole in the wall, he sees idol worship and women weeping for Tammuz, the vegetation god.

Yahweh then orders the execution of the entire city – men, women and children. Only those who grieve for the loss of true faith are spared by a mark placed on their foreheads.

Following this, Ezekiel sees the strange vision of the domed chariot and the glory of God leaving the Jerusalem temple, and Ezekiel is returned to Babylon (Chapter 11).

In a series of acted parables, Ezekiel takes the part of a refugee, breaks a hole in his house wall, walks blindly with his hands covering his eyes, and trembles and shakes when he dines.

He claims that even if Noah, Daniel and Job were living in Jerusalem, they could save only themselves by their goodness - no one else.

Local prophets reject the messages of Jeremiah and Ezekiel, believing Jerusalem to be impregnable.

Jerusalem is described in horrific terms (Chapter 16) as a repulsive baby squirming in its own blood as an abandoned waif.

God saved the child, washed away the blood, covered her nakedness and helped her to grow into the young woman He was to marry.

It is a "rags to riches" story, where the prophet in a crude and indelicate manner describes how God's covenant wife turns to rampant idolatry and human sacrifice – lust, prostitution, nakedness, murder and doom are all pictured in this judgement of Jerusalem.

The sixteenth chapter of Ezekiel is not one to be read in public!

The proverb "Like mother, like daughter" is used of Jerusalem. Jerusalem is related to Canaanite cities and follows the evils of her "sisters", Samaria and Sodom.

In fact, Sodom will be made prosperous again (this is one of the most remarkable prophecies – the raising of Sodom from the dead is an idea behind the conversion of the heathen nations who will share in future glory).

Then, at the end of a blistering chapter of destruction, evil and total ugliness, comes the repeated promise of a new eternal covenant.

"The Sovereign Lord says, "I will treat you as you deserve, because you ignored your promises and broke the covenant. But I will honour the covenant I made with you when you were young, and I will make a covenant with you that will last for ever" (16: 59- 60 GNB).

Further denunciation follows. But a new idea comes into being. "The parents have eaten sour grapes, but the children got the sour taste," says God (18:2 GNB). There seems to be a doctrine of heredity – that a person's life is affected both for good or evil by the influences of his family.

Children do suffer the consequences of their parents' sin. The punishment of exile did not come because of each person's individual sins, but because of the evils of the rulers. It was the behavior of kings and priests who sealed Israel's doom.

Now that the nation has been punished, the idea of individual responsibility comes into immediate operation.

Each person stands before God and is free to determine his or her own relationship with the Sovereign Lord. Individual sin can now be forgiven by personal repentance. Should the son be punished for his father's evil?

"The answer is that the son did what was right and good. He kept my laws and followed them carefully, and so he will live. It is the one who sins who will die," says the Lord (18:19- 20 GNB).

God does not enjoy seeing the evil perish, but would rather see repentance lead to life.

"When an evil man stops sinning and does what is right and good, he saves his life" (18:17 GNB).

I am reminded of the words of the educational philosopher John Dewey, "A good man may be a bad man improving. An evil man may be a good man deteriorating."

With this in mind, God calls on all Israelites to do good and "get yourselves new minds and hearts...I do not want anyone to die...Turn away from your sins and live" (18:30-32 GNB).

A tragic poem concerning a lioness whose cubs are trapped in a pit, a parable of Judah and her children (kings of Judah) trapped by Babylon (Chapter 19), completes the first section of Ezekiel.

Prophecy gives way to history from chapter 20. Beginning with the Exodus from Egypt, through the wanderings in the wilderness up to the present, Israel has been in total rebellion against Yahweh.

This first section is an even more bitter denunciation of Israel's sin than that of the previous prophets. All Hebrew action leads to judgement – The Day of the Lord!

As Jerusalem is besieged, Ezekiel's wife suddenly dies. Ezekiel enacts a parable by refusing to mourn his wife's death. The grief and agony the prophet hides is the same as Jewry feels for the loss of Jerusalem.

Terrible predictions of judgement are given against surrounding nations – Ammon, Moab, Philistia, Tyre, Sidon, and Egypt throughout the next nine chapters.

Then suddenly the Day of the Lord becomes the joyous return and restoration of the Hebrews to their own land.

Chapters 33-48 reiterate the earlier promises in Chapters 3 and 18. The Exiles hear that Jerusalem has fallen, and Ezekiel recovers his lost voice in order to encourage his people.

The land of Israel will become fruitful and well-populated, destroyed cities will be rebuilt. And God will give his people a "new heart and a new mind" and will put his spirit into his people (36).

The Jewish people had been totally cured of idolatry. From now on they were to be completely monotheistic.

They had "new hearts and minds", but this theme was to be taken up, along with many others, by the writers of the **New Testament**.

Ten years later, having given up hope, the nation is apparently "dead". It is then that Ezekiel sees a valley of dry bones that join themselves to other bones. The dry bones turn into living skeletons onto which sinew and muscle are "breathed" by Yahweh to become a living army (37).

God tells Ezekiel that the dead will rise from the graves in a glorious resurrection. In addition, the two lost kingdoms (Israel and Judah) will become a new nation under a new king: "a king like my servant David" (37: 24). The new kingdom will have a new covenant and an eternal temple, which will stay in the land "for ever".

I found these prophecies confusing. Israel has never had a Davidic king, there was no new covenant, and the rebuilt Temple was totally destroyed in A.D. 70.

The New Testament writers claim these prophecies are fulfilled in Jesus Christ and that the full blessings of this future golden age, following the Day of the Lord, will come with the Christian concept of the Kingdom of God, as taught by Jesus.

A great battle under Gog and Magog is now predicted (Chapters 38 and 39). These were Indo-European people living in the Black Sea and Caucasus regions on the northern edge of the known world.

A great battalion from the Steppes of Russia, supported with armies from Sudan, Persia and Libya, will fight against Israel and Judah.

The armies are so large that when God defeats them, the Jews use the captured weapons as fuel for seven years. It will take seven months to clear the carnage and bury the corpses, after which the Jews will be restored to their land for all time.

Later, the writer of **The Apocalypse** chooses Gog and Magog to represent the hosts of evil who oppose God in the last great battle at the end of time (**Revelation** 20:8).

The remainder of **Ezekiel** (Chapters 40-48) was written fourteen years later and covers the rebuilding of the Jewish Temple. There are a number of problems with the details, which cannot be taken literally.

The size is too great to fit on top of Mount Zion (which is a rock-hill on the east side of Jerusalem), the animal sacrifices, which were restarted, were discontinued after the fall of Jerusalem in A.D.70, and **New Testament** writers seem to take these predictions as symbolic of the Church.

Ezekiel's temple is clearly different from the old one, but it may have been meant as the blueprint for a new restoration temple or an ideal restoration (for it was never built as described). Some commentators even believe it may even be a symbolic prophecy of the State of Israel. Certainly, it is discussed again in the **New Testament Apocalypse**.

Reading **Ezekiel**, I realized it had no new insight into the problem of suffering and pain. The prophet was proclaiming the same message as the other prophets. Yet his gross symbolism was often more dramatic in its proclamation of the message.

Wheels with eyes, prophets carried by their hair, babies with bleeding umbilical cords, dead bones knitting together to become an army, huge international wars against Israel, and the strange parabolic behaviour of the prophet make the book different again.

Here was pain and suffering caused by the national evil of kings and rulers. Suffering like this is seen regularly in our modern world, as corrupt rulers bring poverty, enslavement, war and death to their subjects, often for the advancement of their own wealth and status. Such nations may face their own judgement – their own "Day of the Lord".

Yet, despite the horror of coming judgement, there is the promise of future restoration and blessing. The day of the Lord seems to come to us all!

Chapter 19

Apocalyptic Doom

I eventually came to **Daniel**, the last of the **Old Testament** books, to see what it had to say about suffering. **Daniel** is not really a prophecy; it is an apocalypse.

In the Hebrew **Old Testament**, it was separated from the Prophets and put into a miscellaneous group called "The Writings".

Apocalypse means "to unveil" (Greek "*apokalypsis*") or "revealing" (Latin "*revalatio*"). Such writing reveals "secret" or "hidden" insights into God's future purposes.

The secrets of the universe and the last days are revealed in visions, together with symmetrical patterns and symbolic use of numbers like four, six, seven, ten, twelve, thousand and combinations of these numbers.

Wild animals and dragons represent nations, and angels and demons fight each other.

The Book of Daniel is unlike any other. I found the first six chapters contained stories I had heard in Sunday school, such as Daniel's capture in Jerusalem and removal to Babylon. There the youthful Daniel is trained as a courtier, but refuses to serve pagan gods.

Stories of Daniel in the Lion's den, the madness of Nebuchadnezzar, the fiery furnace and Belshazzar's Feast I knew well.

But Chapter seven to the end seems so gloomy, pessimistic and full of unintelligible numbers.

Visions of strange beasts, thrones in heaven, guardian angels of Persia and Greece, and very detailed predictions of wars between Persia, Greece, Egypt and Syria fill this section.

Then at the end is the promise of "a time of troubles, the worst since nations first came into existence" (12:1 GNB).

True prophecy ended with **Malachi** in 400 BC, but something went wrong.

The predictions of a restored homeland and Jewish world rule had not been fulfilled. Not only were the Jews still undergoing persecution, but evil had increased.

The prophecy that the Jews will be restored to their own land had not been fulfilled. Thousands still lived in Babylonia and Egypt, and thousands more were scattered throughout the ancient world. Suffering and pain were as real as ever.

Alexander the Great had brought Greek conquerors to Jerusalem in 332 BC and when he died, Ptolemy of Egypt took over Jerusalem in 320 BC.

Jerusalem see-sawed between Antigonus, a Greek General from Syria, and Ptolemy during the next three years, and Jews were deported to both countries.

During the second century BC the Syrian-Greek leader, Antiochus Epiphanes (whose name means "The Manifest God") desecrated the Temple by sacrificing pigs on the altar.

Mattathias, an old priest in the village of Modin sparked a revolt, which lasted three and a half years. He and his son, Judas Maccabeus, successfully led an uprising to recapture the Temple, which was rededicated in 195 BC.

During the next century, both the Romans and the Parthians captured Jerusalem. Rome finally established itself as ruler of the whole of Palestine and imposed an Edomite king, Herod, as a hated ruler of Israel.

No wonder the Jews felt let down by their prophets. Where was **Yahweh's** judgment? Why did evil powers still dominate God's people? Where was the restored Israel in its full glory and world domination? Where was God's Messiah? Why were the Jews still suffering persecution, evil and pain? Had God deceived His people?

It was to deal with these very problems that numerous apocalyptic writers produced their works between the **Old and New Testament** period. Only two apocalyptic books are found in the **Bible**, **Daniel** in the **Hebrew Scriptures** and **Revelation** in the **New Testament.**

Persian influences can be seen in the apocalyptic writings. The full force of Zoroastrian dualism seems to be taken over by the apocalyptic writers!

Demons and angels fight cosmic wars. Light fights darkness. According to apocalyptic writers the present age is evil and suffering will worsen. Good cannot triumph; evil must run its course. But the end is predetermined - Good will triumph in the end, for the Lord God Almighty remains omnipotent and supreme.

Daniel is the first of these apocalyptic writings (although some parts of the Prophets are written in similar style.) Many scholars believe that **Daniel**, while set in Babylon in the sixth century BC, is really an anonymous work written after the Prophets, possibly during the second century BC, rather than by Daniel, himself.

They point out that its early "history" seems vague, but is clarified in the later chapters when describing the figure and fate of the Syrian ruler, whom they see as Antiochus Epiphanes.

The ideas seem to resemble second century BC thought, such as the concept of angels controlling nations and the resurrection of the dead. Perhaps the book was written to encourage the Maccabean revolt.

Daniel describes four beasts - a lion with eagle's wings and a human mind, a bear with three ribs in its teeth, a four-headed leopard, and a beast with iron teeth and ten horns. A new horn with human eyes and mouth grows to tear out three of the horns (Chapter 7).

While the writer examines the vision, he sees the throne, mounted on fiery wheels, holding the snow-white figure of one who has been "living for ever", ready to destroy the four beasts. One beast is killed and thrown into the flames pouring from the throne, but the others are dethroned and allowed to live for a short time.

A human being ("the son of man") surrounded by clouds is given eternal authority to rule the world. This man is another proclamation of the Messiah, who still has not come.

Later, **Daniel** describes a vision of a ram with two uneven horns ramming the nations of the world (Chapter 8). A one- horned goat charges swiftly from the west and destroys the ram. The goat's horn is broken, but four new horns grow in its place. The goat defies Yahweh and stops the daily sacrifice and desecrates the Temple for 1,150 days.

The Angel Gabriel explains that the ram symbolises Media and Persia (two horns), while the great goat is Greece (Alexander the Great, whose kingdom is divided into four on his death).

Gabriel also explains that the restored temple will occur after "seventy sevens".

"Seventy times seven is the length of time God has put for freeing your people and your holy city from sin and evil. Sin will be forgiven and eternal justice established, so that the vision and prophecy will come true and the holy Temple will be rededicated.

Note this and understand it: from the time the command is given to rebuild Jerusalem, until God's chosen leader comes, seven sevens will pass. Jerusalem will be rebuilt with streets and strong defenses, and will stand for sixty-two sevens, but this will be a time of troubles.

And at the end of that time God's chosen leader will be killed unjustly. The city and the Temple will be destroyed by the invading army of a powerful ruler...that ruler will have a firm agreement... for seven sevens, and when half this time is past, he will put an end to sacrifices and offerings.

The Awful Horror will be placed on the highest point of the Temple and will remain there until the one who put him there meets the end which God has prepared for him" (9:24-27 GNB).

There are many interpretations of the passage. Some see the "Awful Horror" as Antiochus Epiphanes, while some believe the "Awful Horror" to be a future anti-Christ to be revealed after the return of Christ during seven years of "Great Tribulation".

What seems clear are the predictions of the death of God's chosen one, the destruction of the Temple in Jerusalem and the ending of sacrifices.

Seven and seventy are special numbers with symbolic meanings. Seven days in a week and the significance of the "seventh" day as a day of rest after six days of creation may indicate that "seven" signifies completeness or perfection.

Daniel tells of the furnace made "seven times hotter" (3:19), and informs Nebuchadnezzar that he will eat grass like a wild animal until "seven sevens" pass by (4:23).

It seems to me that the "sevens" are symbolic of an indefinite period of time decreed for the accomplishment of God's plan - the perfect period of time when the Messiah would bring about Jewish salvation. (The number "seven", together with "666", and "three and a half," also occurs in the **New Testament Apocalypse**).

I found it interesting that Daniel does not understand his own visions. When told that the "vision refers to the time of the end" (8:19 GNB), he shows his puzzlement saying he "could not understand it" (8:27 GNB).

Furthermore, the angel who orders Daniel to seal the prophecy "until the end of the world" also warns, "many people will waste their efforts trying to understand what is happening" (12:4 GNB).

Then, as the angel informs him that all these things will finish after "three and a half sevens", Daniel again responds that he does "not understand" and asks, "how will it all end?" (12:8 GNB).

In true apocalyptic style he is told, "these words are to be kept secret and hidden until the end comes...only the wise will understand" (12:9 GNB).

It seems to me that apocalyptic literature is not meant to be understood in any literal way. It is unique in its use of language; its symbolism is grotesque and aggressive, and it hits the senses with animal and demonic imagery.

But I can understand the underlying message - Almighty God is on his throne ready to destroy the powers of hell and evil and to preserve his covenant people. The current Age is evil and cannot be redeemed – the bestial must be destroyed forever.

The end of the Age, the end of the World, the Day of the Lord, Judgement Day, the End of the Present Order of things, the end of evil – these are the ideas of Apocalypse.

In one sense the apocalyptic writers are interpreters of the prophets. The Day of the Lord has already come, the Jews have been judged, exiled and then restored to their homeland; but threats from Egyptian or Greek-Syrian invasion remain.

The work of the apocalyptic writers is to show that God will judge in righteousness, bring about a new created world order and rule through his Messiah.

The value of Daniel is in linking the **Old Testament** message with the **New Testament**. It offers hope and encouragement to suffering Jews.

God's people are still suffering, evil powers will still continue to kill and destroy, but God's judgement is sure to come and a totally new order will prevail as God rules from his heavenly throne through his Messiah.

And that is precisely where I found the **New Testament** cuts in!

SUMMARY

I found my study of the **Old Testament** a mixture of excitement tingled with grave disappointment. There was certainly much about suffering and pain, but it failed to answer the most vital questions. The Wisdom writers had asserted that suffering is reserved for the wrong doer, which does not match up with reality.

The prophets showed that evil and covenant breaking result inevitably in national calamity affecting all citizens – the guilty and the innocent.

The **Book of Job** showed new truths, providing a partial solution. One can trust the Creator of the Universe, who knows what He is doing. He comes to his created beings and is willing to listen to their cries. Human beings are not controlled by evil powers.

Job shows that men and women are free beings who can make their own choices. Those who suffer can still worship Almighty God.

So far, I had discovered that suffering could be a test of one's commitment, a necessary discipline, a way of moulding character or a punishment for wrong doing. Sometimes suffering aids faith and causes believers to cling to God in their pain and need.

To the Jews, suffering was the result of breaking a blood-covenant and living sinfully. A terrible day of judgement, "The Day of the Lord", was coming, when evil would be judged, suffering cease and the faithful Jews restored to their own land to rule the world in righteousness.

A special individual, "The Messiah" descended from King David, would rule eternally under God. He was to suffer in a vicarious manner, and bear in some way the suffering of others.

Yet, I could see that prophecy remained unfulfilled. The doom and gloom of the prophetic "Day of the Lord" had given way to the awful pessimism of the apocalyptic writers. There was no hope in this life – evil continued unabated.

And my most pressing questions were unanswered. How could a loving, all-powerful God allow human suffering and pain?

Perhaps the **New Testament** would provide a solution! Perhaps hope lies only in the New Age to come! I was soon to find out.

Chapter 20

The New Testament: Is Prophecy Really Fulfilled?

*E*ven trying to read **The New Testament** has its problems.

I found two: where to start reading, and how to accept the **New Testament** interpretation of **Old Testament** prophecy.

I had read the **New Testament** many times, but trying to come afresh in order to seek answers to the questions of suffering and pain meant that I just did not know where to start.

The twenty-seven **New Testament** books contain history, letters to churches, personal correspondence, a Jewish theological essay to the Hebrews, four specialist books called "Gospels" and an apocalypse.

Paul's letters to the Corinthian, Galatian and Thessalonian churches appear to have been written first, and it is even possible that all Paul's letters were written before any of the **four Gospels**.

The book to the Hebrews links clearly to the **Old Testament**, while **The Apocalypse (Revelation)** links **Daniel**, the **Major Prophets** and other parts of the **Old Testament** with the future. These two seemed to be good starting places.

Eventually, however, I decided to examine the four **Gospels** first as they deal with the coming Messiah.

The first three, **Matthew, Mark** and **Luke** are called the "Synoptic Gospels" ("synoptic" means "one eye") as they each they tell the story of Jesus from one particular viewpoint. The fourth Gospel, **John**, is very different.

I started with **Matthew** as it was written to Jews to explain the **Old Testament**.

Fourteen times **Matthew** uses the phase, "that it might be fulfilled" relating to the **Old Testament.** The writer also quotes from the **Old Testament** forty-five times and alludes to it a further twenty-two.

The intriguing feature about **Matthew's** use of prophecy is that it doesn't ring true to a modern reader.

The book starts out with a genealogy of Jesus, the son of Joseph. There are only twenty-seven names given from David to Joseph but forty-two different names are recorded in **Luke** 3.

There are also at least three kings missed out in 1:8 (Ahaziah, Joash and Amaziah). **Matthew** lists three sets of fourteen names, one from Abraham to David, another from

David to the Exile in Babylon, and the last from Babylonian exile to the birth of Jesus. Fourteen names in each is clearly artificial.

Matthew's first use of the term "fulfilled" begins with a quotation from **Isaiah** 7:14, "A virgin shall conceive and bear a son," to link it with the birth of Jesus to the Virgin Mary. Even more astonishingly, the writer quotes **Old Testament** passages quite out of context. "Out of Egypt have I called my Son" is used of the baby Jesus, whereas the quotation from **Hosea** 11 actually refers to the Israelite Exodus from Egypt under Moses.

He also quotes **Jeremiah** 31 as "fulfilling" the murder of children under King Herod – "A sound is heard in Ramah, the sound of bitter weeping, Rachel is crying for her children; she refuses to be comforted for they are dead." This passage referred to the horrors of the destruction of Jerusalem in Jeremiah's day.

One "quotation" about Jesus does not even exist in the **Old Testament** – "He shall be called a Nazarene" (2:23 GNB).

It seemed that now was the time to answer the questions that had troubled me earlier when I had examined the Minor and Major Prophets.

Were the prophets really predicting the future? Were the **New Testament** writers imagining ideas that were not meant by the prophets? Did Jesus, as well as **New Testament** writers, arrange his own prophetic fulfillment? Why do The **New Testament** writers interpret prophecy in the way they do?

I found my answers through studying another type of Hebrew literature called "Midrash". Midrash, meaning "to examine", is a Jewish-rabbinical method of explaining the **Old Testament.**

The expositional principles the Rabbis used for interpreting scripture included taking inferences from similar passages either with similar words, ideas or conditions and applying them to other passages.

There appear to be four ways in which the term "fulfilled" is capable of interpretation.

1. As prediction, which has been fulfilled literally? This is what most people mean by "prophetic fulfillment". Clearly, some of the predictions have been literally fulfilled. Tyre, Sidon, Jerusalem and Babylon have all perished.

2. As types or shadows. The **Old Testament** sacrifices are seen as shadows or types of the sacrifice of Christ. Joseph suffering in Egypt is seen by many as a type of Christ and his suffering. So is Job.

3. As having a secondary fulfilment. A prophecy may mean one initial thing, yet may be seen as having a secondary fulfilment at a later stage. The coming Day of the Lord was fulfilled by the destruction of Jerusalem, but also referred to the coming of Christ, or the death of Christ, or to future judgement.

4. As being an occurrence that aptly and appropriately expresses something different from that originally

stated. Albert Barnes, a 19ᵗʰ Century commentator, suggested that a fable may be said to be "fulfilled" when an event occurs similar to the one in the fable. The last chapters of **Isaiah** foretell the return of the Jews from Babylon and the circumstances were literally fulfilled. However, the language used is so grand and sublime that it also aptly and appropriately expresses something more important than the original prediction – the deliverance of the redeemed under the Messiah and the universal spread of the Gospel. In that sense, the coming of Jesus and the spread of the Gospel may be said also to "fulfill" the prophecy of Isaiah.

With these examples in mind, I found it much easier to understand Matthew's use of the term "fulfilled" in relation to quotations from the prophets.

For example, Matthew quotes **Isaiah** with relation to the prophecy of the virgin who shall bear a child, "Emmanuel", and sees the words as aptly expressing the virgin birth of Christ. The name, Emmanuel – "God with us" – is appropriate when applied to this new born baby who is revealed as God becoming a human being – "incarnate."

Where the Messiah was to be born, however, is a literal prophecy fulfilled in a literal manner. "In Bethlehem, Ephrata" says Micah.

The parents did not prearrange it, for they could not know their baby was to be a boy, later recognised as the Messiah. If, however, they did arrange to visit Bethlehem because they had been told of the birth by the angel, then that action was clearly approved by the God whose child had been given to the world.

When Hosea wrote that God had delivered his son, Israel, from danger in Egypt, the words are equally appropriate to Jesus, also God's son, who also returned from Egypt after the death of Bethlehem's babies. Hosea's words express both events, and in that sense were a fulfillment of Hosea's words that God had saved his son from Egypt.

The wailing in Ramah originally described the sorrowful departure of slaves assembled in Ramah. Nobles had been slain, the king blinded and Jewish sons murdered by Babylonian soldiers.

Rachel, Benjamin's mother, was buried in Ramah, near Jerusalem and Bethlehem, and Jeremiah's beautiful metaphor introduces the nearby mother weeping over her child, her tribe and Israel's calamity.

Matthew suggests that the nearby mother "fulfilled" the sorrow of Bethlehem's mothers in Herod's massacre. The metaphor used "fulfills" both occasions.

When Jesus returned to Nazareth, the fulfillment of prophecy that "He will be called a Nazarene" is not associated with any one prophet. Chapter 2:23 (KJV) states, "that it might be fulfilled of the prophets" (plural), and the implication is that Jesus would be proverbially despised and held in contempt.

In fact, the term "Nazarene" was a proverbial name for contempt at that time. "Can any good thing come from Nazareth?" (John 1:46 GNB).

I found it vital to understand that my interpretation of the **New Testament** does not depend on the Jewish-rabbinical or Midrash interpretation of the **Old Testament**.

Sometimes I do not accept the **New Testament** writers' use of the **Old Testament** by my own criteria in understanding literature. But that does not in any way invalidate the points the writers are trying to prove, using Jewish methods of argument to convince fellow Jews.

Matthew, Paul and the writer of **Hebrews** each use Jewish-rabbinical methods in "proving" their case to other Jewish readers.

For example, the story of the Virgin Birth in **Matthew** 1 does not depend upon the writer's suggestion that the prophecy in **Isaiah** appropriately fits the facts of the case.

If Mary were a "virgin" as Joseph is led to believe in a dream stated by **Matthew** 1, and as Mary claims to be true in **Luke** 1, then the accounts stand by themselves regardless of the methods used to convince first century Jewish Christians.

The truth of the "Incarnation", that God became a human being, was not just limited to two Gospels. It is revealed in other parts of the **New Testament**.

In fact, I find my knowledge of Midrash gives me an insight into the methods of argument and manner of interpretation used by **The New Testament** writers to convince those who were used to accepting such methods as authoritative.

Every **New Testament** writer indicates that Jesus is in some way part of God. **Mark** opens with the words, "This is the Good News about Jesus Christ, the Son of God." **John**, who calls Jesus "the Word", states, before the world was created "the Word already existed; the Word was with God, and the Word was God...the Word became a human being, full of grace and truth, and lived among us" (1:1 and 14 GNB).

The Virgin Birth is clearly implied in the belief that God became a human being. It was accepted by the early church, and is part of the Apostles Creed.

Paul wrote that "Christ is the visible likeness of the invisible God... the Son has in himself the full nature of God...For the full content of divine nature lives in Christ, in his humanity" (**Colossians** 1:15, 19 and 2:9 GNB).

There is also a reference by Paul to the fact that "God was in Christ, reconciling the world to Himself" (**2 Corinthians** 5:19 KJV).

Paul also wrote, "In the fullness of time, God sent his son, born of a woman." That superfluous phrase "born of a woman" suggests that Paul believed Jesus' birth to be extraordinary. It is so obvious that all human beings have been born of a woman, that for Paul to emphasise that the Son of God was "born of a woman" indicates to me that Paul knew of the virgin birth!

So, while my understanding of the **New Testament** does not depend on the Midrash, or on Matthew's interpretation of prophecy, I can see clearly the way in which the **New**

Testament writers use prophecy and how they interpret the **Old Testament**.

Now to continue my quest. I want to know if God is cruel, callous or incompetent. I need to know if he really is all that powerful. I want to know why suffering and pain exist. And I want to know if God really does exist in the sophisticated, Scientific and technological world of the twenty first century.

Chapter 21

The Puzzles Begin to Resolve Themselves

he whole **New Testament**, all twenty-seven books, is concerned with or connected in some way to Jesus.

Each writer is convinced that Jesus is the Son of God, who died by crucifixion and rose from the dead. They each see Jesus as the Messiah predicted in the prophets and as the "Son of Man," revealed in **Daniel**.

The beginning of the answers to my questions was to be found in a person. But the information given about him is totally different from any other historical person.

I discovered that Jesus was not a particularly exclusive name. Five High Priests had been called Jesus, and there are twenty Jesus's named in the works of the Roman-Jewish historian, Flavius Josephus - ten of whom were contemporary with Jesus of Nazareth.

The prisoner offered for release by Pontius Pilate was himself called Jesus Bar Abbas (Jesus son of the Father). Pontius Pilate offered the Jews a choice: "Which one do you want me to set free for you? Jesus Bar Abbas or Jesus called the Messiah?" (**Matthew** 27:17 GNB).

The name, Jesus, was thus very ordinary. Jesus of Nazareth or Jesus Bar Joseph would be his normal identity – "Bar" meaning "son of" as in "Bar Abbas".

In the **New Testament** he is simply called Jesus over six hundred times, whereas the title Jesus Christ is used on only four occasions in the Gospels (**Matthew** 1:1, **Mark** 1:1 and **John** 1:17 and 17:3).

Yet Jesus was a special name with a prophetic meaning. Jesus literally means "*Yahweh* rescues" or "The Lord Saves" or "God is my rescuer".

Joseph dreamed that he was to name his child "Jesus – because he will save his people from their sins" (**Matthew** 1:21 GNB).

This common name appears to have been given to their sons by parents who believed that God would save His people through His coming Messiah.

The Greek word for Messiah is "Christ". Christ is not really a name, therefore, but a title for *Yahweh's* anointed one – the future anointed prophet, priest and king.

JESUS HAS FULLY ACCREDITED CREDENTIALS

Matthew and **Luke** both start with the story of a Virgin Birth, while **Mark** begins his Gospel with Jesus' ministry. They each recount the last few years of Jesus' life, drawing special attention to his miracles, teaching, execution and resurrection.

Matthew concentrates on Jesus as the long-awaited Messiah and arranges Jesus' teaching into five main sections.

His account of Jesus' ancestry is given in three lists of fourteen names, a device often used to aid memory. It doesn't matter to Matthew that some names are omitted, any more than when he calls Jesus, "the son of David, the son of Abraham".

In fact, Jesus is called "The son of David" on ten occasions in the Gospel, linking Jesus to the Messianic figure from the "stump of Jesse (David's father)" in **Isaiah**. Jesus is revealed as the "Christ" (the Messiah), the man born to be King, even though the title Christ is used only once.

Luke portrays Jesus as a human being and gives the fullest picture of his ministry. Mark shows Jesus doing things, and reveals him as a very active servant figure.

Jesus' power is revealed in miracles. In the **Synoptic Gospels** thirty-two reveal Him healing people, seven show His power over nature, and three demonstrate Jesus' power in resurrection from death.

John reports three extra healing miracles, two nature miracles and the resurrection of Lazarus who had been dead for four days. John also shows Jesus as divine – "the Word", "the Son of God".

Nathaniel, who is introduced to "Jesus Bar Joseph, from Nazareth", first queries, "Can anything good come from Nazareth?" and then acknowledges, "You are the Son of God. You are the King of Israel" (**John** 1:45 and 49 GNB).

Andrew takes his brother Peter to meet Jesus with the words "We have found the Messiah – the Christ" (v 41 GNB). John records Jesus' own claims to divinity - "the Father and I are one" (10:30 GBN) - and the people's response of picking up stones to throw at Jesus because of his "blasphemy."

"You are only a man," they cry, "but you are trying to make yourself God." (10:30-33 GNB). And John also reports Jesus' acceptance by Thomas that Jesus was his "Lord and God" (20:26).

As I read the **Gospels**, I found even greater puzzles, mysteries and paradoxes. Who was Jesus?

Nothing I had believed about Jesus in my childhood seemed the same. His biographers reveal a unique individual. Jesus urged his followers to obey the Jewish Law with integrity, then went and broke it on numerous occasions, himself. He told his followers to "be perfect as your heavenly Father is perfect" and those who knew him claimed that he was the perfect and sinless human being.

Furthermore, he stated, "whoever is angry with his brother will be brought to trial" (**Matthew** 5). Yet four occasions of his own anger are recorded. He rounded on Peter, calling him "Satan"; he called the leaders of his day "serpents", he made a whip to drive merchants from the Temple; and when his disciples would not let children come to him, Mark records that "Jesus was angry" and warned them "that whoever does not receive the Kingdom of God like a child will never enter it" (10:14-15 GNB).

Jesus claimed that he had not come to bring peace, but a sword. He came to set children against their parents (**Matthew** 10:34 GNB). He told his disciples to bring weapons such as staves and swords, yet he also taught the blessedness of the peacemakers.

His enemies accused him of law breaking, of partying as "a glutton and wine-bibber", and of blaspheming by making himself like God.

He certainly did not fit the picture of "Gentle Jesus, meek and mild." He was more of an outcaste, one who had no home - "Foxes have holes and the birds have their nests, but I the Son of Man have nowhere to lay my head", he said. Jesus taught the essential coming of judgement. There would be "wailing and gnashing of teeth", one who called his brother a fool would burn in the valley of Gehenna.

At the end of the world, some would enter the presence of God, while others would burn in the eternal fires of damnation.

Jesus acted like a revolutionary – he called on his followers to renounce wealth and family and to "take up the cross" in following him to the death.

Yet, despite this, he was known for his love and forgiveness. Jesus was a friendly, approachable man. He never refused a request for healing (even though he condemned people for seeking miraculous signs).

On occasions he hid himself, yet was always available when needed. He healed skin diseases, paralysis, haemorrhaging, blindness, deafness and inability to speak, epilepsy, swollen limbs and what was called "demon possession".

Five thousand people were fed on one occasion and four thousand on another. And He began his miraculous ministry by turning water into wine at a wedding.

He was a charismatic leader who revealed his own insecurity and sorrow. He cried when He foretold the destruction of Jerusalem. He wept over the grave of his friend Lazarus.

He appealed to God to deliver him from death while tearfully praying alone in the Garden of Gethsemane – but His prayer went unanswered.

And His agonising cry from the cross, "My God, why have you forsaken me?" reveals Him in **Isaiah's** words as a "man of sorrows and acquainted with grief".

Over three hundred prophecies of the Messiah are said to have been fulfilled by Jesus. I was able to check only about sixty or so predictions.

The life and death of the Messiah had been developed in the Prophets – the place, time and manner of His birth, together with the reaction of his peers, His betrayal for thirty pieces of silver, His suffering and the manner of His death and resurrection are all in the **Old Testament**.

Whether three hundred prophecies or only sixty, it makes little difference. No other person in history has ever been the "fulfillment" of these predictions except Jesus of Nazareth – known as Jesus Christ, the Messiah.

He came into this world with a fully documented curriculum vita. The **Old Testament** writers had seen to that.

Throughout **The Gospels**, Jesus is given and gives Himself many names. He is called Jesus, Jesus Christ, Lord Jesus, Son of David, Son of God and the Word.

He calls himself the Son of Man, the Christ, the Good Shepherd, the Stone, the Bread of Life and the Light of the World. He refers to himself as the Door, the Vine, and the Way the Truth and the Life.

He also called himself The Resurrection and the Life, as well as Lamb of God.

The Gospel writers see him as uniquely a man, a human being who is also "Emmanuel" – *God with us.*

JESUS'S ASTOUNDING MESSAGE

Jesus' teaching was foreign to me. I thought I knew what Jesus had taught – it was to be good, to love your neighbour as yourself, keep the Ten Commandments and obey the Sermon on the Mount.

But as I read the **Gospels**, I realized how wrong I was. Jesus taught people to be "perfect" just as God is perfect, to love God with heart, soul, mind and strength and your neighbour as yourself.

That was far more than my idea of "being good." Jesus taught people to keep all the commandments to extremes - he taught that hatred is really murder and that lust is actually adultery. I found the Sermon on the Mount impossible to live up to. No one can live like that! Furthermore, his message was different from what I had been taught.

Mark says that Jesus preached the Good News from God that: "The right time has come and the Kingdom of God is near. Turn away from your sins and believe the Good News" (1:15 GNB).

He identified with the Messiah predicted by the prophets, and claimed to be the King of the new Kingdom of God. But he turned the Kingdom into "the Kingdom of Heaven" – it was not a physical kingdom at all, but a spiritual kingdom. A kingdom in which God's glory was to be revealed in suffering.

Here was the very idea to which I was seeking my answers.

Jesus told two disciples on the road to Emmaus (**Luke** 24:46 GNB), "This is what is written: The Messiah must suffer and must rise from death after three days."

John records Jesus' words, "I am the good shepherd, who is willing to die for the sheep." And again, "The Father loves me because I am willing to give up my life" (10:17 GNB).

JESUS' PERPLEXING PARABLES

Many of Jesus' parables – the stories he told – were about the Messianic secrets hidden from the people. The parables were not meant to make ideas easy.

When asked by the disciples why he spoke in parables, Jesus replied: "The knowledge of the secrets of the Kingdom of Heaven has been given to you, but not to them (the people) ... The reason I use parables in talking to them is that they look, but do not see, and they listen, but do not hear or understand. So, the prophecy of **Isaiah** applies to them: "This people will listen and listen, but not understand; they will look and look, but not see, because their minds are dull, and they have stopped up their ears and have closed their eyes"" (**Matthew** 13:11-17 GNB).

The secrets or mysteries of the Kingdom were not incomprehensible ideas or doctrines; they were simply concealed, hidden away until it was time to reveal them.

The secrets of the Kingdom were revealed later – they were that the truths of the Good News of salvation from sin and evil were to be proclaimed to non-Jews or Gentiles.

It was the hidden mystery soon to be revealed that the Messiah would die by crucifixion and that the Jewish Temple sacrifices would cease.

The truth that the Kingdom of God would be established on earth. These were the mysteries to be taught in Jesus' parables.

Matthew groups the parables together. In Chapter 13 he gives eight parables. The first concerns a farmer who hand-sows seed in expectation of harvest, but encounters hard ground, thistles, burning sun as well as fertile soil.

Jesus explains the parable as a kind of allegory where the seed stands for the reactions of listeners to his message. Some don't understand the message; others follow it for a short period and then depart; while others follow the Kingdom to the end.

The Kingdom of Heaven is likened to wheat and weeds which are separated at harvest; the Kingdom is like a mustard seed which becomes a tree capable of sustaining nesting birds; it is like yeast; it is like hidden treasure, a precious pearl, a net full of fish in which the bad are thrown away. "It will be like this at the end of the age:" says Jesus, "the angels will go out and gather up the evil people from among the good and will throw them into the fiery furnace, where they will cry and grind their teeth" (47-50 GNB).

These parables of the Kingdom are not easy to understand, even with hindsight. What do the parables of the hidden treasure or the pearl really mean?

Some suggest that the Kingdom of Heaven is so important that a person must sell everything he has, totally change his life in order to obtain the treasure – the kingdom. Others suggest that the last three parables (the treasure, the fine pearl and the fishnet) indicate ways in which people find the Kingdom of Heaven for themselves – some make a sudden discovery that changes their lives (finding treasure in a field), others search for an ideal and slowly come to realize what the kingdom means for them (the merchant who seeks a priceless pearl), whilst others do not know what they want as they sift through life until it becomes clear to them (like a fisherman sifting through his nets, rejecting the worthless fish and keeping the best).

Then there are those who suggest that the parables of the treasure and pearl are about the Messiah – it is He who seeks the treasure - each individual is so precious that Christ has given his all to "purchase" each of us, and it is for us that he has been searching.

No, my Sunday school parables might appear to be simple stories, but they are not easy to understand at all!

One thing, though, is clear - the parables are about spiritual values. The Kingdom of Heaven is a spiritual conquest of the human personality.

The prayer of Jesus asks for God's kingdom to come, His will to be done on earth as in Heaven.

Later, when Jesus rode into Jerusalem on a donkey, as King, John explained how "His disciples did not understand this at the time; but when Jesus had been raised to glory, they remembered what the scripture said about him" (12:16 GNB).

JESUS CUTS THE COVENANT

The kingdom came with the new covenant. Matthew records Jesus' words at the Passover feast. "Then he took the cup (of wine) …and said, "This is my blood, which seals God's covenant, my blood poured out for many for the forgiveness of sins. I tell you, I will never again drink this wine until the day I drink the new wine with you in my Father's Kingdom."

Then Jesus said "This very night all of you will run away and leave me, for the scripture says, "God will kill

the shepherd, and the sheep of the flock will be scattered."
(26:27-31 GNB).

Thus, Jesus claimed to "fulfill" the prophecy of
Zechariah 13:7, and also to be the Son of God who cuts the
New Covenant promised to Jeremiah. This cutting of the
New Covenant is also reported in **Mark** 14 and **Luke** 22, but
it is the writer of **Hebrews** who gives the fullest explanation
of Jesus' blood-cutting covenant.

JESUS' TEACHING: THE KINGDOM HAS COME

After talking to his followers about his death, Jesus explained
that they would all flee, desert him, and weep.

"You will be sad, but your sadness will turn into gladness.
When a woman is about to give birth, she is sad because her
hour of suffering has come; but when the baby is born, she
forgets her suffering, because she is happy that a baby has
been born into the world" (**John** 16:20-21 GNB).

That very night, Jesus' disciples were devastated and
weeping as they saw him betrayed by Judas and arrested. The
following day, they saw Him crucified and die.

Yet their greatest loss became their gain – the suffering
Christ was resurrected within three days and the disciples
began to be joyful at the realization that he had died for
human sin. Jesus' message had been that "The time has
come; the Kingdom of God is near."

How near is not clear.

Jesus said, "the Kingdom is within you", "it is near at hand", "the Kingdom is among you", "seek first the Kingdom of Heaven", "unless a man is born again (or born from above) he cannot see the kingdom of God", "from now on the Son of Man will be seated on the right of Almighty God."

And to Pilate he said, "My kingdom does not belong to this world...no, my kingdom does not belong here" (**John** 18:36 GNB).

As I sought to understand the coming of the kingdom, I found no universal answer.

Some Christians believe the Kingdom came with Jesus and that his first throne was the manger where other kings worshipped.

Some believe the Kingdom started with Jesus' baptism in Jordan, when a dove settled over his head and a heavenly voice said, "This is my beloved son, listen to him" - they see in the ceremony of baptism the anointing of the Messiah.

Others see the death of Christ as the beginning of the Kingdom – the New Covenant inaugurated the Kingdom through shed blood.

Or did the Kingdom commence with Pentecost, when the first disciples were made members of the Church through the coming of the Holy Spirit?

Or was it established when the Temple fell in A.D.70?

Jesus revealed His Messiah-ship and the coming kingdom. God gives the Kingdom gradually. God's Kingdom is still coming as the message of Salvation spreads.

I still pray, "Thy Kingdom come, thy will be done on earth as it is in Heaven," in expectation that God will reveal the Kingdom to others.

The Lutheran Church interprets the Good News, "the Gospel", as the whole New Covenant, the **New Testament** revelation, as contrasted with the **Old Testament** Law.

Jesus taught that the Good News was, "the Kingdom of God is near". Surely the Good News, "the Gospel", is Jesus, himself – his life, death and resurrection. He was and is the King – so the Kingdom is near all of us..

I came to realize that it matters not how, when and where one seeks the Kingdom.

The Kingdom is a moral Kingdom where all its citizens serve God and love Him with their whole heart, mind, strength and soul and their neighbour as themselves.

The Kingdom of Heaven is where the Messiah, the Christ, reigns. His reign has come, people are daily becoming his subjects, and his kingdom is spreading through time and space.

Peter made this clear when he preached his first Gospel message after Jesus ascended to heaven. Using the methods of Midrash, Peter explains that the **Psalms** of King David are prophecies related to Jesus: (e.g. **Psalm** 132:11)

"I must speak to you plainly about our famous ancestor King David. He died and was buried, and his grave is here with us to this very day. He was a prophet, and he knew what God had promised him: God had made a vow that he would make one of David's descendants a king, just as David was.

David saw what God was going to do in the future, and so he spoke about the resurrection of the Messiah when he said, "He was not abandoned in the world of the dead; his body did not rot in the grave."

God has raised this very Jesus from death, and we are all witnesses of this fact. He has been raised to the right-hand side of God, his Father, and has received from him the Holy Spirit, as he had promised...All the people of Israel, then, are to know this for sure that this Jesus, whom you crucified, is the one that God has made Lord and Messiah" (**Acts** 2:29-36 GNB).

If Jesus really is the Christ, the Messiah, the Son of Man and Son of God promised by the prophets then the first answer to my question becomes clear.

If Jesus died as God, or in the words of Paul, "God was in Christ reconciling the World to Himself", then God does care and has shown his love by doing something – entering into suffering and death as the "suffering servant."

I was to learn much more.

Chapter 22

Perfect Suffering

I found the perfect summary of God acting in His world in the very Jewish **Book of Hebrews**. In it I discovered one vital truth that had been missed out of the prophets, but which I had wondered about.

A Messiah was an "anointed one" - usually a prophet, priest or king. The prophets had spoken of a Messiah who was to be a prophet and King, but nothing had been said about priesthood.

None of the **New Testament** writers had mentioned a Messiah Priest (although there are priestly Messiahs in the **Dead Sea Scrolls** literature).

This omission is corrected in **Hebrews.** Jesus is described as the eternal Son of God who was "perfect in suffering"; an eternal priest, superior to the Jewish priesthood; and as the great High Priest, one who can offer full salvation, not available to those indulging in animal sacrifices and other rituals.

The Hebrew (Jewish) Christians appeared to have been facing violent persecution, Jewish believers unsure of their newfound Christian faith. They were a little like old wine-skins holding new wine – Christ being the new brew that threatened to burst their faith.

Whoever the writer was, he expounds the Jewish Midrash in a masterful fashion to show how the Christian faith emerged from Judaism. His message commences in the first verse:

> "In the past, God spoke to our ancestors many times and in many ways through the prophets, but in these last days He has spoken to us through his Son. He is the one through whom God created the universe, the one whom God has chosen to possess all things at the end" (verses 1-2 GNB).

Then follows a résumé of the superiority of Jesus over others. He is the Son of God, the Messiah (1:1-14). He is the perfect man who died for all. "We see him now crowned with glory and honour because of the death he suffered", for God has made "Jesus perfect through suffering" (2:10 GNB).

In addition, the writer declares, "He can help those who are tempted, because he himself was tempted and suffered" (2:18 GNB).

Jesus is the High Priest, superior to Moses and the priests of the **Old Testament** (3:1-6). Instead, He is a priest who learnt obedience through suffering, and who is identified as being a human being, one of the people, identified with humanity.

Unlike other priests who need divine forgiveness even before they sacrifice on behalf of others, Jesus is perfect and sinless. As such, says the writer, He is able to mediate the New Covenant with God by shedding his own blood (7:1-28).

Although Jesus was not descended from the priesthood like John the Baptist, the writer argues that Jesus is a priest after the order of Melchizedek, a Priest of Salem at the time of Abraham.

He performed sacrificial ceremonies before the Jewish priesthood was established.

According to the writer of **Hebrews**, Melchizedek had no ancestry or priestly pedigree (7:3) – his name means "King of Righteousness" and Salem means "peace". He was therefore the King of Righteousness and Peace.

Much of **Hebrews** Chapters 5:1-10 and 7:1-28 is concerned to show that Jesus is the new High Priest of God based on Melchizedek.

The writer explains how the Old Covenant has become useless. "If there had been nothing wrong with the first covenant, there would have been no need for a second one", he states (8:7 GNB).

The writer of **Hebrews** quotes the full words of Jeremiah and shows how the Old Covenant has "become old and worn out and will soon disappear" (8:13 GNB).

The Old Covenant was unable to save from idolatry and sin. "The offerings and animal sacrifices presented to God cannot make the worshipper's heart perfect" (9:9 GNB). That Covenant was unable to help people meet God – only through the High Priest in the Holiest place was God to be found.

Above all, forgiveness was only temporary – the High Priest had to offer annual sacrifices (Chapter 9).

"For this reason," states the author, "Christ is the one who arranges the New Covenant" through his death (9:15 GNB).

According to the **New Testament**, the New Covenant has been cut with "the blood of Christ". He has placed the inner law in the hearts of all believers (8:10). He has revealed God to all (8:11). Furthermore, He has forgiven all sin (8:12).

He is described as the perfect sacrifice whose "blood will purify our consciences from useless rituals, so that we may serve the living God" (9:14 GNB).

All that has happened in the **Old Testament** and all the priestly ritual "are copies of heavenly originals" (9:23 GNB).

Christ is the reality and he has come.

The Apostle Paul also refers to the "secret truth, my brothers, which I want you to know…the stubbornness of the people of Israel is not permanent, but will last only until the complete number of Gentiles comes to God. And this is how all Israel will be saved.

As the scripture says: "The Saviour will come from Zion and remove all wickedness from the descendants of Jacob. I will make a new covenant with them when I take away their sins"." (**Romans** 11:25-27 GNB).

Finally, Jesus Christ referred to the wine at His Last Supper as, "my blood, which seals God's covenant" (**Matthew** 26:28 and **Mark** 14:24 GNB).

It seems that Jeremiah predicted the coming of a New Covenant that was not "cut" or sealed with blood until the coming of Christ.

The Latin word for "covenant" is "*testamentum*" meaning "will" (in English we still use both in the expression "last will and testament").

Thus, the Jewish or Hebrew Scriptures are known as the "**Old Testament**" and the Christian Scriptures as the "**New Testament**". The Old Covenant refers to the laws of Moses, and the New Covenant refers to the grace of Jesus.

In **Hebrews** Chapter 10 the writer urges believers to come near to God. He exhorts Christians suffering persecution with the five-fold exhortation:

> "Let us come near to God with a sincere heart and a sure faith." (22 GNB).
>
> "Let us hold on firmly to the hope we profess. (23 GNB).
>
> "Let us be concerned for one another, to help one another, to show love and to do good." (24 GNB).
>
> "Let us not give up the habit of meeting together." (25 GNB).
>
> "Let us encourage one another all the more, since you see that the Day of the Lord is coming nearer." (25 GNB).

The Hebrew Christians were encouraged to "hold on" to their faith. They had suffered much, had been publicly insulted and ill-treated. Some were imprisoned for their faith, their belongings seized (10:32-35), but they were exhorted to "have faith".

Chapter 11 lists the faithful who endured suffering, torture and death from Abel, murdered by his brother, to Moses at the Red Sea escaping from Egypt.

Jewish heroes fought lions, escaped fires, and fought in battle – weak men and women who gained strength by their faith (34). Others died under torture, or were mocked, whipped, imprisoned, stoned and "sawn in half" (tradition suggests that Isaiah was sawn in two).

Others were poor, persecuted, ill-treated and dressed in goatskins. Some were refugees in deserts and hills, living in caves and holes in the ground.

Yet none of the people mentioned received what they hoped for.

Abraham never saw the great nation promised to his descendants (he died leaving two sons), Moses never entered the Promised Land, and Isaiah never saw the Messiah.

Indeed, it is we in the New Covenant Age, suggests the writer, who can see the fulfillment of promises which ancient saints never understood, "because God had decided on an even better plan for us. His purpose was that only in company with us would they be made perfect" (40 GNB).

God's revelation to humanity was progressive. The entire plan of God's redemptive salvation was not completed at once, or during the lifetime of any one generation.

It was like the two halves of a contract – one part was given to those of faith in the **Old Testament** and the second part was given to believers in the new era of the Messiah when all would be fulfilled - "made perfect".

God's "even better plan for us" which would fulfill the promises to the **Old Testament** faithful, includes seeing these promises fulfilled in Jesus the Messiah, seeing the end of sacrifices by the death of Jesus, the preaching of the Good News of Salvation by faith rather than obedience to the law, the wondrous hope of the resurrection from death, and the wonders of a resurrection and future heaven.

Faith and hope have enabled human beings to endure pain and suffering. No matter how hard the sacrifices, the persecutions and the pains that have to be endured, faith and hope will sustain members of the Messiah's kingdom. That is the essential message of Chapter 11.

Finally, the writer encourages his suffering readers to run the race of life, encouraged by the great sufferers of the past (12:1). He urges the Hebrew Christians to look to Jesus the "one on whom our faith depends from beginning to end. He did not give up because of the cross! On the contrary, because of the joy that was waiting for him, he thought nothing of the disgrace of dying on the cross, and is now seated at the right- hand side of God's throne. Think of what he went through; how he put up with so much hatred from sinners! Do not let yourselves become discouraged and give up." (12:2-4 GNB).

Running the race depends on Jesus who has set the pattern of suffering by his own experience of pain and death. He is the coach in the race, and the help and sustainer.

The Greek word for "race" is "*agōn*", from which the word "agony" comes. It was also used for wrestling matches and included the idea of struggling to succeed.

Endurance, hardship and determination to succeed are part of the agony of competition.

"Run the straight race" or "fight the good fight" is meaningless without discipline and hardship.

The writer urges his readers to cheerfully endure affliction because it is God's way of discipline (12:6 GNB).

His words, "The Lord corrects everyone he loves, and punishes everyone he accepts as a child," are taken from Eliphaz (**Job** 5:17).

The closing statement: "God has raised from the death our Lord Jesus, who is the Great Shepherd of the sheep as the result of his sacrificial death, by which the eternal covenant is sealed." (13:20 GNB), encapsulates the Gospel.

The "Lord Jesus" is the Messiah, God's servant who is King and Lord of his people. He has been raised from death by the power of God who will raise all the faithful to his covenanted Kingdom.

"That Great Shepherd" reminds me of **Ezekiel** 34 where Yahweh promises to be a shepherd to His people.

It also reminds me of the "Good Shepherd" who lays down his life for his sheep in **John** 10; and who leads them through the deepest darkness ("the valley of the shadow of death") in **Psalm** 23.

The message of **Hebrews** is that the Shepherd King is the living guide and sustainer of His suffering people. God does care, and has suffered for His people.

Henry G Ley summarised the book in the second verse of his hymn:

> Run the straight race through God's good grace,
> Lift up thine eyes and seek His face;
> Life with its path before us lies;
> Christ is the way and Christ the prize.

The first part of the puzzle was beginning to be solved. If the writer of **Hebrews** is correct, then the Messiah showed that God does care. He is attempting to do something to deal with suffering and pain.

I still had to read the rest of the **New Testament** before I could take in the full meaning of God's love and concern in a sin-sick, suffering and pain ridden world.

The Suffering God

I t seemed rather strange to come eventually to the letters written to individuals and local churches.

Paul's letters were probably the first part of the **New Testament** to be written.

His first letter to the church at Corinth may have been the first known work to deal with Christianity. It was written to a group of Christians facing the catastrophe of being overcome by evil.

Paul discusses divisions in the Corinthian church (1:10-17), arrogance and boastfulness (1:18-21), the fornication of a man with his father's wife (5:1), speaking unknown languages and giving the impression that the speakers are mad (14:23); and Christians who were taking fellow believers to the law courts over trivial matters (6:1-8).

There was involvement with all forms of sexual immorality (6:5-18), drunkenness at Holy Communion – Christians gorging on food and wine at "agape" or "love feasts", and drinking libations to idols (11:17-27).

Worship was bizarre, noisy and irreverent, so that Paul had to instruct the Corinthian church in worship and especially of the need to develop the gift of love (chapters 12-14).

Finally, they seemed confused about their beliefs in the resurrection, which Paul dealt with in chapter 15.

George E. Gardiner, in **The Corinthian Catastrophe** (Kregel Publications, USA), describes the Corinthian Church as "arrested in development, charismatic in practice, immoral in living and heretical in doctrine."

Unfortunately, the Corinthian church apparently took little heed of Paul's admonitions and failed to survive.

I almost overlooked Paul's teaching on suffering, because his first letter is all about the suffering brought on by the immature, greedy, arrogant and extrovert behaviour of church members - human beings - rather than natural suffering.

That was an error on my part.

Even in this first letter to Corinth, Paul is optimistic about future glory, as he proclaims, "No eye has seen, no ear has heard, no mind has conceived what God has prepared for those who love him" (2:9 NIV).

Paul's later letters deal with some of the most wonderful revelations of suffering in the **New Testament**.

In his second letter to Corinth, Paul outlines some of his own suffering. He is "often troubled, but not crushed; sometimes in doubt, but never in despair" (4:8 GNB).

Also, he patiently endures "troubles, hardships and difficulties", having been "beaten, imprisoned and mobbed… overworked and without sleep or food" (6:4-5 GNB).

On five occasions he was lashed thirty-nine times by Jews; three times by Romans; and once he was stoned.

He was also shipwrecked three times, spent twenty-four hours in the water, and speaks of danger from floods and robbers.

He has known exhaustion, pain, hunger and thirst, with no food, water and clothing (11:22-26).

He also had a strange physical ailment that he prayed three times for God to remove. No one knows what this affliction was.

Each scholar gives his own view -- malaria, poor eyesight, gout, migraine, sexual and emotional feelings, and many other ailments have been suggested.

Whatever the problem, Paul writes that God not only refused to remove it, but also informed him, "My grace is all you need, for my power is greatest in your weakness" (12:9 GNB).

What intrigued me about Paul was not his attitude to suffering. He clearly rejoiced in pain, even praising God in song when incarcerated in a Philippian gaol (Acts 16:25).

But it was his insights into the suffering of nature and the suffering of God that caught my eye.

Paul was a Jewish rabbi, a Hebrew scholar, fluent in Greek and a Roman Citizen. Born in Tarsus in Asia Minor (now Turkey), he was brought up a strict Pharisee and was originally anti-Christian.

Converted through his "Damascus Road experience", he spent three years in Arabia and a further period in Tarsus, before proclaiming the Christian message of Jesus the Messiah.

Being the first to record the meaning of the Gospel, Paul showed the glory of belief in heaven, and also the truth that Jesus the Messiah did not die alone.

Jesus is not a third party who stands between God and us. It was "God in Christ" who suffered and died at Calvary, for Jesus Christ was both human and divine – both man and God.

"Jesus" means "God saves", while his title, "Emmanuel" means "God is with us."

In his letters to Corinth, Paul declares that those joined to Christ are new creations and that "all this is done by God," for "God was in Christ, reconciling the world unto himself" (**2 Corinthians** 5:18-19 KJV).

Later, in his letter to Colossae, Paul explains the love of God, that "it was God's own decision that the Son has in Himself the full nature of God. Through the Son, then, God decided to bring the whole universe back to Himself. God made peace through his Son's sacrificial death on the Cross" (1: 19-20 GNB).

John Stott comments, "What we see, then, in the drama of the cross is not three actors but two, ourselves on the one hand and God on the other.

Not God as he is in himself (the Father), but God nevertheless, God-made-man-in-Christ (the Son).

Hence the importance of those **New Testament** passages which speak of the death of Christ as the death of God's Son… for in giving his Son he was giving himself" (John Stott, **The Cross of Christ**: Intervarsity Press).

God is not only the creator of the universe who allows His creation to suffer, but He is also the fellow-sufferer who enters His own hell of abandonment on the cross. He suffers because He is Love.

As Jesus cries out, "My God, why have you forsaken me?" as he, God the divine Son, experiences His own god-forsakenness, he also shares in the god- forsakenness of all humanity.

Yet, it was at that very moment, says Paul, that "God was in Christ, reconciling the world to Himself."

The Father's own agony as He sees the agony of His dying and abandoned Son, shares the agony and pain of untold millions. This is God, the Trinity – Father, Son and Holy Spirit – involved in the cruel and perverse injustice of humanity.

Paul uses the term "Lord" over 130 times. In addition, he also uses it in combination ("Our Lord Jesus Christ," "Our Lord," "Jesus Christ our Lord") a further 83 times.

"Lord" was the standard title for the Roman Emperor, as well as the title for a judge, the master of a slave and the title of the gods – "My Lord Zeus".

In the Greek version of the **Old Testament** "Lord" is the pseudonym for "*Yahweh*," whilst in the **New Testament** it is used of ordinary people (**Matthew** 21:30).

Of Christ, however, the title "Lord" means something more – it links him to God.

Luke regarded him as the Messiah when he penned the angelic message; "Unto you is born this day in the city of David, a Saviour who is Christ the Lord." (2:11 KJV)

The Apostle Peter refers to the "Lord and Saviour, Jesus Christ" (**2 Peter** 1:11; 2:20 and 3:2 KJV and GNB). The Lord was the divinely appointed king, the majestic, imperial Messiah.

Paul refers to "the Lord" (**1 Corinthians** 7:10) and to the table of the Lord. He writes that true believers must confess, "Jesus is Lord" (**Romans** 10:9 NIV). There is "one Lord, one faith, one baptism" (**Ephesians** 4:5 GNB).

God is also called "Lord" over 150 times in the **New Testament** (e.g. "The Glory of the Lord shone round about them" – the shepherds - in **Luke** 2). Christ and God are inseparably linked.

God is involved with our universe, our galaxy, our solar system, our world, our country and our own lives. He is involved in Christ through and in the cross. He has made human beings with the freedom to live without Him. He has given them free choice with all the risks that involves.

Karl Barth, the Swiss theologian, has stated that the ultimate Lordship of God lies precisely in His own FREEDOM to be and do what He chooses.

As God is in Christ on the Cross, we humans can know a God who freely chooses to humble himself, endure the horrors of Calvary and face death.

God is never more the Sovereign Lord than when he voluntarily goes to the cross to demonstrate that He has the same dangerous freedom of choice that He has given his creation.

In his deep doctrinal letter to Rome, Paul expounds the evil of humanity. He condemns the violence, idolatry, slavery and social dominance of evil people; then he condemns the religious Romans, as well as the Jews who fail to keep their own Laws.

"All have sinned and come short of the glory of God," he proclaims (3:23 KJV).

Furthermore, "the wages of sin is death, but the gift of God is eternal life through Jesus Christ His Son" (6:23 KJV).

Paul explains throughout chapter 8 that Jesus is the risen Christ, which shows there is now no condemnation for those who live in union with the risen Lord. For God has sent His Holy Spirit to deliver us from defeatist attitudes, and to assure us that we really are loved as children of God (1-4). The Holy Spirit changes the way Christians think (5-9); gives a renewed enthusiasm for living (9-11); leads us as children of God (14- 15); and reveals the hope of the future (18).

Christian people are not promised immunity from pain and suffering.

Rather, they are subject to trials, bondage and servitude, attended by pain, sorrow and death.

Paul states that all nature is in the same condition; it is part of the universal system of things; it accords with everything we see – "change and decay in all around I see" – and we should not be surprised if the world in which Christians live is also in bondage, imperfection and sorrow.

All creation is pictured as sighing for deliverance from decay and death. Its agonizing cries, like that of child-birth, suggest intense suffering

Paul states in **Romans** 8, that "All of creation waits with eager longing for God to reveal his children." Creation, condemned to frustration, will one day "be set free from its slavery to decay," (18-22 GNB).

Paul writes with a poetic vision of all nature suffering anguish and pain while awaiting God's glory.

It is this horrific suffering that Paul declares is "not worthy to be compared with the glory that shall be revealed" (18 GNB).

Suffering may be great, but it is incomparable in the light of future glory. Suffering is nothing in degree, or in duration. Suffering is but for a moment, whereas the heavenly condition will last for eternity.

Suffering, according to Paul, narrows into insignificance when compared with God's love. He can conquer the utmost fear, for if God did not spare His own Son, but let Him die in agony and shame, then God's love must surely be beyond comprehension.

As Paul puts it, "Shall trouble or hardship or persecution or famine or nakedness or danger or sword" separate from God's love?

"No!" he exclaims, quoting **Psalm** 44:22, "For [God's] sake we are in danger of death at all times; we are treated like sheep that are going to be slaughtered.

Indeed, the God who loves us, claims Paul, gives complete victory over death. The great crescendo that concludes this passage is among the most lyrical of Paul's utterances:

> "For I am certain that nothing can separate us from His love: neither death nor life, neither angels nor other heavenly rulers or powers, neither the present nor the future, neither the world above nor the world below – there is nothing in all creation that will ever be able to separate us from the love of God which is ours through Christ Jesus our Lord" (37-39 GNB).

Does God care? Is He callous? Paul answers that God loves His creation so desperately that He entered into this world of suffering and pain to experience it for Himself.

He offers hope of the resurrection, hope for the wonders of a future life. He is indeed the fellow sufferer who enters His own hell of suffering and abandonment.

Richard Wurmbrand tells of a prison officer who beat a prisoner, stating: "I am almighty, as you suppose your God to be. I can kill you."

The Christian replied "The real power is all on my side, for I can love while you torture me to death."

God suffers with the tortured. How does God fare today? "He suffers greatly. Our Creator, our Father in heaven suffers," says Wurmbrand. "He is tortured still. What Christians endure becomes His pain. They are His body." (**Where Christ Still Suffers**: Marshall Pickering).

Wurmbrand spent fourteen years in Rumanian prisons, much of it in solitary confinement. Eventually, diagnosed with tuberculosis, he was imprisoned in a hospital where terminally ill patients spent their last tortured hours.

As a Lutheran Pastor, Wurmbrand ministered to the spiritual needs of the patients and praised God for the opportunity to give hope to the dying.

Asked what he had learnt in prison, he said "That God loves me."

And that is the message of the Apostle Paul.

Nothing in this universe, let alone this world, can separate us from the Love of God in Christ Jesus.

This God truly Suffers in and with us.

Chapter 24

The Inexpressible Images that Baffle

In his "Translator's Preface" to **The Book of Revelation** (Geoffrey Bles), J.B. Phillips states, "The translator can hardly fail to sense the urgency of the Seer as he tries to express the inexpressible."

Films such as "Apocalypse Now" or "The Four Horsemen of the Apocalypse" are well known images of war and death. **Revelation** is the Apocalypse par excellence - the true Revelation of the Day of Judgment.

I knew all the symbols of horror and death, bloodshed and famine, lakes of fire and beasts rising from the sea, so I turned to the book with enthusiasm to see what it had to offer concerning suffering and pain.

But as I came to **Revelation** again, I discovered something quite different from all my expectations.

I found the theme of the book revealed in the first verse: "This is a Revelation of Jesus Christ."

Despite its apparent obsession with death and destruction, I became aware of the "Lamb upon his throne", controlling and encouraging the faithful.

The book was written to seven Asian churches undergoing severe persecution.

The writer was exiled to Patmos, an island off the coast of Turkey, noted for its enslaved salt-miners. He had seen his nation (the Jews) utterly destroyed by Roman troops, and probably wrote during the persecutions of the Roman Emperor Domitian.

Like **Daniel,** the book is highly symbolic, expounding dreams and visions with grotesque and inconsistent symbols, such as Jesus pictured as a branch, a lion and a slain lamb with seven horns and seven eyes (**Revelation**, Chapter 5).

Probably the symbolism and imagery used, discouraged hostile readers from attempting to fathom the meaning, for it is self-evident that the symbols used of "Mystery Babylon" and the rise of the Beast represent the Roman Empire, although a Roman censor would probably be confused and not realize this on a first reading.

Almost all the symbols come from the **Old Testament** so would be intelligible only to Jewish Christians.

The four beasts and the New Jerusalem come from **Ezekiel**, the two witnesses from **Zechariah**, the number seven and its synonyms from **Daniel**, the description of the New Heaven and Earth from **Isaiah**.

Numbers are symbols, too. Seven candle sticks, seven horns, seven eyes, seven churches, seven angels, seven vials seven seals, seven plagues and seven trumpets, together with the mysterious mark of the beast (six, six, six) form one such group of numbers.

Twelve tribes, twelve apostles, twelve fruit, twelve precious stones, twenty-four elders, a hundred and forty-four cubits, a hundred and forty-four furlongs and a hundred and forty-four thousand saints on Mount Zion form another.

Ten and its multiples are found in ten days of tribulation, ten horns, one thousand years when Satan is bound (10x10x10), and ten thousand times ten thousand worshippers.

Many fantastic and grotesque interpretations of these symbols have been made by past and present generations.

Halley's Bible Handbook originally saw the vision of "locusts with women's hair" (9:8) as predicting the rise of Mohammed who led his troops from Arabia (the land of the locust) with their long (women's) hair swirling behind them. Others have interpreted the Great Red Dragon (12:3) as Soviet Russia, while Sun Myung Moon, who founded the Unification Church in South Korea, claims the Red Dragon to be North Korea and the woman clothed with the sun and the moon (12:1) to be his own mother, hence "Sun" and "Moon" in his own name.

I was not only concerned with the symbolism and interpretation problems, but also with the question of "when?"

Was **Revelation** written only for the contemporary situation, was it written just for the seven churches named, with no relevance (apart from historical interest) to the

Christian Church of today, or is it a prophecy of the future alone – a kind of prediction chart for the Second Coming of Christ and the end of the World, as **The Schofield Reference Bible** advocates.

Some suggest that it is a continuous prediction of historical progress, with Mohammed, Napoleon, Hitler and others in their supposed respective place in the apocalyptic drama of world events.

Others see it as a beautiful poetic setting for the theme of good triumphing over evil, on a par with Milton's **Paradise Lost** and **Paradise Regained**.

It is clear to me that the book was written for particular Christians undergoing persecution, suffering and pain during Roman oppression.

Yet its principles apply to the universal church of which the seven are a sample – the triumphant and glorified Christ and his church will emerge from the horror of evil and demonic world powers.

THE VISION OF DANIEL'S SON OF MAN

John commences his book with the risen Christ. He sees Him as supreme behind and in the midst of the visions.

The first vision is of the risen Jesus, like Daniel's Son of Man clothed in splendid finery. With white hair (suggesting age and purity), fiery eyes (indicating His all-seeing, penetrating look) and holding seven stars, Christ is seen walking among seven golden candlesticks.

Jesus interprets the seven stars as being "seven messengers" and the seven candlesticks as "seven churches. Jesus is described as "the faithful witness, the first to be raised from the dead and who is also the ruler of the kings of the world" (1:5 GNB).

SUFFERING AND DEATH-
THE VICTOR'S CROWN

Seven letters are written to the churches. Each letter reveals a different aspect of the risen Christ, each promises a reward to the faithful, and each emphasises a different feature of the church – love, suffering, holiness, sound teaching, genuineness, evangelism and humility, suggests Dr. John Stott in **What Christ Thinks of the Church** (Lutterworth).

The second letter, to Smyrna in Turkey, from the "one who is the Alpha and Omega (the beginning and the end), who died and lived again", is the only one concerned with suffering, so I have omitted discussion of the other six.

Poverty, false accusation, imprisonment, trouble lasting "ten days", and ultimately "death" are predicted to the Smyrnan church.

Nevertheless, the Smyrnan Christians are encouraged to "be faithful" for they will be given "life as your prize of victory" and a promise that they will not suffer a "second death" (2:8-11 KJV).

Although only a short letter, every word is meaningful. Christ is the creator (the beginning) and the Messianic King (the end), whose death and resurrection was not unlike the history of Smyrna itself.

Destroyed as a city by Lydian invaders in about 600 BC, Smyrna had lain empty for over two hundred years until Lysimachus rebuilt it roughly 400 years before Christ. It was a wealthy city with daily games in its amphitheater.

There was poverty among Christians who often came from lower sections of society, some even as slaves, and they were falsely accused of heinous crimes.

Many Christians were charged with cannibalism because of their sacrament, "eating and drinking Christ," in bread and wine.

They were charged with sexual orgies because they called the Holy Communion the "Agape", which meant "love feast"; and they were accused of being atheists and traitors because they worshipped an "invisible" God and refused to worship the Roman Emperor.

Nero and Domitian imprisoned Christians on a large scale – "the trouble lasting for ten days". "Ten days" is symbolic of a short period of time or a "complete time". The number ten, like all the other numbers in **Revelation** is not to be taken literally.

One of the Bishops of Smyrna, Polycarp, was martyred in AD 155 after being betrayed by a tortured slave, during the Roman Games. Winners in the arena were awarded a crown of laurel leaves, and the martyrs of Smyrna were to be crowned as victors with a crown of joyous life (2:10).

This would be the end of suffering. The faithful of Smyrna would be raised to life with no "second death". The crown of life brought fullness of living. The term "second death" is found nowhere outside Revelation (20:6,14 and 21:8 KJV).

When the victors reached the end of life and found themselves in the paradise to come, there would be nothing else to hurt or harm.

The Christ who was dead understands the meaning of horror and suffering and has experienced its limits, yet He is also the "risen Christ which was dead and is alive."

POWERHOUSE OF THE UNIVERSE

Following the seven letters comes a vision of the Powerhouse of the Universe.

A beautiful stately throne surrounded by a rainbow holds a Great King surrounded by twenty-four elders who cast their own crowns before Him, then worship Him for His power in creation.

The Four creatures from **Ezekiel** with lion, bull, human and eagle faces, covered by six wings and a multitude of eyes, praise the Lord God Almighty.

The Almighty King holds a scroll with seven seals, but no one is capable of loosening the seals and opening the scroll.

At this point, one described as the Lion of the Tribe of Judah, the root of David offers to open the seals.

John sees that "[a] Lamb had appeared to be killed. It had seven horns and seven eyes" (5:1-6). The Lamb takes the scroll, while the twenty-four elders worship him with harps and incense bowls. The elders sing that the Lamb is worthy to open the seals because he was killed as a sacrifice to bring all beings to serve God.

Ten thousand times ten thousand angels also worship the Lamb, followed by a chorus of living creatures.

One thing that became obvious to me in **Revelation** is the clear repetition not only of ideas, but also of words, symbols and numbers.

The numbers, for example, can hardly be regarded as mathematical or statistical.

Seven is the most used number. The "seven eyes" probably allude to **Zechariah** 4:10, "The seven lamps are the seven eyes of the Lord, which see over all the earth."

Seven also occurs in **Daniel** 12, "Seventy sevens". Here the seven seals, seven angels, seven lamp stands and so on, have been taken to mean "completeness", just as the ancient Hebrews thought of the seven days of creation, or talked of the "seven seas" or the seven colours in the rainbow.

Thus, Christ can see with perfect vision – He sees everything – with "seven eyes".

Four seems to refer to the world itself. There were the four winds, the four compass points, "four corners of the earth." Some have suggested that the four living creatures represent creation or "Nature". **Ezekiel** first introduced the four creatures, covered with eyes – all seeing and ever watchful.

Twelve seems to be symbolic of the church. I use "seems", for no one can be sure or dogmatic about some of these apparent symbols. There were twelve tribes of Israel (God's people) and twelve apostles in the **New Testament**.

Here are twenty-four elders (twelve plus twelve); later on, the number hundred and forty-four (twelve times twelve) is mentioned, the New Jerusalem has twelve foundations, its walls are a hundred and forty-four cubits high and it measures a hundred and forty-four thousand furlongs in each direction.

"Elder" is also a name granted to church leaders, so it seems most likely that the "twenty-four elders" represent the Church of the Old and the New Covenants.

With this in mind, the vision shows the crucified and risen Christ, the all-seeing Lamb ruling the world.

No church or member of Christ's church can suffer distress or persecution, suffering or pain without His knowing, for He has "seven eyes." Only He can break the seals on the scroll.

The scroll seems to hold details of human suffering. Perhaps it is the book of human history or a record of just how the world really is.

None can break the seals except The Lamb, and when He does, all Hell breaks loose, resulting in death, bloodshed and famine.

The sovereign Lamb is in total control. Nothing can happen unless He breaks the seal; nothing can happen without Divine permission.

The powerhouse of history, the control of the universe, the authority and meaning of suffering and pain in each generation are seen in the slain Lamb who controls world events.

This is no prophecy of doom and gloom. Here is wonder, awe and hope in the permissive power of the creator of the Universe.

John's first visions set the scene for cosmic intervention in human affairs.

THE HORSEMEN OF THE APOCALYPSE

Four deadly horsemen come with the breaking of the first four seals. The first pale rider on a white horse conquers with military aggression (6:1-2 GNB).

A bright red horse shedding human blood and causing men to engage in warfare follows.

Death and famine follow a black horse, and then a pale horse holding "Death" in its saddle destroys a quarter of the earth's population through "war, famine, disease and wild animals" (6:8 GNB).

When the Lamb breaks the fifth seal, we are immediately aware of the nature of the suffering.

Faithful witnesses, martyrs for their faith, cry out: "Almighty Lord, holy and true! How long will it be until you judge the people on earth and punish them for killing us?" (6:10 GNB).

They are given no answer, just told to rest until the complete number of their fellow Christians has been killed.

The sixth seal brings violent earthquakes, darkens the sun, turns the moon blood red, and causes the stars to disappear and the earth to tremble.

Rulers, military commanders, and all humanity hide in caves calling for deliverance from the judgement of God, as the Day of the Lord becomes "The anger of the Lamb".

Four angels stand at the four corners holding the four winds so that God's people can be sealed on their foreheads. Those bearing the seal number "a hundred and forty-four thousand" (12x12x100), and as John looks, he sees "an enormous crowd – no one could count all the people" (7:9 GNB).

Every nationality is lined up with palm branches to praise the Lamb and cry; "Salvation comes from our God, who sits on the throne, and from the Lamb."

An elder informs John that these multitudes "are the people who have come through the terrible persecution (or the great tribulation). They have washed their robes and made them white in the blood of the Lamb.

Never again will they hunger or thirst; neither sun nor any scorching heat will burn them, because the Lamb, who is in the centre of the throne, will be their shepherd, and he will guide them to springs of life-giving water. And God will wipe every tear from their eyes." (7:14-17 GNB).

Finally, the seventh seal is broken and there is silence in heaven for about half an hour.

INTERPRETING THE FOUR HORSEMEN

My first consideration was to examine the vision of the seven seals and interpret it as I would any other piece of literature. It seems to me that many writers interpret the Bible according to their own prejudices and beliefs. So many interpretations of **Revelation** seem to me to be as absurd as the text itself appears.

In the vision of the broken seals, only one seems to link clearly with the teaching of Jesus himself. When the Lamb breaks the sixth seal, the description given of the coming catastrophe is similar to Jesus' teaching in **Matthew** 24, where Jesus refers to the Coming of the Son of Man.

In attempting to interpret the vision of the seals, therefore, I felt it necessary to begin at the end, with the known, and work backwards.

When Jesus had foretold the destruction of the Temple, his disciples came to him privately to ask when these things would happen and "what will be the signs of the time of your coming and the end of the age?" (**Matthew** 24:3 GNB).

Jesus informs them that numerous false Messiahs (antichrists), false teachers and deceivers will come (**Matthew** 24: 4,5,11 and 23-26 GNB).

There will be wars, rumours of wars, death, famine and earthquakes (6-8). Many will fall from their faith as a result of persecution (9, 10 and 12), and the "Awful Horror of which Daniel Spoke" will stand in the Holy Place. In those days everyone should run to the hills and hide in caves.

Finally, the Son of Man will come like lightning, "the sun will grow dark, the moon will no longer shine, the stars will fall from heaven…and all will see the Son of Man coming in the clouds of heaven with great glory, the great trumpet will sound and he will send his angels to the four corners of the earth, and they will gather his chosen people from one end of the world to the other" (29-31 GNB).

When these things will happen is not disclosed. "No one knows when that day and hour will come," says Jesus, "not the angels in heaven; the Father alone knows" (36 GNB).

Is this a description of the end of the world? Jesus said, "Such things must happen, but they do not mean the end has come…all these are like the first pains of childbirth" (6-8 GNB).

In other words, the future offers warfare, persecution, famine, death, cosmic upheaval and earth-shattering events. These are commonplace events in our world and have always been so.

All these signs have been in the world since the foundation of the Christian church. There have always been wars and rumours of wars just as there have always been earthquakes, famine, pestilence and plague.

The gory appearance of the horsemen of the first four seals reveals events which happen daily all over the world. The four horsemen have been riding over the earth since the dawn of recorded history and will continue to do so.

The angel marks the hundred and forty-four thousand children of God. They represent the church – God's people from Old and New – the same "great multitude which no man could number".

The church has "come out of great tribulation."

It has been delivered from the suffering and pain of this present world, and redeemed by "the blood of the Lamb" (a wonderfully picturesque way of referring to Christ's atonement on the Cross.)

But there is no respite for those suffering pain and persecution. The seals inform us that the church is not protected – certainly not in this world - only at the end, when "the full number of fellow servants and brothers have been killed" (**Revelation** 6:11)

It seems clear to me that the promise in **Revelation** is that sin and evil, suffering and pain, and persecution by demonic powers will continue both in the world, and especially in the church, throughout the entire period of the **New Testament**, from Christ's first coming until his second coming.

Those redeemed at the second coming of Christ (seal six) praise and serve God, who promises no more hunger and thirst.

Pain and suffering cease forever as God wipes away their tears (7:17 GNB and KJV).

The seventh seal results in silence in heaven. Why? I can only speculate.

Silence to contemplate the glory and wonder of the scene disclosed? Or amazement and awe that renders one speechless? Or does John need to get his breath back after the shock of his visions?

All seven seals show that suffering and pain, persecution and natural disaster are part of the world in which we live, and are subject to the authority of the Lamb who controls world events.

THE TRUMPET BLASTS

Seven angels prepare to sound their trumpets. Chapters 8 to 11 reveal the third vision of death and destruction. It follows the prayers of the church, and appears to be a repetition of the vision of the seals.

I had already noted John's use of repetition. For example, John repeats his doxologies. Four times he praises God, but adds to his doxology each time as follows:

- "To Jesus Christ be the glory and power for ever and ever. Amen" (1:6 GNB).
- "Our Lord and God! You are worthy to receive glory, honour and power" (4:11 GNB).
- "To him who sits on the throne and to the Lamb, be praise and honour, glory and might, forever and ever" (5:13 GNB).
- "Amen! Praise, glory, wisdom, thanksgiving, honour, power and might belong to our God forever and ever! Amen!" (7:12 GNB).

John repeats a similar progression in his titles of Jesus:

- "I am the Alpha and Omega, the beginning and the end" (1:8 GNB).
- "I am the First and the Last" (1:17 GNB).
- "I am the alpha and the Omega, the beginning and the end" (21:6 GNB).
- "I am the Alpha and the Omega, the first and the last, the beginning and the end" (22:13 GNB).

This repetition of words, ideas and visions suggests to me that the trumpets warn of the same sufferings that followed the breaking of the seals.

Hail and fire, mingled with blood, fall to the earth destroying one third of it, as the first trumpet warning sounds.

At the second, the sea turns to blood as a volcano is cast into the ocean. The earth's water supply is polluted by a falling star, and many are poisoned on hearing the third trumpet, while the day shortens as the sun darkens in the sky on the sound of the fourth. Here an eagle flies across the sky shouting:

> "O horror! Horror! How horrible it will be for all who live on earth when the sound comes from the trumpets that the other three angels blow" (8:13 GNB).

As the fifth angel blows his trumpet a bottomless pit is opened by a "fallen star" from which locusts looking like horses with men's faces, lions' teeth and women's hair, covered with breastplates and armed with scorpion stings, torture those on earth who are not sealed by God for five months (presumably the life span of a locust plague).

Abaddon or Apollyon – "The Destroyer" is the leader of the locusts (9:11).

John describes evil and horror at its worst, borrowing his images from **Joel**, whose first two chapters described the invasion of locusts as an army attacking on the Day of the Lord.

Here evil, devastation, torture and pain make life on earth fearful and unendurable. But more horror is to come.

As the sixth trumpet sounds, four evil angels are released in order to destroy a third of mankind. They are accompanied by two hundred million mounted troops (9:16), a number of such magnitude that they are really uncountable.

The horses have lions' heads, from which come fire, smoke and sulphur, and snakehead tails that bite to hurt people.

It is here that Christ appears to return. He is called "mighty angel" or "mighty messenger", but the description of a cloud-covered rainbow, "his face like the sun", and the scroll open in his hand suggest the same vision of the "risen Lamb" as at the beginning of **Revelation**.

Roaring like a lion, this angel is answered by seven thunders.

John is told not to write what he hears – perhaps it was too awful to record. The end has come, and John is commanded to eat the scroll, which tastes like honey.

John then measures the temple and is informed that the heathen will take over its outer courts for forty-two months.

Two witnesses will proclaim God's message for 1,260 days. Then the beast will come from the abyss and kill them in the city of Sodom, or Egypt "where their Lord was crucified". They will die for three and a half days, and then be raised to life and taken up to Heaven.

A violent earthquake will leave 7,000 people dead.

Just as the horrors of the first trumpets repeat in intensity so do those of the seals. In this sixth trumpet we have the return of Christ.

Here the two witnesses appear to be symbols of the church.

Jesus sent out his disciples in twos (Luke 10:1), and Jesus promised that his faithful followers would be made pillars in the temple of the New Jerusalem (3:12). There were only two pillars in the Temple.

The witnesses come from **Zechariah** 4 where by the side of the seven lamp-stands ("the seven eyes of the Lord") are two olive trees described as "the two men whom God has chosen and anointed to serve him, the Lord of the whole earth" (verse 14).

These two candlestick-witnesses shining before the world signify the church of Jesus Christ, and their function is to witness to the world, informing all people that the calamities of their age are Divine warnings.

The description of the witnesses dying in Sodom and Egypt "where also our Lord is crucified" shows that the vision is to be understood figuratively, for Christ was not crucified in Sodom or Egypt.

Instead, it seems a reminder that the church must bear the sufferings of Christ in a sin-ridden world. As Christ was rejected in his day, so will the church be in a world that is no different from Sodom and Egypt, places associated with evil in the **Old Testament**.

The reason why these two places are mentioned as the site of Jesus' crucifixion instead of Jerusalem appears to be that Jerusalem always stands for "The New Jerusalem" (the Church) in **Revelation**, whereas the literal city of Jerusalem had been judged by God and destroyed in AD 70, as corrupt as Sodom and Egypt.

The church, however, is raised to life – raised with Christ – the triumphant and victorious church that the Roman Empire could not destroy.

Measuring the Temple is also mentioned in **Zechariah** 2, again symbolic of the church, which is the new Temple of God.

First it is counted, then measured, both emphasising the security of God's children. This measuring of the Temple also takes place in a later vision.

The use of time is also symbolic. Forty-two months, and 1,260 days are each three and a half years. The witnesses die for three and a half days. Later there is a mention of "time, times and half a time" (three and a half again?). Each of these periods is half Daniel's "sevens". If "seven" is completeness, then three and a half is complete time cut in half. Perhaps it is the second half of history, the period of the New Covenant, or again the period of the church; just as the first half was the period of the Old Covenant, the period of Israel's history.

Finally, as the seventh trumpet sounds, the end of the age comes.

The Lord and his Messiah reign forever, and are worshipped by the twenty-four elders who throw themselves face downwards to worship as the time arrives for God's faithful ones to be rewarded and those who corrupt the earth to be destroyed.

The new Temple is seen opened in Heaven, again referring symbolically to the church, and the Covenant Box is shown as a reminder of God's New Covenant (11:19 GNB).

THE SEVEN-HEADED DRAGON FIGHTS THE TWELVE-STARRED WOMAN

A totally new series of visions appears in the heavens. A woman, dressed in the sun with the moon under her feet and wearing a crown of twelve stars, is heard crying with the pain and suffering of childbirth.

Before her is a huge red dragon with seven crowned heads and ten horns who destroys a third of the stars with his tail.

The dragon is waiting to eat her new born child, but the son who is born to "rule over all nations" is snatched away to the throne of God, while the woman flees to the desert where she is protected for 1,260 days (the three- and-a-half-year period again).

Once more, I was reminded of the words of Jesus that wars will be fought, and famines and earthquakes will be "like the first pains of childbirth" (**Matthew** 24:8 GNB).

I also wondered if John had taken his vision from the story of Joseph in the **Old Testament**, for Joseph dreamed of the sun and the moon with eleven stars bowing down before him. It was a dream of the whole family of Israel.

Here the link with the Joseph story suggests that the woman symbolises Israel as well as the church, for it was from an Israelite girl, Mary, that Jesus the Messiah was born.

The child taken to God must be the Messiah and the woman in the wilderness is thus the persecuted church for the Gospel age.

A second vision reveals war in heaven between Michael and his angels who defeat the red dragon and his angels.

The dragon is identified as the ancient serpent, the Satan (the accuser in **Job**) who is cast down to earth.

There is a reference in the "ancient serpent" to the story of Eve and the serpent turned out of Paradise. There is a cry from Heaven that the accuser of the Christians, together with all his angels, is thrown out of heaven.

God's salvation has come, and the power of the God-king and His Messiah is revealed. The earth continues to suffer for a "little time" (the three and a half years?).

Now the dragon begins to pursue the woman who has given birth to the boy, but she is given two eagle's wings to fly to the desert where she is comforted for three and a half years.

The dragon attempts to drown the woman with a flood from his mouth, but the earth opens up its mouth to swallow the water and save her. The dragon is so angry he fights the rest of her descendants (i.e. the church).

It appears that these three visions are repetitions of the previous visions. John repeats himself time and again.

The church is constantly suffering with Christ and endures persecution, but the Satan is a defeated foe. Surely this powerlessness of the evil one is the same as the millennium of chapter 20 when Satan is bound for a thousand years – an indefinite period of time, here shown as "three and a half years."

Malcolm Muggeridge once said, "Satan is a defeated foe – the war with evil is over - but we (the church) are still engaged in a bitter mopping-up operation."

No matter what the trial, hardships, persecution, suffering and pain, the powers of evil are powerless against the advance of the Gospel – for the Lamb is on the throne. The church may be in the wilderness, but it is there protected from annihilation by the power of God.

THE MARK OF THE BEAST – 666

The dragon stands by the sea, from which emerges a beast with ten horns and seven heads with blasphemous names written on each.

The beast is a leopard with a lion's mouth and bear's feet. One of the heads seems fatally wounded, but the wound has healed (13:3).

As the dragon gives his power and authority to the beast, everyone on earth worships the dragon as well as the beast. The beast has authority for forty- two months, (three and a half years) during which time it curses God and defeats God's people.

The Saints written in the Lamb's Book of Life refuse to worship the dragon or beast. They are encouraged to endure and exercise faith, for many will surely be captured or killed (13:10). As the beast has already been mentioned in John's earlier vision (11:4), it seems self-evident that the events recorded are not chronological, but repetitions of earlier visions from Different perspectives.

This beast reminds me of the four beasts that came out of the sea in **Daniel** 7. One had four heads and another ten horns – they stood for nations or empires with powerful armies.

So many interpreters look for predictions of the future. I am sure that John's Jewish readers would recognise how much John is quoting from the Prophets and the **Old Testament Apocalypse.** They would see the beast as a contemporary evil empire, notably Rome.

A second beast rises from the earth. This one has two horns like a lamb, but with a dragon's voice (13:11). This false lamb uses magic to force everyone to worship the first beast. All people have to receive a mark on their right hand or forehead in order to buy or sell.

John states: "This calls for wisdom. Whoever is intelligent can work out the meaning of the number of the beast, because the number stands for a human name. Its number is 666" (13:18 GNB).

So much has been written of the number "666". Tolstoy, in his War and Peace suggested that the value of the letters in the name "Emperor Napoleon" added to 666. The Reformers suggested that 666 referred to the Pope. More recently, the astronauts on Apollo 8 were called 666 because Lovell, Anders and Borman each had six letters in their names.

Similarly, Ronald Wilson Reagan has six letters in each of his names.

The earliest mention of 666 comes from Irenaus who claimed that the letters of "Lateinos" (Latin Kingdom or Rome) added up to the mysterious number, while others have tried to link the number to Nero ("Neron Kesar").

But numbers in **Revelation** are not usually taken to have secret, mystical and coded puzzle meanings that sap human intelligence. They are grouped according to patterns already known.

"Seventy sevens" from Daniel; three and a half and 1,200 days which are half of "seven"; twelve and twenty- four and a hundred and forty-four; together with tens, thousands and thousands of thousands – these are consistent throughout the book as symbols which are clearly understandable.

Six is one short of seven, the perfect number. If seven symbolises "completeness" and "perfection" then six is "incomplete" and "imperfect". Surely 666 is a trinity of imperfection - failure upon failure upon failure.

It is described as the number of a man, for man was created on the sixth day. Here, 666 is a coded symbol for the beast, just as 7 is the coded symbol for the whole history of the world from Israel's Old Covenant to the end of the Church Age.

Seven is a "spiritual" reality, perfection - six is merely human, imperfect.

There is no doubt in my mind that the false beast requiring worship refers to the Caesar Cult and Emperor worship.

Christians were forced to worship the Emperor and those who refused faced execution. Priests of the Caesar cult were fond of charms and conjuring tricks.

Jesus had warned his own disciples that false Messiahs and false prophets would perform miracles and wonders to deceive God's people (**Matthew** 24:24).

REASSURANCE IN A PAIN-RIDDEN WORLD

If apocalyptic literature tends to be only pessimistic and gloomy, that cannot be said of **Revelation**. The setting is the Risen Lamb, the Messiah ruling from his throne. After a series of horrendous visions, John takes his readers back in Chapter 14, to the Lamb standing on Mount Zion with the 144,000 saints, the four beasts and the twenty- four elders all singing a new song of redemption.

This company have had their sins forgiven and are treated as perfect, sinless human beings.

Three angels appear. The first proclaims good news to the whole world that God will judge wrongdoing. The angel proclaims the "Gospel".

There is only one Gospel – it is the good news of God's redeeming love, and the message that evil cannot triumph as the Lamb is in control.

Next, an angel announces the fall of Babylon (which seems rather early as Babylon is not introduced until the next set of visions), while the third warns that those who worship the Beast will suffer torment in fire and sulphur in front of the holy angels and the Lamb. The smoke of the tormenting fires will smoulder forever without relief of any kind.

All who die in God's service, however, are promised rest and happiness.

SEVEN LAST PLAGUES

Then the second coming of Christ is proclaimed (14:14) as the world is harvested to save the good and destroy the bad. The grapes of wrath are squeezed in "the winepress of God's furious anger" and the blood pours from the press in a flood

1,600 furlongs long and as high as a horse's saddle. Such horror can only indicate total and complete judgement.

The Christians to whom John was writing would know nothing clearer than that the power of Rome was slowly destroying the life of the church.

To them were given visions of Satan and the State trying their worst, only to be thwarted by the power of the Lamb, showing that no power on earth could stop the advance of the Gospel.

Even those who understood the message and endured to the end did not realize how short a time would elapse before the whole Roman Empire was to become nominally Christian!

Now seven angels appear with seven last plagues, held in bowls. Again, they are similar to the seven seals and trumpets.

The outpoured bowls produce painful sores, maritime calamities, rivers of blood, burning from the sun, darkness and pain, a dried up river and the final judgement of God.

Again, during the sixth plague, when the Euphrates dries up, the second coming of Christ takes place "like a thief" (16:15), just as in the sixth seal and trumpet.

THE GREAT PROSTITUTE

A new vision of a prostitute sitting on a red beast with seven heads and ten horns raises her goblet of obscenity and immorality. She is clothed in scarlet and drunk with the blood of God's people. She has been responsible for the persecution and execution of the faithful.

The angel informs John that the seven heads are really "seven hills on which the woman sits. They are also seven kings: five of them have fallen, one still rules, and the other has not yet come" (17:9-10 GNB). In addition, the ten horns are kings who will rule "for one hour".

The Lamb, who is "King of kings" and Lord of lords, together with his faithful, chosen followers, will defeat them. The sea is described as the "nations, peoples, races and languages" (17:15 GNB).

After this amazing scene a cry arises: "Great Babylon has fallen" (18:2). While the world laments the destruction of the woman, the saints are told to rejoice because God has avenged them (18:20).

Again, the twenty-four elders and four beasts return to praise God for his righteous judgments.

The scene now changes to the marriage supper of the Lamb (which does not come to fruition until the next vision) where John sees the wife of the Lamb arrayed in white.

A white horse with the faithful and true one (Jesus) is to judge with a sharp sword coming from his mouth to destroy the armies of the world. Armageddon is to take place again. The dragon is taken and bound for a thousand years.

The martyrs reign with Christ for the thousand-year period, and then Satan is released to deceive the nations but is devoured by fire, and cast with his troops into a "lake of fire and brimstone" together with the beast and the false lamb.

Finally, a great white throne appears and the entire world is judged. Those not in the Lamb's book of life join the dragon in the lake of fire.

Here the visions of judgement end.

I feel sure that the persecuted and suffering Christians for whom John wrote could find nothing more stimulating, exciting and at the same time so encouraging as visions of this nature. The clear inference is that the powers of evil will meet with their destruction by the hand of the risen Saviour.

The woman on seven hills was Rome. Rome was "drunk with the blood of the martyrs." John uses the language of **Isaiah** 13 – the fall of ancient Babylon – to describe the fall of Rome. The kings were the Emperors of the Roman Empire.

Of course, John had to be careful, at a time of severe persecution from the Roman authorities, not to mention Rome or the Empire by name!

John told his readers to work the meaning out for themselves. He states, "This calls for wisdom and understanding. The seven heads are seven hills" (17:9 GNB).

Rome will rule "only for a little time" (17:10 GNB), and the kings "for one hour" (17:12 GNB). John was emphasising the short, negligible period of time before "Great Babylon" – Rome – would fall.

Nothing quite matches the utter horror of the war in which the Lamb destroys the beast and false prophet and casts them and their followers into the lake of fire.

Yet to the suffering church, such a vision brought comfort and joy. The Saints understood their Lord and Saviour would triumph over the powers of hell.

Saint Augustine referred the binding of Satan for the thousand years as being the same as Jesus binding the strong man in **Matthew** 12:29.

There is no logical reason for taking the thousand years as a literal period of time, given that all other numbers in this apocalypse seem to possess symbolic meaning.

The "thousand" years is not a millennium, it is another way of expressing the length of the New Covenant age of the church on earth in the same way that the "forty-two months" or the "three and a half years" do.

Satan bound for a period also suggests the same circumstances depicted in the vision of the dragon in Chapter 12, where the serpent opens his mouth to devour the church but the ground opens up to save her.

Both visions reveal the powerlessness of evil to stop the spread of God's Kingdom. Satan's influence is curtailed so evil is unable to prevent the spread of the Gospel.

Those who are martyred, reign with Christ for the same period. They are with their Saviour during the continuance of Christ's church on earth.

It must be realised that, when Satan is released and gathers the nations to war, all the followers of the beast have already been annihilated (in Chapter 19). This battle and the judgement before the throne must, therefore, be another aspect of the previous visions.

Again, I could only recognize the overlapping repetition that occurs.

John has only one thing in mind – the complete destruction of all evil whether the Imperial forces of Rome, anti-Christian forces of Emperor worship, sinful humanity or the Devil himself. They are all condemned and destroyed by the power of the risen Christ – the Lamb.

The victory of a great, righteous, holy and omnipotent God is one to inspire and encourage the faithful.

But the greatest vision is still to come.

THE NEW HEAVEN THE NEW EARTH

When I first read John Milton's **Paradise Lost**, I found his description of Satan to be among the best in literature. So powerful were the images of innocence and light, that when I eventually read **Paradise Regained**, I found it tame and vastly inferior to the previous epic.

Following on from the multiple repetitive visions of judgement, I found nothing to compare with the final vision of **Revelation**.

John ends not with a negative image of utter destruction of evil, but with the ultimate joy, victory and wonder that awaits the saints of God.

The sea of evil has disappeared, and a New Heaven and New Earth appear. The New Jerusalem descends from Heaven dressed as a bride.

A promise issues from the heavenly throne "I will make all things new" (21:5 GNB). God promises to dwell eternally with His people, removing all tears, pain and death. The Saints will inherit all things and be called God's children.

Transported to a mountain, John witnesses the descent of the New Jerusalem encompassed by God's glory.

He describes the city in a remarkable way, composed entirely of multiples of twelve. There are twelve gates, guarded by twelve angels. The names of the twelve tribes of Israel are written on the gates. Twelve foundations containing the names of the twelve apostles are described.

Then the city is measured. The length, width and height are each twelve thousand furlongs, while the city wall is a hundred and forty-four cubits high. Twelve precious jewels sparkle from the foundations of the city. In the centre of the street from which flows "living water" there are twelve different fruits from the tree of life.

Once in an antiquarian bookshop I saw the grotesque plans of a pyramidal city built 5,000 miles long, by 5,000 wide and 5,000 miles to the apex pointing into outer space.

One wide street spiralled from the apex 5,000 miles high in descending concentric circles to eventually traverse the huge base. Such a city could only be built in the United States of America, proclaimed the author as he interpreted John's description literally.

Clearly, we are dealing with symbolism. Constant repetition of "twelve" and "a hundred and forty-four" show that John means the church.

He makes it even plainer by references to the names of the twelve tribes of Israel (21:12) and of the twelve apostles of the Lamb (21:14). The church is built on the foundation of the apostles. But the church is continuous with the revelation of the **Old Testament**, hence the names of the twelve tribes on the gates.

William Barclay suggests the twelve gates surely stand for the catholicity of the church. There are twelve ways into the city of God. Not one but twelve. There is no one exclusive way into God's kingdom (**The Revelation of John**: Volume 2, Saint Andrew Press).

This seems similar to the meaning of the parables of the Kingdom of Heaven mentioned by Jesus in **Matthew.** While human salvation is only available through the crucifixion of Christ, there may be a dozen ways through the gates of the Kingdom.

The Lamb promises to "come quickly" and to reward everyone according to his work.

Then the spirit and the bride say, "come", while the Lamb again promises, "Surely, I come quickly. Amen."

Finally, the whole book finishes with the prayer of faith, "Even so, come Lord Jesus" (22:20 KJV).

Since the fall of mankind into sin, humanity has failed to enjoy true fellowship with God.

Here the promise is that in the New Jerusalem, all will once more enjoy the fruits of the tree of life, lost in the original Paradise, and know and enjoy fellowship with the God and Father of all.

To a suffering and persecuted church, this is the ultimate climax - to know and understand that their labour, suffering, pain, persecution and patient endurance are not in vain.

This vision amplifies in multimedia-imagery the Pauline statement that the sufferings of this present world are not worthy to be compared with the glory that shall be revealed.

That glory is nothing less than the eternal fellowship with God, Himself.

To John's readers the message was simple, "Surely, I come quickly", and the heartfelt prayer of the suffering faithful can be summed up in "Even so, come Lord Jesus."

SUMMARY

I had found new meaning in suffering.

Suffering results from evil world systems and uncontrollable evil powers. It is inevitable in a godless world, and the church is called to endure suffering and pain in identifying with the slain and risen Lamb.

At the same time, God is still in control. He and the Lamb are on the throne of the Universe, and eventually good will triumph, for God is supreme, guiding and guarding the church from annihilation. Eventually the powers of evil will be destroyed, and the faithful will know the wonder and glory of the revelation that Christ has in store for His church.

Christ is revealed as the slain and risen Lamb. The two witnesses, the church, die with their crucified Lord. While Job learnt to love and worship and trust a God he knew little of, the early Christians to whom John wrote had learnt to love, worship and trust the God who had come to this earth to tread the path of suffering, pain and death Himself.

Everything in the last vision is "new". Just as Christian conversion is said to make people "new creatures" and Jesus spoke of the "new birth", so "all things are made new".

This is the "new heaven and the new earth", together with the "new bride". It is fresh, holy, unspoiled, and pure like a new bride.

How inadequate are the words used to describe the inexpressible!

* * * * *

My study of the **Bible** had ended. The puzzle was beginning to reveal a picture of God's love.

The Old Testament has shown how suffering was often a test of piety and goodness as well as being a punishment for sin or evil. It revealed God's way of moulding spiritual and moral character, and showed it was possible to trust God without understanding His eternal designs.

God is not only beyond human reasoning, but he is omnipotent and wise in new and exciting ways.

Job showed that outside forces do not control us – we each respond in our own way. We are free to choose. There is no dualism in our universe, no spiritual schizophrenia.

The leaders of Judah and Israel lived lives of opulence and greed, causing the prophets to increasingly predict coming Judgement, "The Day of the Lord."

Much of this was self-fulfilling prophecy in which human action reaps its just deserts.

Injustice, oppression, arrogance, moral corruption, fertility prostitution and child sacrificial murder made the politically and morally lax state ripe for outside intervention.

The climax of **Old Testament** answers comes with the revelation that God is His own suffering servant in **Isaiah**. The Day of the Lord now becomes not Judgement Day, but The Day of Salvation.

The stump of Jesse regrowing in dry ground, the remnant to be used for salvation, the young woman about to give birth to "Emmanuel" - the child born, the son given, the wonderful counsellor, the everlasting father, the Prince of Peace, the one from David's line – all predict the coming of God's Messiah, His servant, who paradoxically comes in the form of God, Himself.

Jesus of Nazareth claimed to fulfill these prophecies. The Kingdom of God is not physical but spiritual – it becomes the Kingdom of Heaven in which God's glory is revealed in His own suffering.

Jesus claimed to be the Messiah, the Christ, as "The Good Shepherd who is willing to die for His sheep."

Jesus revealed that God does care. He entered this world of suffering and death as the suffering servant. God is a fellow sufferer who enters His own hell of abandonment as He causes His only beloved Son to cry, "My God, why have you forsaken me?"

The question was not answered, for it is unanswerable. The God who apparently abandoned His own Son, was in reality, "in Christ" suffering with and for His creatures.

To those philosophers who think of God as immutable, without feeling, comes an even greater surprise.

God not only feels pain, suffering, torture, and abandonment "in all points like us;" but He also feels joyous excitement.

Jesus told numerous parables about the happiness of God. He is a father who "rushes to meet His prodigal son," a wife who shouts for joy and calls in her neighbours because she finds a lost coin from a wedding bracelet, a shepherd who calls a party to celebrate the finding of a lost sheep.

Jesus spoke of wedding feasts, of a king who invites the lowest of the low to his banquets, of wise virgins keeping vigil for the bridegroom.

The very God who created the universe has dared to make His own choice, to die in agony and enter into the suffering of His creation.

In Jesus He showed that suffering and death are transitory – the resurrection was to reveal, "The best is yet to be!"

Here was my Biblical answer. But could such insights stand the acid test of twenty-first century thinking?

Is God really all-powerful? Does He really exist? Or is the Biblical answer really part of a mythical fairy-tale?

Part 3

Twenty-First Century Answers to Natural Suffering, Pain and God

Chapter 25

Living in a Scientific Age-Some Problems in Believing in God

S o far, I have looked in **The Bible** to find answers to pain and suffering. But I am aware that my mindset is not that of an ancient Hebrew or Greek. The mindset of the early Christians was similar to that of medieval scholars.

Modern thought, however, has developed only since the end of the eighteenth century when science and philosophy began to challenge traditional thinking.

Now I understand the value of sharp, critical, non-conventional thought as the mark of the intelligent observer in modern science.

Divergent thinking has led to practical inventions, the Industrial Revolution, the medical sciences, the rise of atomic physics, electronics, biomechanics, and genetic engineering.

New theories have challenged Christian belief. Freudian psychology and Darwinian evolution have opened up the so-called "modern mind".

New philosophies, humanism, naturalism, materialism, and empiricism – all claim to use the "scientific method" in their enquiries.

The new social "sciences" such as sociology, economics, and psychology try to be scientific but they are unable to offer true scientific evidence, rather ideas, thoughts and opinions which often vary from person to person.

Even so, many believe that the "modern mind" is very much a "scientific mind".

Unfortunately, many in the churches appear to have reacted to science in two extreme ways:

1. They either take all new thought-forms on board or become liberal or "modernist" in their approach to thinking about God and religion. They remove the element of supernatural from religion and see God only as something within us.

2. Or they develop a hyper-orthodox, literal or "fundamentalist" approach that is narrow, rigid and dogmatic as it tries to overcome what it sees as false science. The fundamentalist wing of the church has been proved wrong over numerous issues such as anthropological finds, geology, astronomy, the age of the earth, fossil remains and so on.

I am not a scientist, but five subjects I studied at university have helped me to formulate my own scientific thinking – they were anthropology, physical geography (geology), human anatomy and physiology, together with behavioural psychology and empirical philosophy.

In addition, I am an active member of The Hastings Geological Society and was also a member of Christians in Science (UK).

Anthropology was my first introduction to the scientific study of human beings. I studied human anatomy and physiology, prehistoric and fossil remains, archaeology and cultural life-styles.

Like other science students, I used the scientific method of systematic observation, attempting to put these observations and possible explanations together in a systematic way.

Systematic observation is vital, limiting any valid study to what can actually be observed. Although anyone can observe, some observations need specialist training or instruments such as an electron microscope, a telescope or special measuring devices.

The observed information (called "data") is categorised in a methodical way with the possibility of testing and retesting to ensure the information gained is correct and consistent.

When a scientific investigation is complete, it is still always provisional and subject to correction by any new evidence that comes to light.

People often speak of scientific "evidence" and scientific "proof" as though they are one and the same. They are not. Scientific "laws" are not provable. They are seen today as being descriptions of what we expect to happen rather than what will happen. "Laws" held by scientists for hundreds of years may suddenly be shown to be untenable by new observations or new interpretations of past observations.

HOW DO WE KNOW?

As a teacher, I have been fascinated by my studies in epistemology, the theory of knowledge. It covers the whole aspect of how we know and how we know we know!

People accept most information by "faith".

We believe most of what we know about our parents' early lives and family histories because our parents gave us such information in the past.

Much of our knowledge of history and geography is believed purely on the words of other people such as teachers, authors or television presenters.

In fact, most of our knowledge is based on our faith in the trustworthiness of the books, magazines, television or radio programs, or faith in our teachers or professors. We believe what we are told.

Interestingly, Atheists also have faith. They have faith that the "Big Bang" caused the Universe to suddenly begin out of nothing. They have faith that life suddenly began out of dead material.

Also, they believe that human beings have a knowledge of morality – what is right or wrong – which developed by itself.

These are all beliefs based entirely on faith.

There are various kinds of knowledge, which are arrived at by different routes, but these are each acquired through some kind of faith or belief.

Scientific knowledge, or experimental knowledge, is based on close observation and experimentation. It has enabled us to understand the world of nature and biology – including the physics and chemistry of outer space.

Yet scientific observers have faith in the uniformity of nature. They believe that the systematic behaviour that controls the laws of nature with which they are experimenting or observing, also operates everywhere in the universe and has done so at all other times in the past.

Scientists need to have faith both in the regularity of nature and in the integrity of their fellow scientists in order to systematise their findings.

I have seen the skull of a Neanderthal creature in Germany, which I regard as evidence that such proto-humans existed.

My knowledge of other finds and details of Neanderthal life-styles is based on what I have learned from my anthropology professor, various articles I have read in **Scientific American** and other magazines, and from reading textbooks on anthropology. They are all "evidence" which I have taken in faith.

I believe that all things are made up of atoms, minute particles that move in constant motion, attracting each other when they are small distances apart, and repelling each other when squeezed into each other.

How do I know that atoms exist?

Scientists make the **hypothesis** that there are atoms. Some are so tiny that they have never been seen – either by a light microscope or an electron microscope.

However, tiny microscopic particles can be seen continuously "dancing" in water or air, suggesting that they are being bombarded by something too small to be detected (atoms!).

The way particles "dance" in water, or the manner in which salts are dissolved, the way in which crystals form, the way in which materials can change from solid to liquid to gas are just some of the evidences that atoms exist.

Furthermore, scientists predict results of experiments, which should work if things really are composed of atoms. Correct and constant predictions indicate that there is abundant evidence for the belief that atoms exist.

Evidence is information that adds weight to an argument to support a particular conclusion. The more evidence, the more likely (or probable) the conclusion.

Mathematical knowledge is based on logical thinking. We can prove something by pure logic or by the process of reasoning. Proof is not the same as evidence.

Proof is the result of a valid argument based on a set of true premises. The premises must be known to be true by both those offering the premise and those accepting it.

One example is mathematical proof such as "the interior angles of a triangle add up to 180 degrees," or "the area of a circle is *pi* multiplied by the square of the radius." These can be proved to be correct so long as the basic Euclidean premises of triangles and circles are accepted.

Euclidean space suggests that there are three dimensions of length, width and height and assumes that triangles and circles are drawn on flat surfaces. If one assumes those premises then the formulae may be used.

No one is compelled to draw triangles or circles on flat surfaces.

I well remember the head of mathematics in a local school pointing out that if you were able to draw a triangle on the surface of the earth starting at the North Pole and taking it to Singapore and then across to Quito in South America (both almost on the Equator), before linking up to its beginning, you would have a triangle whose interior angles would not add up to 180 degrees.

Similarly, if you take a circle such as the Arctic Circle, the area is not pi multiplied by the square of the radius, but is much larger, as the inner area is slightly spherical rather than flat.

Yet, while the mathematician can prove his knowledge of mathematics, it is no more than knowledge of what takes place in the axiom system that he has himself created. Everything the pure mathematician proves is based on faith.

All his proofs are based on the belief that everything he does is meaningful. He can, for instance, draw graphs to show numbers squared. Such a graph could show, inversely, the square root of any number.

It would be possible to show the square root of "2" on the graph, even though no such number as the square root of "2" exists.

Because it can be discussed and shown on a graph, such a number is known as an "irrational number", meaning that it cannot be expressed as the ratio of two whole numbers. (Incidentally, we use the symbol "π" to stand for this irrational number, as there is no real number that defines the relationship between the radius and circumference of a circle.).

C.S. Lewis in an edition of the BBC Brains Trust on 18 April, 1944, said that if the solar system were brought about by pure chance, then all life is an accident and all our thoughts are accidental by-products of the movement of atoms.

"I see no reason for believing that one accident should be able to give us an account of all other accidents," he stated.

Belief in rationality, meaning and mathematical logic is just that – "belief" - an act of faith.

Legal knowledge is based on evidence and clues that suggest meaning and motive. A crime may be committed with no witnesses, yet clues, circumstantial evidence, the suggestion of motive and other observations enable juries to find defendants innocent or guilty.

Sometimes new evidence comes to light, which overthrows previous verdicts. Yet most people have a belief or faith in the jury system.

What lawyers call "proof" is merely a weight of evidence. It is not proof in the mathematical or logical sense of the word.

Historical knowledge is very similar to legal knowledge. Scholars interpret clues, documents, artifacts, burial mounds and numerous other pieces of evidence.

They have faith in their own abilities to interpret the evidence, even though propaganda, exaggeration or personal bias in written accounts is difficult to judge.

Personal knowledge, or experiential knowledge, is the knowledge or experience encountered by us in our daily lives.

Meeting people, experiencing emotions, social intercourse and self-revelation are part of human relationships.

We can "know" other people only if they express their thoughts and emotions to us and if we express our own thoughts and feelings in return.

Personal knowledge is not based on evidence and experiment, but on experience. Yet, such experience is based on faith – the belief that other individuals experience feelings similar to our own, and think as we do.

All relationships are based on this **personal knowledge** or **experience** of entering into the minds and emotions of others, and letting the other delve into our own minds and feelings. The more intimate, the deeper the experience, the greater the faith – the trust – one has in the relationship.

CAN I KNOW GOD?

How can I know if God exists? The answer depends on my epistemology. How do I know anything?

Ancient philosophers like Plato and Aquinas used logic to attempt to "prove" the spiritual.

Later, in 1660, Rene Descartes wrote his **Discourse of Method and Meditations,** in which he attempted to "prove" the existence of God by using his mathematical logic.

It seems to me, though, that there is currently no way in which I can prove God by mathematics or logic, as the axioms on which I might base my own "proofs" are not acceptable by all. I might be able to "prove" the existence of God to another Christian, Moslem, Jew or Sikh only if he accepts my religious axioms.

Similarly, there is no scientific proof that God exists, just as there is also no scientific proof that he doesn't.

If God exists, then he cannot be observed by the scientific method because he is not part of physical nature – and observation is essential in science.

God is spirit, totally outside human comprehension. Christians believe we cannot understand God apart from the life and teaching of Jesus Christ.

That does not mean that scientific knowledge may not assist me in knowing God.

Professor Paul Davies, a theoretical physicist, in **God and the New Physics** (Pelican Books) argues that science offers a surer path to God than religion.

Even Sir Fred Hoyle in his book, **The Intelligent Universe** (Richard Joseph) acknowledges an intelligent design behind the Universe.

Perhaps my knowledge of science enables me to understand something of the mind behind and motivating all nature.

Some believe that God cannot be known through science at all - whilst others believe He can be known only by a "leap of faith" into what is called, "religious existentialism".

The latter see the spiritual world as being outside the material universe, undetectable except through an irrational leap of faith.

Soren Kierkegaard, a nineteenth century theologian in Copenhagen, believed that faith begins where reason ends. The virgin birth and the incarnation offend reason, showing that faith and reason cannot be reconciled. Knowing God requires a leap beyond the rational. To Kierkegaard there was no such thing as evidence, only "the miracle of faith."

I am too scientifically minded to reject evidence, and could not believe in something that ran against the evidence. My faith needs to be "rational".

If God exists as the creator of the Universe, then he must be part of it in some way. For me, science and religion are "twins", so that investigating God and the Universe help me to understand the wonder of each.

Professor David Ingram, former Vice Chancellor of the University of Kent, told a story that illustrates this. He suggested that three highly intelligent people who had never before seen a television set were placed in three separate rooms with a television monitor and asked to report what they made of it.

- The first expressed his amazement at its construction – he described the properties of plastic and glass, the makeup of transistors, wiring, weight, size and use to which the item could be put.

- The second investigated the television waves that came through the aerial, worked out the circuitry, the voltage, amplification and signal input, together with the physics of colour input and pixel size in the production of the image.

- The third wrote a complete explanation of the plot of "The Avengers", and linked the struggle for survival to the ingenuity of the characters overcoming their various conflicts leading to a startling climax. Comments were recorded about visual highlights, sound and music.

Each account, suggested Professor Ingram, can be correct, meaningful and complete, yet they do not overlap at all. Each could be considered a complementary alternative. Such seems to be similar in the realms of knowledge.

Mathematical formulae, logical systems, scientific analysis, historical and legal understanding can all operate in different spheres or they may be synthesized into one whole.

My personal relationships, my own experiences, may be correct, meaningful and complete without ever overlapping other forms of knowledge. I may know love and experience a whole gamut of emotions that are meaningful and complete, without my having any knowledge of the biological and neural functions that are also at play in my body.

In our world nothing appears to be exactly what it is. Nothing, for example, is ever still – everything in the universe is moving. Not just atoms, but also the earth, planets, stars and galaxies are moving in space.

Science has also raised a number of issues for Christians through the insights of quantum physics and relativity theories.Max Planck, around 1900, demonstrated that the Universe is made up of particles smaller than the atom. He showed that such sub-atomic particles behave randomly - with light, for example, being made up of waves and particles that act unpredictably. Such unpredictable behaviour on the part of individual atoms, neutrons and sub- atomic particles is known only in terms of probability.

But such random behaviour of sub-atomic particles did not fit into Albert Einstein's understanding of the Universe. In his **Special Theory of Relativity**, Einstein viewed nature on a macroscopic scale in which concepts like"absolute space" and "absolute time" do not exist.

Everything is relative to some arbitrarily chosen point of reference. A wave may have the appearance of movement to a person standing on a beach, but a person in a large ship being carried along by the wave may detect no movement.

Similarly, astronomers often find it useful to imagine that the Sun is stationary while the planets and stars move in relation to it.

Yet the Sun is moving at vast speeds around the centre of the Galaxy, which is itself travelling at great speed within other moving galaxy clusters, all of which are moving away from a suggested centre of the Universe.

Einstein showed in his General Theory of Relativity that the Universe contains only a finite amount of energy that resides in mass. All action and creation are summed up in his equation "$E = mc^2$". Such equations bring humanity "closer to the secrets of the Old One", as Einstein termed God.

In fact, Einstein believed there was a meaning to human life and also "organic life all together".

His approach to understanding the world was very much "holistic" in that each part (each atom or sub-atomic particle, each "quantum") must be seen in relation to the whole – the whole is much more than the sum of its parts.

For Christianity, the two apparently contradictory theories of quanta and relativity suggest that our understanding of God must be both cosmic as well as personal.

If God does exist, and if He is, as ancient philosophers proclaimed, "the greatest conceivable being, the sustainer of the Universe who moment by moment keeps all its components in place," then both quantum physics and Einstein's theories enable us to understand something of the greatness of His being.

Science is coming to new understandings. The apparent contradiction of Quantum Physics and Relativity Theory is accepted as a paradox.

Both are seen as completely true. It may also be that the interpretations of Max Planck, Einstein or a Christian theologian concerning the Universe are each correct, meaningful and complete, yet with no overlap.

One final problem is that many philosophers believe statements about God are meaningless. Christians may describe God as an eternal, omnipresent, infinite spirit, or the Absolute, Ground of Existence or Life Force, yet also describe "him" as a male walking in the Garden of Eden, speaking to the prophets, laughing in the heavens and having a son.

The philosopher, A.J Ayer, believed that such talk about God is meaningless unless it can be verified through sensory experience, which it clearly cannot.

If God is unique, a spirit with no body, then how can analogies in which God is compared to human characteristics– all based on human action, thought and speech – have any meaning?

In a radio interview on "Good Morning Sunday" (BBC Radio 2), Magnus Magnusson was asked if he believed in

God. He replied that he couldn't answer a meaningless question, for he had no idea what the word "God" meant.

When Christians, Moslems or Jews discuss God, they use poetry, prose, allegory, metaphor and analogy, especially anthropomorphism to discuss or describe God.

Anthropomorphism is a way of describing a non- human entity in terms of human characteristics, for example saying that my car "doesn't like cold mornings".

In the same way, God, who is assumed to have no gender, can be described as a mother or father figure.

Christians and Jews see God as the creator who fashioned human beings in His own image. Human beings mirror in some minute way the character of their creator.

Thus, analogies are not attempts to define God, so much as attempts to show how human beings may be imperfect shadows of God.

Some Christians have used the idea of a clever dog mirroring Einstein. The dog is "clever" only in the way appropriate to a dog (it may be able to open a door by jumping up to the door-handle), whereas Einstein is clever in a way appropriate to scientists.

A wise man is wise only in a way appropriate to human beings; whereas God is said to be wise in a way that is only appropriate to God.

Professor John Hick of the University of Birmingham suggests that human love, wisdom and goodness are merely very weak shadows of God's nature.

We each assume that knowledge is either true or false.

But knowledge is not always concerned with "facts" so much as "beliefs" or "emotions".

Knowledge of the world varies according to our culture, family upbringing and the way our thought processes have developed.

Thus, the knowledge of the world seen through the eyes of a Hindu, a Buddhist, a communist, a Japanese Shintoist or even two Europeans brought up in a Catholic or Protestant tradition can seem quite different from each other.

It may be possible to talk "meaningfully" about an indescribable fear, ecstasy or joy, even though the listener may not fully comprehend the emotions being expressed.

Imagine a number of scholars asked to examine a piece of bread and a goblet of wine and then to assess their meaning.

How might a chemist in his laboratory, a poet writing for a competition, an artist thinking of spatial and emotional feeling, an anthropologist in Central America, or a Christian Cleric explain their significance?

Their conclusions might appear meaningless to each other, and it might seem that they were each speaking a different kind of language. What they say might bear no similarity in meaning or vocabulary yet each may express truth.

So, it may be with religious and scientific language – they may both express the same truth and meaning, even though they express that truth and meaning in totally different ways.

As I look at science and scripture, I see a God who reveals himself in both. In each I find a self-revealing and a self-concealing God who makes Himself known only to those who diligently seek him. "Seek and you shall find" seems to aptly fit both nature and scripture.

I once saw it expressed in this way: "In (God's word and His works) we find stimulants to faith and occasions for unbelief; in both we find contradictions, whose higher harmony is hidden, except from him who gives up his whole mind in reverence" (Neander).

In my journey to discover if God even exists, I travelled through three areas of evidence – philosophy, history and the revelation of Jesus Christ.

• Philosophy:

I had studied general philosophy, philosophy of religion, philosophy of science and philosophy of education, and in all of them "God" had been a factor to be reckoned with.

There were arguments about design in the Universe suggesting a master designer at work in nature, arguments about "Mind" and "Intelligence" behind creation, and arguments about first causes – "something must have started it all off" - and that "something", philosophers called "God".

There were discussions about the place of beauty, about the miracle of life and about moral consciousness. I learnt about the implications of such consciousness, of human reason, of memory and meaning.

While I found such thinking fascinating, I learnt that traditional philosophy does not provide "proof" of the existence of God, although it seemed to offer strong evidence for the possibility that God may exist.

Sir John Houghton, Professor of Atmospheric Physics at Oxford University and Director General of the Meteorological Office, suggests "The size, the complexity, the beauty and the order we find in the Universe are expressions of the greatness, the beauty and the orderliness of the Creator." ("A God Big Enough", **Real Science: Real Faith**).

He further points out that the atmosphere is a chaotic system only because of the limits to our practical ability to measure or observe. If, as is sometimes suggested, a butterfly's wings may affect the weather thousands of miles away, meteorologists have no instruments sensitive enough to even begin to measure or observe such a process.

Chaos Theory represents a new scientific discipline, according to Roy Peacock, Professor of Aerospace Science at the University of Pisa.

Discussing disorder in nature, he notes that even in chaotic breakdown there can still be symmetry and harmony, as when wakes shed from ships and aircraft produce beautiful spirals of patterns, intricate vortices, and fractal images with repetitive patterns.

"Somehow", suggests Professor Peacock, "the Solar System is being held together when it should be flying apart". Perhaps the designer, God, is an interventionist. ("**Credibility and Credo**" in **Real Science: Real Faith**).

Although we think in twenty-first century terms of the scientific method of thinking about problems and solving them, there are areas which science does not deal with. Although science, for example, reduces colour and sound to "wave lengths," I remember a blind pupil who learnt all about the physics of light and the spectrum, although unable to see.

Similarly, a deaf person can pass examinations on the physics of sound and even photograph patterns of musical scores.

But the ability to comprehend, to be conscious and to experience the qualities of life is beyond the Scientific method. It is obvious that scientific knowledge and **personal knowledge** do not necessarily overlap.

Science can deal only with the stable and repeatable.

In my anthropology lectures we "stabilised"individuals through categorizing "racial characteristics", "medieval thought", or we discussed "the average Englishman or Scot" or "working class and middle-class attitudes", as though each individual in each group exhibited the same characteristics. There was no place for the individual as such.

Individuality must give way to statistical averages.

One anecdote regularly quoted to show how deceptive averages can be, is of the boy who had his head in a freezer and his feet in a fire, so on average he felt comfortable!

Human beings are unique among animals. Our power to reason, to read and write, and interpret phenomena are far beyond mere brain-size and neurology.

And our understanding of meaning and purpose go beyond our limited perceptions (a dog, for instance, can perceive more in terms of hearing sounds and smelling even long deposited scents than any human being, yet a human can understand meaning far better than any dog). It thus seems that there is much more to nature than science can detect.

Science observes, quantifies, tests and orders its observations into systematic ideas, hypotheses or theories.

It seeks to explain how and what. And science does an excellent job at finding answers to the "how" and "what" of nature.

One thing science cannot do is explain the "why" of nature and its phenomena. It can deal with observed phenomena, but not with meaning or purpose.

The scientist cannot differentiate between an accidental and purposeless universe, and one created by a super-intelligent being.

The "why" of the universe is explicable only in an understanding of religion? The alternative is quite simply that the Universe is meaningless with no purpose. And if that is so, then suffering and pain have no meaning either.

If this is true, then how do I know which religion is true, anyway? What if there is no God, and all searching is vain? And just what do I mean by "God". I can certainly understand Magnus Magnusson: "What do you mean by God?"

I soon came to realize that God couldn't be understood by the scientific method, or by any of my sense organs. If there is such a being as God, then I can only know about him if he were to reveal himself to me. Such revelation is part of **personal knowledge**.

What can I learn about God - if he, she or it really exists?

I have learnt quite a lot about God from three different sources.

• History

Religion is about relationships and personal encounters with the divine. Yet for me, my own faith in Christianity is strengthened by my knowledge of Jewish history, the **Old and New Testaments** and especially by my knowledge of Jesus Christ, a historical person.

In the **Old Testament**, God is revealed as a Father in Heaven, and as a Mother to her people Israel. The history of the Jewish people is told as the history of God's first revelation to the world.

With my understanding of Ancient history, I knew how the Jewish nation had developed. The Jews endured slavery in Egypt and then claimed to have been miraculously delivered under the leadership of Moses, who through a series of "miracles" established the new nation. He also gave them Ten Commandments plus hundreds of religious laws.

The new primitive nation comprised twelve families who developed into clans or tribes, plus a priestly caste that led the worship and administered the laws.

Later they developed into twelve nations. The nations were attacked, subjugated, led into exile and subjected to numerous pogroms. Yet one nation which stayed true to God survived, which is part of the miracle of its history – the Jewish Nation.

For an almost continuous period of 1,500 years or more, Jewish history was concerned with God's revelation to Israel. Over forty different authors from every stratum of Jewish society, writing in different forms, styles and genres, with different messages and concepts of God, revealed a unified interpretation between them. They produced the **Old Testament** scrolls, and later the **New Testament.**

Israel's prophets revealed deep human insights. They taught moral duty and obligation to a God who was separate ("holy") from humanity. They introduced different concepts of the Divine character and (as already noted) they predicted future events.

Prediction is a notable feature in Jewish scripture. It is not only peculiar to the **Bible**, but covers the entire **Bible**, not just the period of the prophets. Jewish prophecy is unique in being fulfilled without the trickery and ambiguity often associated with ancient religions.

Oracles of ancient Greece were known for their duplicity and vagueness.

Hebrew prophecy, on the other hand, is specific. It foretells the fall of Israel and then Judah, names particular individuals, predicts the fall of surrounding nations, and promises the coming Messiah with astonishing clarity and precision (especially in **Micah** and **Isaiah**).

The later eschatological prophecies relating to the coming Kingdom, with their grotesque symbols, are not quite so clear.

The prophets warn people to be morally responsible for their actions, they remind their listeners that God is the Ruler of History, and they predict in very minute detail people, nations and events not even existing at the time of the prophecy.

• Jesus of Nazareth

If God can be revealed in nature and through human inspiration, for me the most important revelation comes through my understanding of the person, teaching and work of Jesus Christ.

Jesus claimed to be God dressed in human form. His character is as unique as His teaching. His miracles are simply recorded, He appears to fulfill prophecy as the Messiah, and His death and resurrection are well attested.

Professor J.N.D. Anderson, Head of Oriental Law at the University of London, and Director of the Institute of Advanced Legal Studies, has analysed the evidence for the resurrection of Jesus Christ to evaluate its relevance, honesty, ability to convince and whether it is susceptible to any naturalistic interpretation.

Dealing primarily with six witnesses (Matthew, Mark, Luke, John, Peter and Paul,) supported by the whole primitive church, he shows the contemporary nature of the evidence, arguing that Paul's detailed resurrection account in **I Corinthians** 15 was written between AD 52-57, although Paul writes that he had previously given the information orally to the Corinthian church (about AD 50).

Professor Anderson shows that the testimony of Mark may be as early as AD 44, and that Luke is also early. In addition, equally authoritative eyewitness accounts come from Matthew, Peter and John.

Such early eyewitnesses argue strongly against the accounts being legend or later inventions.

In fact, suggests Anderson, no forger would possibly think of having the risen Christ appear first to a woman (Mary Magdalene) rather than to a leading church leader like James (to whom no record is given) or Peter.

There appears no doubt that the tomb of Jesus was empty. Professor Anderson discusses the possibility that Jesus' body was removed from the tomb.

But he makes the point that, if the authorities stole the body, why did they not say so, to nip the preaching of the resurrection "in the bud"?

Within seven weeks, the whole of Jerusalem was seething with this preaching, and thousands became Christian through the preaching of Peter.

Anderson explores the possibility that Jesus merely swooned on the cross and was buried while still alive, to recover in the coolness of the tomb to confound his enemies for a few weeks more.

But could a being who had stolen half-dead out of the sepulchre, who crept about weak and ill, then died (presumably needing bandaging, medical care and close attention) have given his followers the impression that he was the conqueror of death and Hell, the Prince of Life.

Furthermore, he points out that the tomb was not actually empty. The linen "clothes" and "napkin" were still there when John and Peter entered the tomb.

Professor Anderson argues that the Christian Church traces its history back to the resurrection; that Sunday (the resurrection day) became the centre of new worship of Christian Jews who were fanatically attached to the Sabbath (Saturday); that the success of the apostles in founding the church only "a stone's throw away from the empty tomb" is highly significant; and that the awkward period of seven weeks between the event and its first proclamation makes no sense unless the risen Jesus was with his disciples during that period, as they all proclaimed.

Finally, he points out that Christ foretold his own death and resurrection: the apostles – all cowardly men – were transformed into formidable missionaries.

According to legend all but one died for something they claimed to have seen with their own eyes.

Their faith makes sense only if Jesus Christ really is God manifest as a man (**Evidence for the Resurrection:** Intervarsity Press).

I found both the historical evidence and the legal evidence concerning Jesus Christ to be powerful in the argument for God's existence.

For the resurrection of Jesus does far more than indicate that a man once defeated death. If such an event occurred, then the implications are immense.

Jesus claimed to be divine; the one who came to die that others might know God in an intimate and personal way. And if that is so, then it means that God may be known through a personal or experiential relationship, which is what Jesus taught.

I believe that it is possible to know God.

By God, I do not mean an invisible, powerful, spiritual being undetectable by scientific measuring instruments – although he is that and more – which Magnusson rightly call "meaningless".

God is a personal being revealed by Jesus as My Loving Heavenly Father. We have something in common because he made me in His image.

God is the force that created nature and constantly holds it in being.

He has a moral character totally opposed to evil, while his attitude to me is one of self- giving love. "He so loved the world," says John, "that He gave his only Son that whoever believes in Him will not perish but have eternal life" (John 3:16 KJV).

Knowledge of a God like that can come about only through a two-way relationship – a relationship of faith and trust.

Chapter 26

Can Top Scientists Believe in God?

*M*any people believe that real scientists are atheist. Surveys suggest that almost half are either unsure or agnostic, while many believe in some kind of creative mathematical mind behind the Universe.

A survey by James Leuba in the early part of the 19th Century discovered that around 40% of scientists believed in a creative God.

Amazingly, later in 1996 Edward Larson and Larry Witham found that the percentage of scientific believers in a personal God had not changed: it was still around the 40% mark. A further 12% also believed in some creative mastermind or master mathematician behind everything.

My Cancer Consultant discussed mutation causing cancer with me. He told me that all mutations caused changes that either died out, or caused problems for those people with mutations. He told me that he believed in mutation, but did not believe in evolution as a theory.

When I told my son, his immediate response was, "Your consultant was obviously a fundamentalist Christian." In fact, my consultant was an Anglican Church member, but he was no fundamentalist.

For many years I was a member of Christians in Science and met many of Britain's leading scientists once a year at a Science Conference.

Professor Sam Berry, previously President of the British Ecological Society, studied genetic changes in animals. His book, **Real Science, Real Faith (Ed),** Monarch (UK), **1995**, explains his belief in science and in the God, who is creator.

He told me that most conflicts between science and belief in God (or faith) are caused either by a misunderstanding of science and nature, or a serious misunderstanding of the **Scriptures.**

Professor Harry Darling was for many years the Head of London University Agricultural Department in Wye. He told me that he believed in the creator God whom we can know personally through the revelation of Jesus in the **Bible**.

I also find it interesting that Professor Sir Ghillean France, Director of The Royal Botanic Gardens in Kew and Visiting Professor at Reading, says that all his scientific research has confirmed his faith in God.

Many astronomers believe in God, the creator of all in the Cosmos. Fredrick Smith, Director of Time at the Greenwich Observatory, was a good friend of mine. He lent me books on science and astronomy and we met weekly to discuss Christianity and science. I knew him as a Life Deacon in my church.

Another Professor of Atmospheric Physics at Oxford University and Chief Executive of the Meteorological Office, Sir John Houghton, CBE, FRS, believes in God. As the Chairman of The Royal Commission on Environmental Pollution he has stated, "Looking after the Earth is a responsibility given to humans."

He believes that Nature teaches us "about God's Creative activity in the Universe" and the **Bible** gives a revelation of this God who revealed Himself in Jesus (**God and the Scientists, M.W. Poole,** CPO – Design and Print).

These are just a few of the 1,500 scientists who served as members of Christians in Science, UK.

There are a similar number of scientists in the Christian group, **The American Scientific Affiliation** in the United States.

During the 1960's I remember reading the conclusions of Robert Boyd, Professor of Physics, University College, London, and Professor of Astronomy in the Royal Institution, about his own faith as "the knowledge of encounter".

He stated, "Christianity is in essence a relationship, the outcome of both an objective, historical revelation and a contemporary, personal encounter. It is a relationship because the revelation is no mere demonstration of the character and attributes of the ineffable Ground of all Being, but a declaration of concern and demonstration of involvement on the part of God in my personal good." (**Can God be known?** Intervarsity Fellowship).

Later, a colleague asked him if he had ever thought "that God probably had to make a universe as large as ours to be able to evolve man?"

In response, as Sir Robert Boyd, he wrote the following poem, which encapsulates his faith:

> The Word of God; Reason, Design and Form.
> Intelligence, whose workshop spans the stars,
> Expressed within the Cosmos and alike
> In what seems chaos; He who works as much
> In randomness as order, who to make
> Man in His Image scorns not to create
> By patient evolution on a scale
> Of craft divine which dwarfs a million years?

Chapter 27

The Age of Aquarius – New Age Beliefs

*T*he twenty-first century started in Europe with an anti-science sentiment. Many Europeans are no longer prepared to trust the scientific world.

Since the last World War, anti- nuclear activists and those opposed to genetic engineering have challenged the sciences.

Although numerically small, the number of vegans, vegetarians, and those connected with animal rights, ecological and green issues and new-age ideologies are increasing.

"New Age" is a term used by astrologists to mark the apparent move of the earth backwards from the Zodiac sign of Pisces to the sign of Aquarius. Such moves, known as "The precession of the equinoxes" apparently occur every 2,100 years.

Patrick Moore (**The Great Universe:** CMP Publishing) points out that the constellations used by astrologers are completely arbitrary because the stars are many light years from each other, so that the apparent patterns in the sky have no meaning whatsoever. He suggests that if we had chosen to follow Egyptian or Chinese star patterns (instead of Greek) we would have no Great Bear, Herdsman or Plough, but rather the Cat or the Dragon.

It is not my purpose to discuss astrological, ethical or ecological aspects of "New Agers", but to briefly examine some "New Age" Attitudes to pain and suffering.

"New Age" therapies are often called "holistic" or "alternative". They are usually critical of modern medical science, which they believe to be disease-centred, rather than person-centred, as medical science concentrates only on sick parts of the body.

In addition, medical science concentrates on smaller and smaller bodily fragments - cell-tissue, DNA and genetic modification - rather losing sight of the patient as a human being.

Holistic practitioners in reflexology, aromatherapy, herbalism, homeopathy, some forms of chiropractic and osteopathy together with new Asian practitioners of acupuncture and Tai Chi massage claim to treat the whole person.

I attended a training session with the local branch of the Institute of Chiropodists on "Reflexology".

Reflexology is founded on what is called "Zone Theory". William Fitzgerald of the USA suggested that energy from the nose causes numbness in the face when the nasal areas are pressed.

Eunice Ingram developed this by suggesting that ten zones run from the tips of the toes to the top of the head, then back down through the arms and fingers.

All bodily organs connect in a zone, so reflexologists claim, to be able to both diagnose and treat bodily complaints by "reading" and massaging areas of the feet.

One of my colleagues claims to be able to treat diarrhea, heartburn, premenstrual syndrome and kidney disease by pressing and massaging in the correct foot zone.

Similar ideas come from **Tai Chi or Tai Chi Chaun**. Practitioners specializing in acupuncture, acupressure or Tai Chi massage believe that all life and material in the Universe originates from a single source "Tao", within which are two opposing forces – "yin", female and "yang", male. Yin and yang always cooperate in harmony, constantly changing and merging with each other, yet always remaining in balance.

It is this constant movement that produces the life force or "chi". Chi thus permeates through "Tao" both surrounding and flowing through all human bodies in orderly patterns called meridians (or zones). Illness results from blockages in the meridians or by unbalanced chi.

Acupuncture specialists insert needles at specific points to divert the flow of subtle energy ("chi") moving through fourteen different meridians in the body. Needles or pressure can change the energy flow. Tai chi practitioners use gentle body movement to channel physical and emotional chi.

Another form of alternative therapy that differs from medical science is homoeopathy, a belief that "like may cure like". Homoeopaths use poisons and minute amounts of substances that in larger doses would actually cause similar symptoms.

Homoeopaths speak of the "vital force", or "body vitality" (just as Chinese practitioners speak of "chi" and Indian practitioners of "prana") and try to stop disease caused by imbalance in the body by introducing minute doses of deadly toxins or drugs to enable the body to call on its own "vitality" to heal itself.

Many medical experts believe that the minute traces of poisons are so microscopic as to be meaningless in treatment. They appear to have a purely placebo effect.

Many other forms of holistic medicine used by "New Age" practitioners, together with "religious" states induced by meditation, yoga, altered states of consciousness and herbal drugs are said to bring back harmony to the Tao.

There is no doubt that human beings are a unity and need to be treated holistically, as whole individuals. "New Age" is about recognising human harmony, natural understanding and spiritual growth.

The holistic perspective on life that takes in mind, body and soul provides a warning that quantum medical theory can go too far.

Human beings are not just cells, tissues, glands, strings of DNA. They are whole people created in the image of the God of the universe. Holistic health sees beyond symptoms to the whole person: the background, stress, ideology, society, family beliefs, diet, emotions and the "life force" within.

Having stated that, I must also confess that I can find no relevance between my own studies of human anatomy and physiology of the leg and foot and the meridian zone theory of my reflexology colleagues.

There appears to be no scientific evidence that zones and meridian lines, or Tao and chi, exist.

Clearly, too, there is a need for balance in the human body and there is a clear need for energy to stimulate living creatures.

Yet scientific medicine has shown that balance is part of all healing processes – balance in blood supply, in body liquid and temperature, in which the liver, kidneys, blood circulation, respiration and lymphatic system all work to keep the body in harmony.

Energy is constantly moving through the nervous systems from the brain to the conscious nerve endings and back again, and in the parasympathetic nervous system.

Such energy can be measured by means of encephalogram and electrocardiogram link-ups. Even thinking and dreaming can be shown to be measurable in terms of electric currents, even though there is currently no way of interpreting the impulses so measured.

Furthermore, an enormous body of evidence exists for viral, bacterial and genetic changes and other pathologies causing disease.

In 1999, a small number of deaths were recorded in the UK caused by the use of unsterile acupuncture needles, and several deaths from kidney cancer in Denmark have been traced to Chinese herbal remedies. Yet so many people appear to be helped by holistic alternatives that I can only suggest at this stage that a person does respond better to pain and suffering when valued as a real person rather than, say, "a kidney problem".

That, after all, is precisely what Job revealed. Friendships, love, relationships, touching and being touched, taking time and making the sufferer feel important are all vital in the healing process of the whole person.

Chapter 28

Is God Competent in the Physical World?

As a student I was once asked by a philosophy professor why I thought God had created people. My reply was that He was probably lonely, a concept that the professor rejected as too anthropomorphic.

God clearly does not think like me. Yet, somehow my own thoughts may be mere "shadows" of the infinite "mind". We human beings are free to think, meditate, reason and mentally explore the universe as creatures with an implant of the divine image somehow within our personalities.

It occurred to me that the creator of the universe might have deliberately hidden Himself from human sense for a valid reason. And in this hiding, He may also have hidden His competency! But why?

THE DANGERS OF TRUE FREEDOM

Suppose the Almighty God of the Universe felt the need to love and be loved. Suppose He really were lonely. He may have existed alone in space.

How could God make a being that did not just serve and obey, but also love and worship entirely of its own choosing? Would such a choice be real? How could a created being really choose to obey or disobey its own creator?

Then I remembered a phrase I had read in a "one-line philosophy."

"**Without danger, there is no real risk**."

It was that first bit that intrigued me – "**Without danger**."

As I thought about it, I began to realize that any concept of "free will" was meaningless without danger.

There was no risk for God unless there was danger. What exactly did that mean? I wondered if God had to create a world of risk in order to give human freedom.

Perhaps God thought about the possibility that a created being might love Him, and even be a member of His own family, entirely because that new being chose to do so entirely of his or her own free will.

But that involved risk.

William I Thompson (**The Time Falling Bodies Take to Light:** St Martin's Press) gives an imaginative account of God's reasoning in Heaven.

God knows how a "perfect" world will function – like an undeviating machine of absolute precision.

Thompson then suggests that such a world would be uninteresting to God, who can predict every possible eventuality, and imagines God thinking of this dangerous risk.

"What if I create a universe that is free, free even of me?" he speculates.

"What if I veil my Divinity so that the creatures are free to pursue their individual lives without being overwhelmed by my overpowering presence?

Will such creatures love me?"

Can creatures that God has not programmed to adore Him forever, still love Him of their own free will? Can love rise out of freedom?

Thompson goes on to show that if God creates in His own image, beings that are free to love good or evil, then that choice makes God take a risk.

God can no longer predict each action – does He respond to evil with good, or does He allow freedom regardless of its consequence?

Or does He join in this limited world of suffering and evil, if it becomes that? Dare God take that risk for love?

It seems to me that God has taken that risk.

He has taken the risk of creating a totally free universe, producing a world that is free to be itself. He has created free life forms that have developed at their own whim, and has finally created a being in His own image that can freely choose good or evil.

Each risk has its own dangers – what if things go wrong?

Only if they are true risks, and the creation is truly free, will God know if His creation will succeed.

But such true freedom can only be at the expense of God relinquishing His power to intervene, for a risk without danger is hardly a risk at all.

If this new creation does not succeed, then God can either destroy it entirely as a failure, or He can plan some other way of redeeming an evil creation.

RESTRAINTS ON TRUE FREEDOM

Yet even a free universe cannot be without some kind of restraint. Total freedom would mean complete chaos. God has appeared to place certain physical, chemical and biological "laws" as controls within the universe.

Equally, the universe appears subject to three limiting forces - gravity, electromagnetism, and nuclear forces. These forces keep creation within certain bounds and limits.

Gravity keeps us on the ground and determines the large-scale structure of the universe, keeping the planets, stars and galaxies together. Every object in the Universe has its own gravity - two fifty-thousand-ton ships by the side of each other on a windless day will be pulled together by their own gravity.

Electromagnetism is the energy that runs our electrical appliances, produces x-rays, sends television signals, and provides the colour spectrum that enables us to see with our own eyes. (It is also the same energy that keeps electrons in orbit around an atom and creates the magnetic fields that keep atoms in place).

Few of us understand the two **nuclear forces**, which determine the behaviour of minute particles within atoms. **Weak nuclear force** controls the behaviour of decay in the neutron of the atom and controls the strong thermonuclear explosions that fuel the atom, while strong nuclear force keeps sub atomic particles tightly bound together around the nucleus of the atom.

Although the Universe is free to expand, mutate and evolve, it nevertheless seems that God has placed these forces to control and limit that freedom, by giving some kind of stability and structure by which all things "hang together."

Gravity is essential for holding the Universe together, yet it can also injure or kill. The Guillotine and the hangman's noose rely on the force of gravity to kill their victims; and mudslides, falling trees and lava flows are affected by gravity.

Misused, x-rays, laser light rays, microwaves and electrical current can also injure or kill.

If humanity is to be really free and not be automatic robots, then it has to live in a world with really free choices, a world that allows real choice between good and evil.

If there were no pain of any kind then human beings would have no choice, because every single thing each of us did could not harm us in any way. We could do anything without consequences – and that is not free choice. If God protected us from the laws of the universe then we would lose our free will for there would be no choices to make.

Choosing to love someone, to be kind to our children, to help a neighbour, to be either sympathetic, humane, merciful or cooperative would be meaningless because doing the opposite would cause no harm – so nothing would be right or wrong – there would be no choice; therefore, no real freedom.

If gravity always works then heavy objects will always fall towards the earth, whether individuals who carelessly lose their footing on cliff tops or stair wells, or meteorites falling from outer space.

The alternative is for God to suspend the laws of gravity every time an item falls that might cause pain or suffering. Objects might fall at different speeds, vaporise, become soft or jellified and magically relieve us of pain or suffering.

But again, we would have no choices. Choice always means to choose consequences of some kind.

The world in which we live is the only one that enables us to choose to love God and our neighbour rather than choose to do evil.

The possibility of making good or bad (sometimes foolish, sometimes evil) choices is only possible where there is pleasure and pain, not only for us but also for other people and animals.

This was part of the risk (the danger) that God took, when He created a universe in which people have real free choice.

UNDERSTANDING GOD'S UNIVERSE

We are so ignorant about our Universe. Specialist Cosmologists and Astronomers are beginning to know more and more about less and less. New knowledge, combined with new theories, only produces greater wonders and mysteries to be resolved.

During the last hundred years, however, there have been three major breakthroughs in our understanding of the Universe.

1. Most important is our growth in the knowledge of the atom. As a schoolboy, I was still taught that the atom was the smallest particle of matter and could not be split! It is the smallest particle of a substance (usually called a chemical element), which still has all the features and properties of that particular substance. About ninety substances or chemical elements occur naturally on earth or in space (and around 20 synthetic or artificial elements have been produced in chemical laboratories). But atoms are not the smallest particles – a whole range of sub-atomic particles such as protons, neutrons, electrons, quarks and leptons are smaller still. Each single element has its own physical properties such as hardness, colour, melting and boiling temperatures, ability to conduct electricity, and method of joining or combining with atoms of other elements.

2.   At the other extreme, Einstein's theory of general relativity has proved reliable throughout the whole Universe and is generally accepted by modern astronomers as the most likely explanation for the measurement and interpretation of space. General relativity is a mathematical concept in which curved space and warped time are used to describe gravitation. It is now known that the Universe is much larger than imagination can comprehend. Not only are there planets and stars, but we also know that billions of stars encircle each other by gravitation to form huge clusters called "galaxies". Recently, it has been discovered that galaxies circle each other so that there are huge "galaxy clusters", but even more astounding is the recent discovery through the Hubble telescope that there are clusters of galaxies encircling each other in "mega galaxy clusters" and even "super clusters of mega galaxy clusters"!

3.   On a different front, there have been amazing advances in observation. Telescopes are extremely limited, but in the second half of the twentieth century the electromagnetic spectrum has provided new ways to explore the heavens. Most new discoveries have come from radio and microwave astronomy. In fact, astronomers are now using gamma rays, X rays, ultraviolet rays, infrared rays as well as the visible spectrum to study outer space. The word "spectrum" refers to the sizes of waves and wavelengths (e.g. x-rays

having smaller wavelengths than visible light) – all of which travel at the same speed (186, 000 miles a second). Telescopes have also been mounted in space to give clear images of distant stars and galaxies, the most famous being the Hubble Space Telescope. Today, images from the very edge of the known Universe are decoded and enhanced by computer technology. Equally amazing are the advances in detecting the ultra- minutiae of sub atomic particles through the use of the electron microscope, computer simulations and nuclear reactors.

These three new branches of knowledge are essential to an understanding of our Earth, quite apart from the Universe.

A believer in God might ask, "Is the Universe intelligently designed, or is it chaotic?"

Is God competent as creator or not? No scientist can answer those questions. How could science possibly know? Science can deal only with observed knowledge, and there is nothing with which to compare the Universe.

A COMPETENTLY DESIGNED EARTH?

One question that may sensibly be considered, however, is: "Has our Earth been intelligently designed so that life can come into existence?" We cannot ask such a question of the Universe at present as we have virtually no knowledge of other solar systems in other parts of our galaxy and no knowledge at all of any other planet like Earth.

Our solar system consists of a huge sun, four enormous planets, our Earth and four smaller planets, over forty moons, over a hundred thousand smaller bodies called asteroids, billions of comets, yet life is found only on Earth.

Fortunately, we do know a lot about Earth.

Is there any evidence to suggest that God created the Earth in a competent manner? Or is it just a chaotic, haphazard rock spinning through space?

Earth is a "perfect" size - were it larger it would contain too much free hydrogen like Jupiter and Saturn, yet if it were smaller its atmosphere would escape as it has from Mercury and the Moon.

Earth's gravity is also just right. If it were more powerful, human beings would find it difficult to walk, and air pressure would be difficult to cope with, but if it were even a little weaker, our atmosphere would gradually escape.

Our Earth is also a "perfect" distance from the Sun. The Sun's energy radiates heat that provides life and warmth.

Venus, our next planet is nearer the Sun with an average temperature of 460° Celsius (860° Fahrenheit) over four and a half times hotter than boiling water. It produces too much carbon dioxide and has an atmosphere 93 times greater than our own.

Mars, our nearest neighbour away from the Sun is quite cold, with an average temperature of −60° Celsius. As a result, Mars has a very thin carbon dioxide atmosphere.

Our proximity to Jupiter is fortunate. Jupiter is 1300 times larger than earth, made up mostly of hydrogen. Its magnetic field, over twenty times that of Earth, traps deadly fast-moving particles, while its gravity pulls asteroids and comets towards itself that might otherwise hit Earth.

Jupiter traps dozens of asteroids into its orbit, saving Earth from such cosmic bombardment.

The tilt of the Earth's axis is just right for providing the Seasons. Without seasonal variation, both Poles would not only be permanently frozen, but so would much larger areas within the Arctic and Antarctic Circles which now have plant- growth during the summer seasons.

The Moon is unique in its responsibility for tides. (It is also possible that the Moon has been responsible for continents and the Pacific Ocean basin.)

Also, the chemical elements seem designed for life on Earth. Hydrogen is essential to life. It binds with other atoms, and is necessary for muscle contraction. It combines with oxygen to form vapour, gas or water (H_2O). In solid form the combined H_2O is unique in floating and expanding as ice, so marine life is able to survive below a solid frozen surface.

Oxygen is also unique. Not only does it easily combine with hydrogen and carbon, but it is also found in large quantities in its uncombined state. And as O_3 it also becomes Ozone, which sterilises water, purifies air and absorbs high-energy solar ultraviolet rays in the ozone layer surrounding our atmosphere.

Carbon atoms form enormously strong chains, which give structure to both plants and animals; and nitrogen in combination with other atoms, possesses the power of becoming positively or negatively electrically charged, apparently making reproduction possible by enabling chromosomes to build up exact patterns of themselves out of the material in which they are placed.

Finally, it is only necessary to note that many trace elements like iron, calcium, sodium and iodine, which also appear essential for life, are found in abundance on Earth.

Fred Hoyle suggested in the 1950s that the Universe seemed perfectly designed for the emergence of life.

Most of these elements were created in the intense heat of a star, perhaps our own Sun, a passing star or the remains of a star-explosion (a supernova).

All living things contain approximately equal numbers of carbon dioxide molecules and oxygen atoms. Oxygen is also contained in rocks and soil.

Hoyle pointed out that if the strength of the nuclear forces were only very slightly different, the balance of carbon dioxide and oxygen would have been quite wrong and the Earth could not have sustained life.

Again, he suggested that the force of gravity appears to be "fine-tuned" in relation to electromagnetic and atomic forces. If gravity were slightly stronger, then the "big bang" would not have been so big and the expanding hydrogen and helium would have slowed down, stopped or even collapsed.

Conversely, if gravity were weaker the gases would have thinned too quickly for stars to appear.

A very strong case can be made for a competent and intelligent mind behind the whole Universe, but certainly of Earth, if one considers the claims of living creatures.

GOD'S SELF-LIMITING POWER IS ESSENTIAL FOR TRUE FREEDOM

If God has allowed His creation to be truly free then God has also chosen to self-limit His Divine power. He has chosen to give us the gift of true freedom. In fact, He appears to have given all creation the power to be truly free to the extent that it is appropriate to the proper character of each part of His creation.

Christians react in different ways to the concept of God the Creator. Many believe that God just holds the Universe in being. They see Him as an unchanging God - the same yesterday, today and forever – a kind of passive God who faithfully keeps everything in motion.

G. Jantzen has suggested that the Universe is an embodiment of God.

Just as human beings inhabit our own bodies, he sees the Universe almost as a living organism (G. Jantzen, **God's World, God's Body: Dalton, Longman and Todd).**

Others see an active God, urging His creation towards particular outcomes by interacting with both people and atomic particles.

I imagine God "guiding" evolution either through a process of continuous creation or by a process of theistic manipulation.

Furthermore, I also see Him acting through divine influence on people. Perhaps He influences the human psyche through inspiration and encouragement. Just as ancient prophets were inspired to write of moral issues and the triumph of Good over Evil through Divine Messianic intervention, so He may inspire secular creativity and scientific or medical insights.

That, surely, is why many Christians pray for their leaders and decision makers, or for the skills and insights of surgeons and other medical practitioners.

But God's "urges" and "inspiring power" are just that – they are not predetermined, Calvinist "Sovereignty".

God allows free choice both to human beings and to His created Earth (and I presume, the Universe). All are free to resist His urges and His divine inspiration.

The creative genius (Homo sapiens) is free to debase his abilities or "gifts" and use them for evil or selfish ends, to ignore them through laziness, or to use them for the betterment of mankind and the planet on which he lives.

In his review of Max James' book' (**Einstein and Religion:** Princeton,1999), Andrew Pinset suggests that we are all "in the position of a little child entering a huge library filled with books in many languages.

The child knows that someone must have written these books. It does not know how. It does not understand the languages in which they are written. The child dimly suspects a mysterious order in the arrangement of the books, but it does not know what it is.

"That", states Pinsent, "is the attitude of even the most intelligent human being towards God." (**Physics World: June 2000**).

ARE NATURAL DISASTERS "ACTS OF GOD?"

Yet why do so many natural disasters take place?

They are, as I have already stated, an essential part of the physical laws that make up our freedom.

All the physical changes that take place on our Earth are linked to the constant forming, breaking up and changing form of rocks through surface weathering and internal pressures.

The three forces that control our universe and prevent total chaos in a free universe (gravity, electromagnetism, and nuclear forces) are the primary forces that cause these changes.

John Polkinghorne (**Belief in God in An Age of Science: Yale University Press**) suggests it is the nature of dense snowfields that they will sometimes slip with the destructive force of an avalanche – they are free to do so.

This is the necessary cost of a creation that has been given by its creator the freedom to be itself.

He writes: "The cruciform pattern of life through death is the way the world is, not only in the familiar tale of biological life on earth but also cosmically.

We are here today because some five billion years ago a star died in the throes of a supernova explosion, scattering into the environment those chemical elements necessary for life, which it had made in the nuclear furnaces of its interior." (page 14).

Our Earth is a giant ball of rock about 8,000 miles across that spins through space.

Its internal heat causes constant changes in the Earth's surface through earthquakes and volcanic eruptions.

Nothing on earth is permanent.

Our atmosphere, oceans, land-forms and living creatures all change over time.

During my time as a geography undergraduate, the first real evidence for plate tectonics was discovered.

Between 1967 and 1970 undersea studies were undertaken of ocean trenches and sub oceanic mountain chains on which were located numerous volcanic islands.

Such volcanic "islands" became progressively submerged as they were traced down the slopes of ridges. It almost appeared that they were being carried away from the ridge crests on a gigantic conveyor belt. Ocean floors are not static, but mobile with continuous spreading taking place away from the ridge crests.

The ocean floor was found to be moving at the rate of four inches (10 centimetres) each year. The ridges were apparently created by volcanic activity.

In the Atlantic Ocean a ridge of mountains runs the whole length from Iceland to the Antarctic, rising about 9,800 feet (3000 m) above the ocean floor level and flanked on both sides by numerous parallel ranges and broken at right angles by gigantic fractures and rift valleys.

As the two sides move apart, molten rock from under the Earth's crust rises, cools and solidifies. On some occasions the molten rock reaches the ocean surface and new islands are formed.

One such island rose off the coast of Iceland at 6.30 am on 14 November 1963. Now named Surtsey, the island reached 30 feet high by the following morning, by the 16 November it was 130 feet high and by 19 November it was 195 feet high and about 2000 feet long. Since a further eruption in 1967 the island has grown even more.

Eruptions occur frequently along the ridge near the Azores, Fayal in The Ascension Islands and Tristan da Cunha.

Even larger mountain ridges and deep trenches were found underwater in the Pacific Ocean, encompassing a ring of volcanoes from the Gulf of Alaska, across the Bering Sea to Siberia, turning south through Japan, the Philippines, and Indonesia. Breakaway ridges travel south from the Aleutian Islands through Hawaii, while others snake around the Coral Sea through New Zealand.

As molten rock breaks through the Earth's under sea crust, so new volcanic islands have formed throughout the Pacific Ocean on the ridges of the expanding mountains.

Because our Earth is not expanding, the ocean crust must be recycled.

Old, heavy seafloor sinks back into the Earth's interior at deep ocean trenches, often sucking vast amounts of ocean water with it. No one knows how far water seeps into the underlying crust (perhaps miles) but it erupts back through the seabed as scalding jets of water.

These hydrothermal vents have been discovered only since 1977, the first almost three hundred miles northeast of the Galapagos Islands. Since then, similar vents have been discovered along the eastern side of the Pacific and also in the Atlantic Ocean.

EARTHQUAKES AND VOLCANOES

Insurance companies refer to earthquakes and similar natural phenomena as "Acts of God", as though God is to blame for them.

Yet they are events free to happen in a freely designed universe that is controlled by the three forces. The very forces that keep our universe together, that keep atoms in check and that have produced a world where life is possible, also prove dangerous in other situations.

Just as fire can be a servant, so it can be a master. It can help and bless, keep us warm, destroy harmful bacteria, but also burn, maim and destroy human beings.

One amazing observation is that the great ridges and seeping molten materials from the earth's core that produce earthquakes and volcanoes are largely under the oceans, or in non-populated areas. Perhaps this, too shows competence and intelligent creation?

But earthquakes and volcanoes are not simply haphazard "Acts of God". Only recently have scientists discovered their cause to be the nuclear force responsible for radioactive decay within the earth.

As long ago as the seventeenth century, Francis Bacon had noticed that the west coast of South America was the mirror image of the east coast of Africa, and pointed out that the "nose" of Brazil would fit into the Gulf of Guinea, and the bulge of West Africa would fit into the Caribbean.

Geologists now believe that the Earth's crust is made up of several large rigid plates, which move as a result of temperature changes within the Earth's mantle and the forces of gravity, and that at one time South America and West Africa were joined together before being forced apart.

The energy causing such tremendous heat comes from radioactive decay.

The six major continental plates and about ten or more smaller ones sometimes slide past each other, causing earthquakes; or they may move away from each other, as happens on the ocean floor.

Or they can collide with each other to cause volcanoes and mountains to form. Sometimes volcanoes erupt in the middle of plates as enormous pressures push molten rock up through weak areas in the Earth's crust. Earthquakes occur many times a day along the edges of continental plates. There are continuous plate movements along the west coast of America (from Alaska through the Rocky Mountains, Mexico and the Andes as the Pacific plate pushes both under the American plate and also slides sideways.

One fault or crack that goes through San Francisco (The San Andreas Fault) is over a thousand miles long.

In the Mediterranean, the African plate is pushing under the Eurasian plate, causing earthquakes and volcanoes to erupt in Italy, Greece, The Balkans and south of the mountain ranges throughout Turkey, Iraq and Iran.

Why has God permitted earthquakes and soil erosion? Perhaps there is a reason and a competence behind such phenomena.

Over 8,000 earthquakes occur every day, but few are particularly harmful.

There is a noticeable increase in earthquake activity when the combined gravitational pull of the Sun, Moon and other planets (especially Jupiter) cause tides of solid earth to produce small sequential variations in the diameter and shape of the globe. This "Jupiter effect" also affects weather patterns every seventeen years or so.

Without earthquake and volcanic discharge, we would have no soil or rocks, for all rocks are caused by fire.

Rocks are melted and re-melted, put under intense pressures and heat, and then eroded and broken down by tremors, water and weathering into the soils that feed plants and enable life to develop.

Without volcanic and tectonic forces, we would have no life, no plants, insects, reptiles, birds, fish or animals – certainly no human beings.

Only now are geologists aware of the amazing manner in which fertile soils are created.

Erupting volcanoes certainly can cause great loss of life. One of the worst eruptions in May 1902 covered the city of Pierre, Martinique, killing 30,000 inhabitants – there was only one survivor to the tragedy.

On the other hand, when Mount Bezymyannaya, Siberia, erupted in March 1956 and exploded 24 billion tons of rock (enough to bury Paris under 32 feet of debris), no one died as the area is so sparsely populated and warnings of an impending eruption were heeded.

Four out of five land volcanoes are located in a belt called "The Ring of Fire" around the rim of the Pacific Ocean (including Mount St. Helena in Washington, USA, which erupted in 1980). Over eighty per cent of the world's major earthquakes also occur along the "The Ring of Fire".

It is so easy to blame God for the way the world is. Volcanic eruptions may often be called, "Acts of God," yet most never cause human casualties, and those that do are often due to "Acts of Humanity".

Most volcanic activity occurs below the oceans, unknown and unseen except on seismographic equipment.

Of the 516 known volcanoes in the world, only 89 are known to have caused casualties. Often this is because of the large numbers of people who live on volcanic islands (often overcrowded) or near mainland volcanoes.

Despite repeated volcanic activity, many people freely choose to farm on fertile volcanic soil.

Mount Etna, in Sicily, erupts every few days, sometimes destroying houses and whole villages. The farmland is fertile, the climate warm and enjoyable, crops are prolific and people take the risk, which choice entails.

Volcanic islands are not only good for farming, but the surrounding seas are prolific in fish stocks. Even the deep-sea vents of boiling water some miles below the ocean surface produce an astonishing density of life surrounding them.

Bacteria, two-foot-long tube worms, clams, limpets, mussels, snails, totally blind crabs and carnivorous fish, together with many previously unknown species, live in deep lava crevices devoid of any sunlight, surviving only because of the warmth and chemical discharges that nourish the bacteria on which the smaller animals feed.

Earthquakes rarely cause damage or loss of life by themselves. Of the almost three-million earthquakes that occur each year, around forty moderate ones cause damage anywhere in the world; while a powerful earthquake occurs less than once every two years.

Most deaths and injuries in earthquakes result from human error such as falling structures and collapsing buildings, bridges and broken gas or power lines.

Serious loss of life is often shown to be due to shoddy workmanship and inadequate building materials.

Japan, which suffers more than most from earthquakes, has learnt how to build "shake-proof" buildings, as have the inhabitants of the quake zone of the San Andreas Fault. One of the worst disasters in the United States was the San Francisco fire, which burnt for three days following the 1906 earthquake.

Earthquakes may also cause rock falls, ground settling and falling trees, or break down river banks, thereby flooding lower lying areas.

Under the oceans, destructive waves called Tsunamis may build to over 100 feet in height to flood coastal areas many miles from their source.

Yet without the breakdown of rock, life could not exist. It needs finely grained soil for bacteria to survive as the source of the food chain.

Vegetation and minute insect life depend on the bacteria in the soil. Up to 20% of fertile soil (called "humus") may contain bacterial and other forms of living creatures.

Minerals and rock including salt, potash, iron, aluminium, chalk, granite, slate, stone and sand are essential for human existence, as are natural gas, oil, tar and coal - much needed for fuel. All these come from the earth's crust.

THE WEATHER – AN ACT OF GOD?

Floods, blizzards, hurricanes, tornadoes, gales and storms – it is so easy to blame God for the weather conditions. In some countries shamans pray for rain and perform rain dances, while brides and farmers may pray for fine weather.

Worldwide, we see drought in Ethiopia and other "desert" countries; floods in Mozambique, and recently in Europe and Britain; outbreaks of forest-fires in Indonesia, U.S.A., Australia and Canada; hurricanes in the Caribbean and Florida Coast; and snow blizzards in northerly regions. Newspaper headlines underscored the term, "Act of God," when discussing insurance claims for flood-victims in England during winter 2000.

Why does God give us such bad weather? Every planet in our solar system has weather (except Mercury which has no atmosphere), together with Saturn's moon, Titan.

On Earth, weather takes place in our atmosphere, the layer of thin air that surrounds us, mostly quite close to the Earth's surface.

Gravity, electromagnetism, the spinning motion of Earth and nuclear forces affect the air temperature, air humidity, air pressure and wind patterns which give us our weather.

Air temperature is a measure of the energy of the motion of the gas molecules in air, caused by electromagnetic radiation from the Sun and radiation flowing from the Earth.

The Sun's infrared and ultraviolet rays also influence our atmosphere, and warm the Earth's surface.

Our weather systems are classified according to their size and duration. There are large-scale belts of winds that encircle the globe for weeks and small-scale weather patterns such as tornadoes that cover only a few acres.

Wind belts blow thousands of miles. Trade winds (named from early shipping days) blow near the equator; westerly winds blow in middle latitudes (from 30 degrees and 60 degrees north and south of the Equator); while polar winds blow from 60 degrees latitude towards the poles.

Prince Charles has blamed human folly for weather changes – flooding, droughts and freak storms - which seem to be more prevalent in the past twenty or thirty years.

In 1990, The IPCC (Intergovernmental Panel on Climate Change) spoke of "The Greenhouse Effect". Environmentalists urge higher taxes to improve energy efficiency, reduce pollution and save rain forests.

In Britain during the 1970s there were periods of severe water shortage, so a Minister for Drought was appointed.

Later, in 1999 and again in 2000, Britain had so much rain that severe flooding took place throughout the country (1998 was the wettest year in the 20th century, slightly wetter even than 2000).

The great hurricane of 1987 was described by Bob Ogley (**In the Wake of the Hurricane:** Froglets Publications) as, "the most furious gale ever known...this was a hurricane; the omnipotent hand of God tearing at both townscape and landscape and changing it forever."

Most of this century's warmest years have occurred since 1980, or at least since the advent of computers!

It is very difficult to know if human activity does really influence climate. Scientists, oceanographers and meteorologists all have a vested interest in ensuring

Government grants, supercomputers and important status for themselves.

Certainly, detailed and accurate measurements of global climate have been taken only in the last six or seven decades, and climatologists disagree over the information gathered.

Some scientists argue that increases in carbon dioxide will actually benefit humans by enabling faster growing trees and higher yielding farm products. Even the effects of El Nino are uncertain outside Peru.

Jan Nukk of National Weather Service in Monterey, California, states that in the eight heaviest El Nino years, California experienced drought in 1965 and 1991, while around one third increase in rain was observed in other El Nino years. There is also no evidence that El Ninos are either caused or made more intense by CO_2 emissions, the usual explanation for warmer climate.

Other scientists point out that volcanoes pour far more CO_2 into the atmosphere than all of human industry; and that a major source of methane gas, which may be far more potent that carbon dioxide in causing "greenhouse" effects comes from enormous increases in world farming of cattle, pigs and other herbivorous animals.

As for lakes at the North Pole, evidence from the US space agency suggests that wind and waves often cause fissures to occur in polar-ice during summer months. Claire Parkinson of Goddard Space Flight Centre states, "It happens many, many times every year."

Some openings can be hundreds of miles long. And gulls are regular visitors to the Arctic Ocean whenever there is open water, because that is where they get their fish, explains John Bianchi of the Audubon Society.

Again, a British weather forecaster, Martin Rowley, has analysed every August Bank Holiday period since 1955 (plus 1948). Most were stormy with hail, gales and floods – some even with frost!

On 25 August 2000, Mr. Rowley stated in **The Times**, "All this moisture is being sucked up by high vertical velocity into huge clouds. It basically means heavy rainstorms. **But it is nothing unusual**." (Emphasis mine!)

At any given time, the weather is sunny and warm in some places, and raining or snowing in others. Air circulates according to wind-belt patterns, but mountains and ocean radiation greatly affect its behaviour.

As wind blows through mountain ranges, tropical rain forests, steppes, pine forests, glaciation areas, dry deserts, over lakes, seas or vast oceans, so weather patterns can change in minutes.

Knowledge of Geography and Meteorology suggests that forces from the Sun and the oceans are the main controllers of climate.

Oceans circulate with the spin of the Earth and absorb vast quantities of the Sun's heat. The ocean surfaces circulate north, while cold polar currents migrate under the ocean back towards the Equator.

Huge "coronal mass ejections" from the Sun, carrying billions of tons of searing hot gas from the Sun arrive on Earth. One bubble of gas over thirty times the size of planet Earth was detected by the European Space Agency and NASA on 12 August 2000.

Taking about three days to reach Earth, such nuclear charged gases disrupt radio communications, blind satellites, cause surges in World power grids and damage space weather warning systems.

Many British people, who have seen national flooding during the winter of 2000, believe such flooding to be unprecedented.

Historical evidence reveals, however, that equally severe flooding occurred in 1903 and also in 1947. During January 1953 over 250 square miles of farmland were flooded and 307 people died in England, with a further 1,850 in the Netherlands.

Great storms in Europe killed 50,000 people in1287 when the Zuider Zee flooded. Hardly a century has gone by without great storms, intense flooding, and heavy loss of life.

Weather is clearly controlled by forces outside human control, yet people do affect local weather conditions.

Construction of cities creates dry and warm areas where storm waters are carried away to further swell rivers.

Solar radiation heats concrete and buildings, while motor vehicles, heating (and air cooling) systems, and industrial heat exchange make cities warmer than the surrounding countryside.

Downwind of cities there are more clouds and rain as chimneys and vehicle exhausts produce water vapour and dust particles that rise and form clouds.

Deforestation (the removal of trees for industrial or home use) affects local weather patterns in Brazil and Panama.

Since trees have been cut down for up to 100 miles each side of the Panama Canal, there has been less rain in the Canal area, and there has been a steady increase in silt levels in the Canal itself.

One example of weather change that is clearly an "Act of Man" is to be found in Northern China where desert is moving towards Beijing, China's capital.

Overgrazing, over logging and overpopulation in farmlands north of Beijing, together with lack of water, have produced huge sand dunes, which were creeping towards Beijing at about two and a half miles a year.

Large dams, water conservation excluding farmland from irrigation, and the needs of Chinese industry are destroying farmland.

A thousand tons of water can either grow a ton of wheat worth $200 (US) or expand industrial production by $14,000, according to Lester Brown of the Worldwatch Institute.

Industry clearly takes precedent.

According to a report in 21 August 2000 issue of **Newsweek**, Lester Brown has predicted that the Yellow River will become "an internal river, never even reaching the sea".

The Chinese Prime Minister, Zhu Rongji, called on Chinese farmers to grow trees, stop farming hilly land and keep all live-stock in pens to prevent ecological disaster – something that poor farmers could not afford.

Now with over 22% of the World's population, China has only 7% of the World's fresh water. In Beijing 20% of the annual water supply is lost through leaky faucets and other wastage.

Yet the Yellow River and the Yangtze regularly flood, and in 1939 half a million people died when all Northern China's rivers overflowed.

Again in 1948 the Min overflowed in Fukien Province in Southeast China.

During the 21st Century it seems that China's rivers are drying up as part of weather pattern changes, bringing crop failure, unusual sandstorms and locust plagues – all caused by the drought.

The Chinese government planned to pump water from the Yangtze almost 800 miles across mountains and desert to the Northern plains, in 2010.

In addition, 700,000 ducks and chickens were trained to chase and eat locusts at the sound of a whistle in an effort to combat locust hordes that thrive in dry weather conditions. So many of China's desertification problems seem man-made rather than "Acts of God."

Another country where weather seems to bring constant famine as rains fail annually is Ethiopia where millions die annually – another "Act of God?"

But rain does reach Ethiopia every year. Here famines are caused more by "Acts of Man".

During 1999 Ethiopia actually exported surplus crops grown in the Northern plains and hills. Some parts of Ethiopia have produced substantial harvests with their fine weather and improved agricultural techniques.

During 2000 Ethiopia produced 10 million tons of cereal crops. Yet, despite its internal famine, much was sold abroad to raise money for weapons to fight Eritrea.

It is in the dry south-eastern corner of the Ogaden Desert that famine exists. It hardly ever rains in the Ogaden, as rainwater falls on the northern and central areas of Ethiopia.

But the famine was caused by Ethiopia's war with Eritrea in the north. Ethiopia quadrupled its military spending between 1997 and 2000 to fund its war, and commandeered civilian lorries used for transporting food to the Ogaden, for war use. Clearly this is an "Act of Man."

CAN HUMAN BEINGS CONTROL WEATHER?

Much damage to the environment affects local weather patterns. Although there is no direct evidence that this will result in long-term climate change, there remains the possibility that it may.

So called, "Acts of God", which in reality are the normal consequences of physical laws, may often be made worse by thoughtless and foolish "Acts of Man."

The 1989 US Environmental Protection Agency (EPA) highlighted the difficulties of knowing what might happen in the future.

Hundreds of scientists, studying the effects of global warming on Egypt, used four separate "supercomputer" models from the Meteorological Office of Great Britain, the Goddard Institute of Space Studies, Oregon State University and the Geophysical Fluid Dynamics Laboratory.

Depending on which model was used the conclusions differed immensely. One gave a 30% increase in Nile run-off, while another gave a reduction of 77%. There were other wide discrepancies in forecasts for such things as crop production and forest cover.

A number of suggestions for changing weather patterns may seem nonsense. They range from killing all farm livestock (cows and pigs) in the world to eliminate methane gases - a politically unattainable goal - to painting white all roofs, roads, parking facilities and even vehicles in order to reflect the Sun's rays.

One scientist, chemical engineer Dr Michael Markels, believes in sowing iron to increase microscopic phytoplankton in the oceans. These use the Sun's energy to take carbon dioxide from the sea and convert it into carbohydrates. At present, sixty percent of such plankton is found in only 2% of the ocean rich in iron.

Such an increase in carbohydrates would increase fish stocks.

Five experiments in sowing iron have resulted in quite astonishing phytoplankton growth. It is obvious that phytoplankton needs to make both chlorophyll to harness sunlight and also DNA, the molecule on which life depends.

Two oceanographers from the Moss Landing Marine Laboratories at Monterey Bay, California, spread half a ton of iron in three doses in iron-depleted areas of the Pacific Ocean in 1995, and plankton increased by a factor of 27 within a week.

Dr Markels conducted similar experiments in the Gulf of Mexico in 1998, where he added over three tons of iron pellets to three, twenty-three square miles of water. Within 32 hours the plankton had multiplied by up to seven times.

By seeding America's East Coast Gulf Stream, he claims he could increase plankton by up to a thousand times, which would not only dramatically increase the World's fish stocks, but also enable the plankton to remove carbon dioxide and reverse the "greenhouse effect".

Other oceanographers are sceptical. Tinkering with the seas on such a large scale could have unforeseen consequences.

Sediment cores extracted from the South Atlantic reveal that during the last ice age, there were enormous amounts of iron in the ocean. Enormous amounts of phytoplankton destroying carbon dioxide may have been partially responsible for the ice ages.

Human beings may control some local weather. Human control of future climate is quite different. No one knows!

CONCLUSION

The competence of God does not apply to the physical world if God has allowed His creation the freedom to be itself.

A God who "controls", "takes over", "orders things to happen" and "breaks his own laws of physics, chemistry and nature" is one who runs a robotic and deterministic universe.

A God who wants to know and share love with His creation, must allow each individual total and complete freedom, together with all the risks that involves.

There can be no risk without danger. There is a risk in freedom. To be free is to be totally free one's self. In the case of Nature, freedom means to be free to be itself.

The Earth's crust is free to move according to the pressures produced from within the Earth's mantle and core. Thus, it is free to produce tremors, earthquakes, or volcanic discharges.

Wind patterns must be free to blow where they will as the natural spin of the Earth, the radiation from Sun and ocean, and the forces of gravity act upon them.

Droughts, heavy rain, thunderstorms, hurricanes, floods, tornadoes, blizzards. and a host of other conditions are the natural results of freedom to move over different kinds of terrain and water.

Forest fires, lightning and natural combustion are free to be themselves, and to act according to their own natures and the laws of physics and chemistry.

Either there is total freedom to be and act, or freedom is controlled.

Yet nothing is completely free in the sense of chaotic unpredictability. All nature is subject to forces, which can help to control and predict future events.

Gravity, the electromagnetic field, and nuclear forces all control the otherwise free actions of all creation. Even that which appears haphazard is not really so. Random particles that split from atoms as they decay are subject to the same laws that indicate the half-life of the particular atom.

While human beings may never be able to predict "chaotic" atomic disintegration, perhaps an all-knowing omniscient God can.

Where then does God fit in?

God may at times lure or entice His creation from complete self-destruction, or stir people to new insights and heights of creative thinking.

He may even inspire people to help others, to answer their own prayers and even prompt them to love and worship Him - but such stirrings are not compulsion.

Human freedom is just as real and just as limited. Birth, health, upbringing, wealth, need of food and shelter and a host of other things limit us.

Physical and chemical forces also limit our freedom. Yet we are free to use those very forces to destroy others and ourselves, to deliberately or carelessly wreck nature itself, or to manage our planet and its resources, help living creatures, and support other human beings as creatures made in "the image" of God.

God is the one who gave creation its freedom to be itself. But no freedom can be called such, unless there are choices with real alternatives. And such alternatives must offer real choices, which by their very nature must also involve suffering and pain.

If we cannot choose to hurt ourselves, to hurt others, to seek to learn and attempt to coexist or control nature, then human beings are not truly free.

God upholds the laws of physics and chemistry, thus allowing true natural and human freedom. That is His supreme gift of love

Chapter 29

What About Disease and Decay?

The deaths I have seen as hospital chaplain were caused by illness. I witnessed friends and strangers in their last years, months or days of life. Some were in pain, generally relieved by medication; some were resigned to death's inevitability. Every emotion was prevalent – anger, anxiety, fear, happiness, contentment, bitterness - to name just a few.

I offered my love and friendship. Mostly I listened to patients anxious to relieve their feelings. I would pray, give the sacrament, talk about faith in God on occasions, but my primary task was to stay and listen, to hold hands, touch heads and be still.

Meeting patients in a haematology ward suffering from blood disorders, leukaemia and infectious disease I had many unanswered questions. Why do people fall ill? Why is there cancer? Why do bodies deteriorate? Where is God in all this? I had to find answers.

First, I decided to examine the world of genetics, and then look at the causes of disease.

THE LATEST DISCOVERIES IN GENETICS

Since the beginning of the twenty-first century it has been difficult to open a newspaper without finding the words "genetics", "genes", "genetically modified", "GM", the "chromosomes." "Human Genome Project", "DNA", or "RNA"

Nothing seems to be what it appears. The physical world is made up of atoms and molecules, and the world of plants and animals is made up of cells.

Every living thing is made of cells. While some organisms may consist of only one cell, the human body contains more than ten trillion (10,000,000,000,000), most of which contain a nucleus.

The nucleus holds the cell's genetic programme that controls everything the cell does. In the nucleus are structures called chromosomes. They are long, threadlike strands of a substance called chromatin, consisting of a chemical called deoxyribonucleic acid (DNA) and other proteins.

Each human chromosome contains a DNA molecule about 5 centimetres long (if the entire DNA from one person were laid end to end it would reach to the Sun and back 600 times!).

Normally there are two sets of chromosomes in each cell, one from each parent. Following fertilization, when sperm fertilises the egg in most animals or pollen fertilises the ovum in plants, the cell divides into two identical copies of itself, each containing exactly the same unique combination of chromosomes identical in each new cell.

This inherited DNA contains all the information needed to manufacture and reproduce each living body.

The individual instructions that make up the blueprint for the DNA are called genes.

Each gene gives instructions for just one particular characteristic of the living creature, using four chemical bases (adenine, thiamine, guanine and cytosine) known as A, T, G and C. The entire code of instructions may be huge and sprawling, with some genes consisting of numerous characters combining these four chemicals in some sort of coded message, such as GCTGTTCACCACTAATAGGTA AGAAATCATTCC.

One anthropologist describes the human body in this way:

"The genes themselves are like sentences. Several genes together make a paragraph, and many paragraphs of gene clusters make a chapter, and many chapters make a book called a chromosome.

There are 23 chromosome books to make the whole encyclopaedia of instructions. An encyclopaedia specifies a man. This is duplicated to make an identical copy so that the body has two encyclopaedias – in other words 46 books or chromosomes in each human cell." (Dr. E.K. Victor Pearce: **Evidence for Truth: Science:** Chapter 5 "God's Amazing Word Processor: The Genetic Book of Man**": Eagle Publishing).

DNA never leaves the nucleus in order to make proteins. This is done by a chemical cousin of the DNA, made from the nucleus of the cell, called RNA.

In the nucleus an RNA copy of the DNA blueprint is made. Then the RNA leaves the nucleus, duplicating the DNA instructions to produce protein, including hormones and enzymes, which may work within or outside the cell.

DNA controls life by determining the form and function of the cell, the proteins produced, and passing on all hereditary information from one generation of cells to the next.

One of the first total genetic messages to be translated was that of a sub microscopic bacterial virus (called PhiChi174). Containing 5,375 instructions, it was first described by Frederick Sanger and Alan R. Coulson of the British Medical Research Council Laboratory of Molecular Biology in Cambridge in 1975.

The complete set of instructions was described in "The Nucleotide Sequence of a Viral DNA" in **Scientific American, December 1977.**

Scientists have spent ten years attempting to sequence the human genetic code in the Human Genome Project.

Dr Anna Gloyn, geneticist, explains in an article in **Diabetes Wellness Letter,** March 2001, how Research scientists took blood and sperm samples from anonymous donors, removed the DNA from the cells, combined it and made thousands of copies of minute sections of DNA, during which the sequence of the four-letter code was determined.

In the year 2000 the project workers announced the successful decoding of the genetic make-up of human beings. For one individual to read the genome like a book would take over nine years, as it would be equivalent to reading about 200 telephone directories.

Each instruction tells a cell how to make a protein from amino acids. These proteins produce the size and shape of the brain, heart, intestines, muscles, eyes, glands, bones and everything that makes a living creature.

Research has revealed some astonishing things about human genes.

In **"Numbers" (Time,** February 26, 2001), the following statistics were revealed.

1. 99.9% of genes are identical in every person.
2. 40% of our genes are similar to those of a nematode worm.
3. 60% are like those of a fruit fly.
4. 90% are similar to those found in mice.
5. 99% are similar to those in a chimpanzee.

Indeed, it seems that the DNA Code is used by every living creature, whether an organism like a bacterium, an insect, plant, fish, reptile, bird, mammal or human being.

WHAT CAUSES HUMAN DISEASE?

Natural disasters or "freaks of nature" are one thing. But what about the pain caused by disease and decay? I had seen both in my roles as medical orderly and later as hospital chaplaincy assistant.

In London, 68,596 deaths were recorded by plague during 1665-6.

When Christopher Columbus returned from the New World in 1492, over 10 million people died of syphilis in Europe within twenty years.

An outbreak of 75 million cases of malaria was documented in India in 1947 (with a million recorded deaths), while 3 million deaths through typhus were recorded in the USSR following the First World War.

Today the spread of AIDS is mostly unchecked in Africa, and is spreading throughout South America and Asia with many millions suffering from its effects.

Traditional religion usually blamed the devil, demons or demonic powers for pain and suffering.

When clergy and monasteries were wiped out by the plague in 1348, William Edendon, Bishop of Winchester, said, "A voice in Rama has been heard...this cruel plague... man's sensuality...has now fallen into deep malice and justly provoked the Divine wrath by the multitude of sins."

German Monks ("Brethren of the Cross") often called "Flagellants," chastised themselves with metal-studded whips three times daily for thirty-three days in extreme penance to placate God's anger.

In the German town of Oberammergau, the inhabitants pledged to perform a passion play as a sign of their remorse and repentance over the suffering and death of Jesus, in an attempt to pacify God's fury in sending the plague.

Since 1634 the play has been performed every ten years (in the first year of each decade since 1680) apart from 1770 and 1940.

There is, however, no one cause of disease. Today's medical scientists know of numerous answers to the questions about the origin of disease.

Living organisms – parasites, pests, bacteria, or viruses - cause some ailments.

Chemical reactions, poisons, injury or malnutrition produce others.

Personal folly such as drinking excess alcohol, drug taking, fasting, over eating, carelessness or accident also occasion ill health.

Genetic defects or perinatal circumstances cause illness and deformity in some children.

And it is self-evident that the aging process itself causes sickness, decay and death.

Medical science strives to overcome the causes of disease, to eliminate or alleviate the effects of illness, and to lengthen life whenever possible.

But why is there illness and suffering in the first place?

Professor Richard Dawkins believes that illness is a natural phenomenon brought about by nature and the breakdown of genetic replication. He sees human bodies as "survival machines" and DNA as a kind of photocopying "Replicator" that reproduces itself in the gene.

In his book, **The Selfish Gene** (Oxford), Dawkins states: "We are survival machines – robot vehicles blindly programmed to preserve the selfish molecules known as genes" (Preface to 1976 edition).

For Dawkins, God does not come into it. While he cannot prove there isn't a God, Dawkins suggests that the same is true of fairies and Father Christmas.

"If... there are no traces of God's involvement in the universe; if God did indeed set things up so that life would evolve, but covered His tracks so brilliantly that no clues remain; if He made the universe look exactly as it would be expected to look if He did not exist, then what we have is not an argument from design at all. There can be no argument from design if the universe is expertly designed to look undesigned."

Of course, Dawkins is right to say that God cannot be proved by science. As has already been stated in chapter 21, God is not known through the scientific method but through His own revelation to the **Old Testament** writers, through the life, work, teaching, death and resurrection of Jesus the Christ of Nazareth, and through the personal experience of those who accept Him by faith.

An illustration of the way science and experience differ from each other is given by David Wilkinson (**God, The Big**

Bang and Stephen Hawking: Monarch), in his four different descriptions of a kiss:

1. The approach of two pairs of lips.
2. The reciprocal transmission of carbon dioxide and microbes.
3. The juxtaposition of two orbicular muscles in a state of contraction.
4. The sign of betrayal, love, greeting etc.

The first three descriptions define kiss in "scientific" terms, whereas the fourth explains the "why" - the purpose behind it.

Science explores cause and effect, and simply ignores purpose and meaning. It seeks to investigate and explain the universe in terms of our senses, and by definition and choice it leaves out the concept of God.

Science deals only with what can be perceived by the senses, and never attempts to examine the spiritual or the supernatural. They are excluded from its remit.

Purpose and meaning do not contradict science, they merely explain our universe, our world, and our own lives from a totally different viewpoint.

Medical science can explain the causes, give detailed descriptions of observations and offer some remedies for disease and suffering, but it cannot supply details of the "mind" behind disease – the real "why?"

It is essential, then to look at the causes of disease from a scientific viewpoint before seeking an explanation that might satisfy a believer in a good, rather than a perverse, God.

GENES CAUSE SUFFERING

Richard Dawkins explains life through the metaphor of "The Selfish Gene". He calls his book "a gene's eye view of nature" and fully understands that he is using a mere figure of speech, just as when he discusses "ruthless" genes.

The fundamental agent of life is the gene, the DNA replicator, which produces an individual body or sex machine, the vast majority being bacteria, microscopic life consisting of a single cell.

Larger organisms like human beings or elephants are rare in comparison with bacteria or insects.

Even Dawkins, however, accepts that the whole body is much more than multiple genes.

A living body or organism is coherent, integrated, intensely complicated with a conscious unity of purpose.

Human beings can reason and seek to understand something of the "why?" as well as the "how?" of creation.

Sickness, deformity, pain and suffering are sometimes clearly linked to genetic factors. Genes make us grow, develop, mature and age. Genes cause our muscles, nerves, bones and all organs to develop as they do. But often we fail to realize the huge number of genes involved in any one function.

Dawkins gives an example of haemoglobin molecules in the blood. As chaplain's assistant in a haematology ward, I found this particularly fascinating. Haemoglobin or red blood cells each contain 574 amino acids, and are created at the rate of 400,000,000 per second. A further 400,000,000 are destroyed each second. The gene responsible for haemoglobin reproduces each cell as an exact copy of every other cell.

With such huge numbers and the speed of replication, accidents can occasionally happen. Sometimes a piece of chromosome detaches itself at both ends - and turns head-over-heels to reattach itself in the inverted position. Such changes or mistakes in gene sequence (a mutation) can lead to the production of a protein that does not work, or stop production of that protein entirely.

Cystic fibrosis is caused by mutations in a gene that encodes a protein called CFTR whose function is to regulate membranes in tissue such as lungs. The gene mutation disrupts this process and the lungs become prone to infection.

Dr. Anna Gloyn points out that Chromosome 22 carries genes linked to at least twenty-seven diseases, including some cancers. Gene mutations, or misspellings of the code for a protein, can cause disease such as diabetes, which can be passed onto future generations. Some genetic defects are not found in just one gene, but may be caused by different combinations of mutations in different families.

These new discoveries are not the end of our knowledge about genetics, but just the beginning. Millions of scientists throughout the world in genetics, medicine, pharmacology, microbiology and allied fields are seeking to learn more about human genes.

Despite my school biology lessons about simple cells, I soon discovered that there is nothing "simple" about anything. Even with my own little knowledge of biological sciences, I marvel at the staggering complexity of life apparent from its very beginning.

The flu virus PhiChi174 contains 5373 nucleotides in its DNA. There is nothing "simple" in that. While there are only 66 genes in a red blood cell, there are over 22,000 in a white blood cell. There are 6,000 genes in a heart cell, and the same in a testes' cell, but over 30,000 in one single brain cell.

No wonder, that with such immense numbers of genetic instructions being given to the cells of the human brain, most genetically inherited diseases affect the nervous system. That is why Down's syndrome, cystic fibrosis, Huntington's disease and Alzheimer's disease are so prevalent.

With so many instructions, the genes controlling the functions of the brain need only the slightest error to cause brain defect.

If over 30,000 people were all passing on instructions every second, we would accept that the occasional error would be made. Or if more than 30,000 machines were producing products, we would expect the same.

I began to understand the causes of leukaemia. With 22,000 or more genetic instructions in the leucocytes (white blood cells), again occasional errors are more likely during the lifetimes of some individuals.

In a world where genetic make-up varies with each union with a new partner, errors are bound to occur. When people enter a sexual union with someone with very similar genes to themselves (such as brothers, sisters, cousins or parents) similar genetic weaknesses can wreak havoc on a child of such a union.

INHERITED AND ACQUIRED DEFECTS

One of the smallest ethnic communities on earth is the surviving group of Samaritans in Israel.

Before the Six- Day War of 1967 the Samaritans had been divided into two communities, one group numbering about 250 living in Nablus, with a similar number living south of Tel Aviv. Thus, the total Samaritan population stood at 500. They appear to have remained within their own families, and kept their religious rites unchanged for over 2000 years.

Living for years under Moslem rule, the Nablus' Samaritans have survived virtual exclusion, in a typical "ghetto" situation. They still speak Aramaic, the language of Ancient Israel, together with Hebrew, and keep to their own cultural traditions.

The Samaritan community south of Tel Aviv has integrated somewhat into Israeli society since 1948, although it has resisted religious assimilation.

Because the Nablus' Community is isolated, its members tend to marry first cousins (as do the Samaritans near Tel Aviv).

Studies since 1963 by Batsheva Bonne of the Tel Aviv School of Medicine, have shown that this inbreeding has resulted in three specific genetic defects.

Around 27% of Samaritans (i.e. 135 out of 500) suffer from colour blindness (most belonging to one extended family near Tel Aviv). Another extended family has chronic shortness of breath resulting in respiratory deficiency; while an extended family of Samaritan priests at Nablus, together with another family, has a high incidence of deaf-mutism.

Genes clearly cause a large number of illnesses through accidental instructions or breakdown, in-breeding or through other means.

OLD AGE CAUSES DISEASE

It is also obvious that over time everything deteriorates

The heart pumps almost 300 thousand tons of blood throughout an average human lifetime, enough to fill a decent sized oil tanker, according to Steve Jones, **In the Blood**. After a number of years, the heart stops beating. Fat fills up the arteries, stopping the blood, causing a stroke or cardiac arrest.

Our joints deteriorate over time. Simple mechanical failure plays a part – old age is programmed into life itself. In fact, it is programmed into our genes.

Professor Jack Cuzick, of Imperial Cancer, says that he looks at cancer not so much as a disease but rather as part of a process, like aging. The longer an individual lives, the more likely is that person to develop cancerous cells somewhere. Cancer is not a new disease. Tumours have been discovered in 3000-year-old mummies.

All life eventually decays and dies. As the hymn writer puts it:

> Swift to its close ebbs out life's little day;
> Earth's joys grow dim, its glories pass away;
> Change and decay in all around I see…

INDUSTRIAL POLLUTANTS CAUSE DISEASE

Roughly a third of the population in industrialised countries develop cancers of some kind. During the eighteenth century, many chimney sweeps died from cancer of the scrotum. German scientists discovered that lung-cancer was greatly increased by smoking. Smoke and poisons from industrial processes also produce cancers.

Radiation is a known cause of cancer. Madam Curie and many of those working with early X-rays died from radiation. Too much sunlight and sunburn in early years are contributory causes of skin cancer.

Chemical pollutants in water supplies, release of chemical wastes in the atmosphere, increase in carbon monoxide and other waste materials may poison our food, air, water or general environment.

VIRUSES CAUSE DISEASE

A number of my hospital congregation suffered from viral diseases. Viruses are tiny lifeless particles that are not made up of cells, so they cannot reproduce alone.

Once inside a living cell (of a bacterium, a plant or an animal), however, they become active and can reproduce themselves within twenty minutes, one virus producing 16 million others in a day.

They infect cells and may cause diseases such as influenza, the common cold, AIDS, yellow fever, or poliomyelitis in humans, or foot-and-mouth disease or rabies in animals.

God appears to have made provision for viral invasion. The body protects itself from viruses through its phenomenally sophisticated immune system.

White blood cells destroy diseased cells, or produce antibodies to prevent the virus spreading.

In addition, heat can prevent viruses reproducing, so the immune system produces high fevers to combat disease. The body also produces extra supplies of mucous in the nose and throat, which not only traps viruses, but also expels them through coughing, sneezing or blowing the nose.

Modern scientific methods of immunization with vaccines result in the immune system producing antibodies that fight the virus when it first enters the body.

Scientists are currently learning more about viruses and how to control them. Already viruses are used in insect control, in cell research, and in the development of vaccines and other medicines.

In addition, viruses are used to genetically engineer bacteria to fight infections. A Scot named Robert Swan was reported to have an inoperable brain tumour into which a herpes simplex virus was injected through a hole drilled into his head.

After four years, the tumour had stopped growing, the viruses were still confined to the tumour cells, and the patient was alive and attending football matches.

There is hope even for those suffering from HIV.

Over 130 prostitutes in Southern Africa have been found to possess a rare natural immunity to the AIDS virus.

Despite copulating with up to six male clients daily, one woman and her daughter are both immune. Their blood contains specialized white cells from which vaccine has been made in Oxford.

While years of trials are needed before large scale treatments become available, there is cautious optimism that AIDS will eventually be cured or prevented.

BACTERIA CAUSE ILLNESS

Microbes surround us. A thousand billion live on us, as well as in us. There are about 10,000 on each square inch of our bodies (much more in "sweaty" areas such as the feet, crotch and armpits).

Most bacteria are harmless, but even harmless ones may cause infection if the body is weakened in some way (infection does not mean contamination – it means the multiplication of microorganisms in or on the tissues of the body).

Rarely do microorganisms enter intact healthy skin. Entry is through the nose, eyes, mouth, damaged areas such as abrasions, ulcers, cuts, bites, puncture wounds and areas weakened by excess moisture (including profuse sweating).

Every person is completely colonised by a huge number of microorganisms, especially the skin, mouth, upper respiratory tract and the large intestine.

Most of these colonies are beneficial for they prevent the establishment of "foreign" bacteria, or help in such functions as digestion.

In weakened bodies or in damaged areas infection can turn to contamination and serious illness.

Harmful bacteria come from numerous sources. Infected people shed skin cells, breathe or cough bacteria, and produce harmful bacteria from infected sites such as boils or ulcers.

Animals such as domestic pets, rats, mice or cockroaches may harbour harmful colonies of such bacteria. And large colonies of microorganisms thrive in wet conditions such as still water, leaky pipes or in wet containers.

Dry areas of blood, faeces, skin or nail debris, together with dirt and dust from clothing and shoes may also host harmful bacteria. Bacteria do not attack people on their own.

They must be transmitted in some way. The science of infection control seeks to prevent such transmission.

Just walking within range of an infected person can be enough to pass on infection. Human droplets from breathing and skin particles can fall up to two metres from the source, or can be blown by winds over large distances. Contact with clothing, dust, vermin and insects may also spread infection.

When I visited patients with infectious illnesses on the haematology ward, I was required to wear a plastic overall, hat, gloves and facemask. These I wore regularly on my chaplaincy visits to patients in "isolation" areas.

Fortunately, there is a whole science of hygiene, sterilization and disease limitation that can prevent much spread of disease, if only it were properly adhered to.

LIFESTYLE CAUSES ILLNESS

Genes and bacteria are not the only causes of disease. **The New England Journal of Medicine** studied 89,576 identical and fraternal twins from Sweden, Denmark and Finland to analyse the causes of eleven different types of cancers; correlating the incidence of cancer between the identical twins and the fraternal twins.

The researchers concluded that genes account for only 42% of prostate cancer, 35% of colorectal cancer, and 27% of breast cancer. The risk of developing breast cancer if one's twin sister has it is less than 9% (or 13% if the twins are identical and share the exact same genes).

In "Stop Blaming Your Genes" (**Time Magazine**), Sharon Begley points out that the environment – what we eat, drink, breathe and smoke; how we live and what chemicals we are exposed to – accounts for roughly twice the risk of cancer as genes do.

Professor Jack Cuzick, Head of Mathematics, Statistics and Epidemiology for the Imperial Cancer Research Fund, discussing five major cancers (lung, bowel, breast, stomach and prostate) at a lecture in Brighton (in 2000) suggested that most were caused by lifestyle.

Excess smoking is a cause of lung, head, neck, bladder and pancreatic cancers. Diet can affect colon, breast, stomach and lung cancer.

Excess alcohol encourages cancers of the esophagus, head and neck, liver and breast.

While lack of exercise can cause colon, breast and heart cancers.

Cancer is not a disease so much as a process, rather like aging, he suggests. Growths such as polyps and moles occur much of the time, with some growths in the gut (polyps – adenoma carcinoma) developing over 10 to 30 years before they need medical treatment.

Living in poverty, in war conditions; living in perpetual fear of enemies, insects, wild animals or even the local shaman; or feeling inferior, lonely, rejected or unfulfilled – can all cause stress, depression and even physical illness.

Poisons and other chemical reactions, alcohol and drugs, overeating and failure to eat a balanced and adequate diet are all causes of illness and disease.

WHAT HAS GOD GOT TO DO WITH IT?

If disease is the result of genetic accident, poisons, bacteria, viruses, radiation or other factors like overeating, alcohol or drug taking, or societal problems like pollution, malnutrition, war or oppression then God is clearly NOT the primary cause at all.

It is no different from the suffering caused by natural disasters.

If God has created a world in which all is free to be itself, then the result is that each virus, bacterium, insect, plant or animal is free to express itself in a logical and natural manner. That is how creation is!

Why does God let these things happen to people? Why do people become afflicted with blood disorders like leukaemia? Why does God inflict cystic fibrosis on one child but not another? Again, is God incompetent, inadequate, uncaring, cruel or non-existent?

The Biblical accounts of creation (and there are many references to God's creative activities outside **Genesis** 1 – for example: **Genesis** 2 and 3, and 8:22; **Jeremiah** 5:24 and 31:35- 36; the whole of **Psalm** 104; the great passage when

Almighty God meets Job in chapters 38-41; and **Proverbs** 8, to indicate just a few) distinguish themselves from all other ancient accounts by their complete lack of animal and plant mythology.

The heavens declare God's glory and all nature is regarded as a "glorious tribute to the power, majesty, wisdom, splendour and benevolence of God" (as Professor Bernard Ramm expressed it).

There is no Hebrew word for "Nature" in the sense of a creative and regulatory power involved in life. The Jews had no "Mother Nature", but "Father God", "The Creator", "El Shadai" (God Almighty), who produces and preserves life. The laws of nature are the laws of the Creator.

The fundamentalist or the creationist will believe that God has "created" all life as it is. But that is not the only way to understand life.

The Creator might have created the world of living organisms exactly as they are today, if He so wished; but the evidence from biology, anthropology and geology suggests that many life-forms in the past have been extinguished, while new forms have arrived later.

The Creator may have designed the very laws of nature that include genetic codes for replication and reproduction. I find it every bit as honouring to God, to believe that he created life forms capable of self- development.

Michael Poole, Visiting Research Fellow at King's College, London has stated, "Indeed it could be argued that evolution by natural selection is a clever way of ensuring that available ecological niches are occupied; and that if climate and food supplies change, provided the changes are not too rapid, populations of living things are likely gradually to adapt to these changes, rather than dying out."

He also points out that Frederick Temple in a Bampton Lecture suggests that God "did not make (animals)... but He made them make themselves."

The idea that God has created the Universe, allowing it to develop (another word for "evolve") to its present state, where a particular galaxy produced a particular solar system with a particular planet that itself developed the necessary ingredients for life, and then developed various life forms until human beings were created, is as valid as the assumption that everything there is has developed on its own by random chance.

To me, God is the "life force" who brought about the original miracle of life.

Since then, He has been the force behind its development – its evolution – through new life forms until the creation of human beings.

These new life forms were not just chance gradual development over long periods of time, but were often sudden and novel in appearance.

While some Christians take the Garden of Eden story literally, I rather like the Jewish interpretation of the story.

In his book, **When Bad Things Happen to Good People (Pan Books)**, Rabbi Harold Kushner explains that as a child he thought Eve was a naughty lady who stole God's fruit from a tree and was punished for it.

Now he sees the story as symbolic of the truth that human beings made in God's image are different from animals. The forbidden tree is "the knowledge of good and evil," and it this knowledge that differentiates humans from all other life.

It is the knowledge of moral issues that makes us human. Animals are programmed to behave by instinct.

Humans have to grapple with right and wrong. God did not "punish" Adam and Eve.

Their own behaviour brought its own "consequences." Consequences that they and their offspring had to deal with – consequences that still affect us today.

Sex and procreation are natural for all animals. Females come into heat and males are attracted to them. Instinct controls.

But human sex is different unless we want to behave like animals, as some humans do!

Human sexuality is bound up with love, friendship, tenderness, sharing of affection, responsible commitment; and only humans, states Kushner, know the pain involved in love and commitment.

Sex is about choice - choosing to love, commit and be responsible - in contrast with the animal instincts of those in society who rape, bully and control weaker members of the community.

Even the choices of bringing up children or abandoning them, teaching one's culture, language and values or choices of sacrifice before personal selfishness all make human sex and child rearing different from pure animal instincts.

God has designed us to be free, in His Image, and we are free to choose good, or we can choose evil instead.

Animals eat food, hunt for survival, seek shelter and water, mate and exist.

Human beings make moral choices to work for food, to steal it, to kill others, to share protection and shelter, to marry or stay single, and to prepare for their own deaths, because humans have the "knowledge of good and evil."

To Rabbi Kushner that is what the Garden of Eden story is all about. It is a parable of human choice based on knowing "Good and Evil."

And with that knowledge humans can destroy, maim or torture others. They can be complacent and uncaring in a world of suffering and death.

Or they can ennoble their race with selfless acts, heroic efforts, thoughtful research, loving care and compassion, and all that is good in life.

It is in seeking the good in life that human beings have been able to help the sick and dying with loving care, medical attention and research, the development of hospitals and pharmaceuticals together with all the therapeutic developments of modern society.

Such developments in medicine are the results of individual human beings making choices to research and share their discoveries with others.

Richard Harris, Bishop of Oxford and former Dean of King's College, London, points out that God did something far more sophisticated than creating our world. "He has made a world that creates itself."

"He gives everything in the universe, the sub-atomic particles of which matter is composed, through electrons, atoms, cells, up to multi-cellular structures like ourselves, a life of its own…God has given the basic elements of matter a life of their own and has weaved the universe from the bottom upwards through the free interplay of millions of forces. In all this interplay what we call accidents occur the whole time." (Richard Harris, **Evidence for the Love of God**: Mowbray).

God may have included predatorial behaviour to prevent pain in injured and starving animals. Far more death and decay would be seen if sick, injured, dying and dead animals were not quickly removed.

Humphrey Primatt, writing over two centuries ago, suggests that God created beasts and birds of prey as a kindness to animals!

He believed that we would be daily tormented by the sight of numerous birds and animals "dying by inches and pining away through accidents, infirmity and old age."

Numerous dead bodies would cause disease and offensive smells. But, says Primatt, God has guarded against the evils of broken wings or legs, or of cubs starving to death having been forsaken by a parent, or unable to feed themselves: for "God's creatures relieve (them) of their misery by putting them to death. A kindness, which we dare not show our own species." (Quoted by Tony Sargent in **Animal Rights and Ways:** Hodder and Stoughton).

"If God had made us so we could observe Him with our senses," suggests Richard Harris, "we would be drawn by his beauty and holiness to be other than free.

In order for us to have real, true, freedom God has deliberately hidden Himself from His creation. We are free to live and die as truly free individuals with the ability to make our own personal choices – to do good and love God with all our being and our neighbour as ourselves, or to be animal-like, evil, cruel and selfish. Only by hiding Himself from human discovery, can we be truly free.

That explains why He made us physical beings in a physical world that puts a veil between the spiritual and us.

It is only as a person is capable of growing out of his self-centeredness, and seeking forgiveness through Christ, that he or she can know the God who can make a difference in a human life. But such knowledge of God is rarely overwhelming and inescapable.

By revealing Himself only through "a flickering, dawning awareness related always to our willingness to know and love God…He preserves our freedom to choose for ourselves and ensures that the pilgrimage we make is our own journey."

God is not sitting on the fence during illness, disease and suffering. He is upholding every electron, proton, atom and cell of the universe in such a way that they can combine to form higher forms of life.

As I discovered in the writings of St. Paul, God suffers with and feels the anguish of His creation.

God, through Jesus, endured the uttermost anguish and pain. Christians and godly people of all faiths have sought to cooperate with God in alleviating suffering. They have founded hospitals, hospices and clinics for healing the sick.

HEALING IN THE NEW TESTAMENT

Healing is very much part of **New Testament** teaching. The Greek word *therapeuo*, occurring 38 times, gives us the word "therapy."

In Biblical times *therapeuo* meant to dress wounds, heal the sick, wash and care for those who were ill.

Two other verbs used are *iaomai*, used 29 times, especially by Luke, as the physician's word for treatment, healing or curing from sickness; and *sozo*, used over a hundred times, translated as save, to preserve from danger or destruction.

In his **Healing and Wholeness in the New Testament** (Crowhurst Occasional Paper) David Howell states that the **New Testament** concept of healing includes the loving care and attention of nursing staff, therapists and all who care for the sick, disabled and disadvantaged, together with the doctor's skill with medical means and remedies, aided by prayer, sacrament and all the means of grace which God has provided through Jesus.

We humans live in a dangerous world of choice.

It is a living world in which all living creatures have choices – animals that hunt to kill, parasites that lay eggs, bacteria that seek to multiply in warm host cells or eat dead or dying tissue, and viruses that can only live in the cell of another living creature.

Yet in all this apparent chaotic state of life, there is a clear "balance of nature." The food chain is circular. Living organisms feed on other organisms, until the larger are themselves eaten by insects and bacteria to form a new part of the food chain for plants and so on.

Christian hope in the resurrection, and an understanding that God enters into our suffering in a vicarious way, gives true meaning and purpose in the face of illness, decay and death. Without God, it would be meaningless.

God is not incompetent or cruel. He has planned the best possible outcome, where we can be truly free to choose the highest and the good. There is much more to life than life.

According to the **New Testament** there is a resurrection and a future where suffering will end, and "God will wipe away all tears."

I must return to that later.

Chapter 30

Does Pain Continue After Death? THE Reality of Hell

The British Evangelical Alliance has produced a theological statement on the reality of Hell. It is clearly taught in Scripture and needs to be addressed, the EA believes.

Is God cruel in sending people to Hell? I now had to discover if Hell exists and, if so, whether it challenges Gods love, wisdom and omnipotence.

My father, following his skin grafts cried that he had "been to hell and beyond" in describing the unbearable agony endured during his four-year recovery period.

The BBC survey of 1000 respondents, Soul of Britain, conducted by Opinion Research Business, reported in May, 2000, that 28% of the population believe in Hell and 32% also believe in the devil.

A letter to the **Baptist Times** (20 April, 2000) by Elma Ibbott strongly objected to the idea of Hell.

She wrote, "Those of us who are continually writing to countries, trying to persuade them to refrain from torture, can hardly believe in a torturing God."

Nor can I!

So, what does the Bible teach? I had to be careful and thorough, and soon found it impossible to examine what I had been taught about Hell without also looking at the Devil, God's final judgement and Heaven, for they seemed to me to stand or fall together!

THE EXISTENCE OF HELL?

My first discovery was that the **Bible** does not use the word, "Hell" in the traditional sense of a place below the earth where souls are tormented by the devil and his demons.

Hell comes from the Saxon *helan*, meaning "to cover." To the Saxons, Hell was "the covered" or "the invisible" place."

It was during the medieval period that theologians developed their concepts of Hell as a place of perpetual fire and darkness (with black flames) beneath the earth to which the wicked were sent after death to be eternally tortured by Satan and his demons.

The puritan translators of the 1611 King James (Authorised) Version of the **Bible** wrongly translated four Hebrew and Greek words as "Hell". These words, *Shoel, Hades, Tartarus* and *Gehenna* referred to graves, the abode of the dead, and to a local rubbish dump.

1. *Shoel* occurs in the Old Testament sixty-five times. It is translated as "grave" thirty-one times in the Authorised Version of **The Bible** (e.g., **Genesis** 37:35; 44:31; I Samuel 2:6).

2. In thirty-one further references it is translated "hell", but the context is clear - it is the place of disembodied spirits, the "congregation of the dead" (**Proverbs** 21:16); the abode of the wicked (**Numbers** 16:33; Psalm 9:17); and also the abode of the *good* (**Psalm** 30:3, 49:15, 86:13). In **The Book of Job**, *Shoel* (the abode of the dead) is described as deep (11:8), dark (10:21) and barred (17:16).

3. *Hades* is translated as "hell" ten times in the **New Testament.** It has the same connotations as *Shoel*. Originally *Hades* was the Greek name for Pluto the god who reigns over the dead. It seems that the translators of the Authorised Version of the **Bible,** in 1611, frequently replaced *Hades* with the misleading Hell. Orpheus visited the underworld, the state or abode of the dead, which came to be called *Hades*. The abode of the dead is described as a prison (**I Peter** 3:19), with bars and locked gates (**Matthew** 16:18 and **Revelation** 1:18). It is downward (**Matthew** 11:23) and the righteous and wicked are separated from each other. The good or blessed are in the part of *Hades* called "Paradise" (**Luke** 23:43), also called "Abraham's bosom" (**Luke** 16:22).

4. *Tartarus* appears only in **2 Peter** 2:4 where sinful angels are thrown into a pit to be kept chained until their judgement. *Tartarus* is a Greek word from early mythology. It is the lowest reaches below *Hades*, where the Titans and giants who rebelled again Zeus, the King of the gods, were sent. A Jewish legend developed that wicked angels had seduced earthly women, producing a race of giants. From this lustful union under an evil angelic leader, named Semjaza or Azazel, the resultant giants became cannibals and were guilty of every evil known to mankind. According to the Apocryphal book, **Baruch** 3: 26-28, these giants died out "because they lacked understanding and the wit to survive." Their end is also mentioned in **Wisdom** 14:6, and in **Ecclesiasticus** 16:7. None of these books is included in The Protestant **Bible**, but they were added to the Greek Version of the **Old Testament.** They were not regarded, however, as part of the Jewish or Hebrew canon of **Scripture**.

5. *Gehenna – Valley of Hinnom.* Eleven times the Valley of Hinnom is translated as "hell" (e.g. **Matthew** 5:22, 29, 30; 23:23, **James** 3:6 KJV). *Gehenna* was the valley outside the southeast wall of Jerusalem. It was used to burn rubbish as the public incinerator. Its smouldering smoke and flames were never extinguished, and loathsome worms (maggots)

bred in the dead carcasses. It was a place of filth, offensive odours and the burning of the bodies of vagabonds, lepers and those who died of pestilence or plague. In **Old Testament** times, it was known as the "pagan place of worship" where children were burnt to death on the arms of the God, Molech (**2 Kings** 23:10 KJV).

One astonishing fact I discovered in checking these references to "Hell" is the total absence of any reference to Hell being the domain of the devil and his hordes. I could find no reference to the devil being the king or leader or Lord of Hell, and I could find no reference to demons or devils in Hell.

Where have such ideas come from? Perhaps from Milton's **Paradise Lost**, which almost glories the beautiful Lucifer? Or did they originate from Dante's **Divine Comedy: Part 1** where Vergil conducts Dante through Limbo and then to levels of Hell descending conically into the earth, before reaching the mountain of Purgatory on the other side?

One thing is certain: they don't come from the **Bible**! Hell in Scripture almost always just means, "the grave".

British culture uses the term "Hell" very idiomatically. A "Hell hole" is an oppressive and unbearable place. "All Hell breaks loose," suggests confusion and pandemonium (Pandemonium was first used by Milton in **Paradise Lost** as the principal fictional city in Hell, "the high capital of Satan and his peers." It was distinguished by its wild, unrestrained uproar - but it is **not** a Biblical concept.)

Human beings can make their own hells. They can create hell for other people, and put animals through hell. They may live in their own private hells of loneliness, despair, addiction or rejection. Those existing without hope or who feel rejected by God may be living in a hell. In that sense my father did go to "hell and beyond". But hell does not seem to come from God.

When Jesus said that certain people were in danger of "hell fire", he was talking about the local rubbish dump - the "Valley of Hinnom" or "*Gehenna*" (**Matthew** 5:22 in early Greek manuscripts).

Jesus said that it is better to destroy the causes of temptation than "go to the Valley of Hinnom where the worms that eat them never die, and the fire that burns them is never put out," (**Mark** 9:44 and 48).

In the same chapter (verse 42) Jesus also suggests that a person who causes a child to lose faith would be better "to have a large millstone tied around his neck and be cast into the sea."

Clearly, neither expression is to be taken literally. They are both symbolic of anger and judgement. Such people are fit only for refuse; they are like the rubbish or garbage of the world, to be cast into the ocean or dumped in the local incinerator.

The symbolism of burning corpses, rubbish, maggots and worms, eternal fire, and depths of the sea all suggest the meaninglessness, hopelessness, rejection, and all that makes human beings exist in a "hell" of their own making. Hell is not a place in the future. It is a state in which people can exist now.

THE PERSON OF THE DEVIL

Having discovered that Hell is not a place, but a state of mind; and that the words translated "hell" mean "grave" or "rubbish dump," I wondered if the devil really exists and in what form.

The early church seemed to accept that Satan was sent by God to act as an agent provocateur, tempting people, very similar to his tempting of Job, states Dennis Wheatley in, **The Devil and All His Works: Peerage Books.**

Another school of thought, says Wheatley, saw Satan as a fallen angel who was jealous at Adam being created in God's image. Others identified him with Lucifer in **Isaiah** 14.

Later, during the Middle Ages, the devil "was amalgamated by the church with the old god, made a creature of bestial appearance, with horns, the cloven hooves of the lecherous goat, scaly wings and a spiked tail. Thus, was the Devil born" (Wheatley).

Milton writes of Satan as the most beautiful of angels, Lucifer, who fell from heaven through his pride.

Yet, the passages, which he uses to describe this beautiful fallen creature, are addressed not to Satan, but to the King of Babylon (**Isaiah** 14:4, 9 and 12).

Predicting the time of Israel's siege and capture by Babylon, **Isaiah** explains how Yahweh (God) will punish Babylon and allow the Hebrews to return from Exile. The king is called "Lucifer the Light Bearer" (or "bright morning star") who has fallen from heaven after conquering the surrounding nations.

He "thought he "would sit like a king on that mountain in the north where the gods assemble" and "climb to the tops of the clouds and be like the Almighty." Instead, the king of Babylon has "been brought down to the deepest part of the world of the dead" (v 13-15 KJV). The death of The King of Babylon is clearly predicted – his body will be "thrown out to rot" and cast "into a rocky pit and trampled down," together with his dead soldiers.

Similarly, the picture often used of Satan "puffed up with pride, claiming to be God" (**Ezekiel** 28:1-10 KJV) is a parable spoken to the king of Tyre.

"Tell the ruler of Tyre what I, the Sovereign Lord, am saying to him," says the prophet. The King will be "brought down to the pit" and as Tyre was an island, he will be like people "slain at sea" (v 8), and he will "die like a dog at the hand of godless foreigners" (v 10).

Nowhere is Satan mentioned in **Isaiah** or **Ezekiel**, yet **The Moody Handbook of Theology** states, "although Satan is not so- named in **Isaiah** 14 and **Ezekiel** 28, these passages are understood with good reason to refer to his original state and subsequent fall" (page 292).

I see no good reason for taking statements about the arrogance and pride of Babylonian and Tyrean Kings as secretly referring to Satan, even though some early church ideas came from allegorising passages of scripture to produce complicated and mysterious occult concepts.

One unclear reference to Satan occurs when he leads David to take a census (**I Chronicles** 21:2 KJV). This contrasts with an alternative account which states that "God told David to number the people", rather than Satan (see **II Samuel** 24:1-2 KJV).

Apart from this, Satan is mentioned only twice, as an accuser or adversary in the heavenly court. He is mentioned as the Accuser of Job, and later as the Accuser of the nations before God (**Zachariah** 3:1-2 KJV). Apart from these two references where Satan is an official prosecutor or accuser in the Courts of the Almighty, he is not mentioned elsewhere.

The word *Satan* occurs in other contexts. Translated "adversary" it is used of King David when the Philistines complained that David might become their adversary (a satan) in battle (**I Samuel** 29:4 KJV). Solomon claimed that he faced neither "adversary (satan) nor misfortune" (**I Kings** 5:4 KJV). And the psalmist states that "an accuser (a satan)" might charge his enemy with some crime (**Psalms** 109:6 KJV).

It seems that the Hebrew concept of Satan as God's court official changed after the **Old Testament** was written.

The concept of the devil came into Hebrew thought only after the Exile, possibly under the influence of Persian Zoroastrianism between the two **Testament** periods.

In the Apocalyptic (Hidden) writings between the **Old** and **New Testaments**, an evil, diabolical figure emerges called Beliar, Mastema, Sammael and Smyaz.

The Dead Sea Scroll Community Rule refers to the power of evil as "The Angel of Darkness."

The New Testament uses a number of titles to describe evil. Hebrew *Satan* becomes Greek *diabolos*, from which our word "devil" is derived. *Diabolos* literally means slanderer, accuser and adversary, the same as Hebrew.

Three Gospels record Jesus' temptations as a contest between Christ and the Devil.

Yet Christ was "tempted in all points like us". We do not see a satan in our temptations but are tempted in our thinking.

Perhaps Jesus was tempted in thought or word or deed, like us. In his hunger, Jesus may have toyed with the idea of turning stone to bread, but rejected it as contrary to the Scripture.

Perhaps he was tempted to use his miraculous powers to force people to follow him, but realized that was not God's way.

Did he think of using force to fight Rome in order to gain the loyalty and admiration of the Jewish Nation? Was that the temptation to capture all the cities of the world by force of arms? If so, he rejected that too.

In overcoming His temptations, he was described as the "one without sin."

Later, in writing about his trials, the Gospel writer put them into more cultural terms – fighting with Satan – a symbol of all that is evil and bad.

Jesus seemed to do the same when he stated that his friend, Peter, was Satan (**Matthew** 16: 23 KJV).

It is interesting that Jesus does not tell Peter that his thoughts come from the devil. Jesus specifically says to Peter, who had objected to Christ dying and rising again, "Get away from me, Satan! You are an obstacle in my way, because these thoughts of yours don't come from God, but FROM MAN" (Capitals mine). These thoughts were human, not demonic.

Apocalyptic symbols are highlighted in **Revelation**, where the Dragon is called "Satan, the deceiver of the whole world" (Revelation 12:20).

Clearly, in the **New Testament**, understanding these figures of evil enabled the early Christians to grasp the enormous power of evil, violence and corruption in the world.

The symbols and their destruction, however, showed them that Christ and God were in total control.

So many **New Testament** expressions or names for this evil are used.

In **Revelation** it is called, "Apollyon" or "Abaddon", "the Destroyer" (9:11); "The Accuser of the Brethren" (12:10); "The Angel of the Abyss" (9:11); "The Deceiver" and "serpent" (12:9); and "King" (9:11).

Other references to this personification of evil are "antichrist" (1 John 4:1-4), "Beelzebul" or "Beelzebub," "the dung god of the Ekronites", translated as "Lord of the Flies" or "Lord of Filth" (**Matthew** 12:24 and 27 KJV); "Belial" or Worthless one" (II Corinthians 6:15 KJV); "the Enemy" (**Matthew** 13:39 KJV); and (in **II Corinthians** 4:4 KJV), "the God of this world"

Jesus used the titles "liar", "tempter", "thief" and "wolf" to describe evil in John's **Gospel**.

Such a multiplicity of terms and titles for evil and wickedness only convinced me that these are symbolic representations of evil.

Just as we today might speak of "Uncle Sam", or "The Jolly Roger", or "John Bull" to stand for countries or types of people; or as we might sing "Rule Britannia" we would know that Britannia is not a real person. These figures represent other values or ideals.

The **New Testament** also seems to use such cultural expressions to express the evils of its day.

The book of **Job** had already convinced me that there is no dualism in the universe. There is no weakened God struggling with a demonic being.

Evil and corruption are in the hearts and minds of people like you and me. We are the ones possessed by sin.

And it is God, the only omnipotent power in the universe, who has allowed humanity the right and privilege of being able to choose for itself to follow good or evil.

We cannot stand back and blame the devil for the evils of mankind. Evil is in the heart of man.

No one knew that better than Sigmund Freud. In "The Anatomy of the Mental Personality, Lecture XXI," in **New Introductory Lectures on Psychoanalysis:** (Norton 1964,)

Freud describes the devil and the angel in the human mind.

He described the unconscious mind (which he called the "Id") as a devil figure. It was "a cauldron of seething excitement with no organization and no unified will, only an impulsion to obtain satisfaction for the instinctual needs in accordance with the pleasure principle".

Freud saw the "Id" as the source of all aggression and desire. Unchecked, it would lead to destruction, including self-destruction, to satisfy its desires for pleasure. It is the untamed passion, the selfish desire for pleasure regardless of the consequences.

The second was the regulatory agent in the human mind, the "Super-Ego". This was considered by Freud to be a largely unconscious censoring agent, controlled by conscience and pride.

Using religious language, one might say that the "Id" is devil- dominated; the "Super-Ego" would have us behave like angels (or worse, as creatures of social conformity.)

In psychotic individuals, said Freud, there are few or no controls on the passions of the "Id" (the unconscious mind), but for most people the conscious mind usually has a rational way of thought based on reason and cultural upbringing.

In popular language, Freud would say that the conscious mind (which he called the "Ego") "stands for reason and circumspection." He saw the rational mind of a "healthy" individual, the "Ego", as standing between and coordinating the evil "Id" and the "angelic" Super-ego. The Id, as defined by Freud, is identical to the Devil as defined by theologians.

Although I do not accept the three-part nature of the human mind as outlined by Freud, there is no doubt that he deals with evil and "the devil in all of us" in a rational manner.

The "Id" represents to me, sin and evil and animal passion that acts impulsively and selfishly with no thought for what is good or morally right.

The Devil not only personifies human evil, however, but also personifies the evils of Society, multi-nationalism, institutions and political world systems. The links with Satan, the Dragon and Great Babylon in Revelation are connected to the political and economic systems of Rome. Yet they go beyond the Roman Empire.

Leon Morris in **"Revelation: Tyndale New Testament Commentary**, states, "The great city (of Babylon) is every city and no city. It is civilized man, mankind organized apart from God. It has its embodiment in every age."

The apostle Paul made little of the devil. Rather, he personified political systems, sin, the law and death.

Paul writes of "Principalities and Powers", "powers in high places", or "the rulers of this Age". Such ambiguous references surely point to the power of Rome, and evil rulers.

Paul S. Fiddes suggests that we can recognize the earthly face of principalities and powers in every single system and institution that claims ultimate authority, whether it be Rome, in the case of Paul, or the Church, Communism,

Nationalism, or any economic, social, religious, political or bureaucratic organization that makes individuals feel powerless or forced to conform in order to survive.

Any power that dehumanises or depersonalises human beings is thus "demonic". (**Past Event and Present Salvation:** Darton, Longman and Todd).

Paul also personifies a range of concepts: "Sin" pays wages, enslaves, controls, has its own sting, and leads astray. "The Law" is a schoolmaster, a slave owner, a destroyer, a king who rules over us. "Death" has a sting in its tail, it is the last enemy, and we are enslaved by the fear of death.

We can be enslaved by numerous demons – fear of nuclear destruction, drug dependency, and even by the mind control of leaders in fanatical religious orders, churches or cell groups.

Just as Neptune is a personification of the ocean or Mother Nature of all biological functions, so Satan or the Devil is the personification of all individual and corporate evil.

So much pain, suffering, fear, animal behaviour without responsibility, helplessness and despair originates in the devilish behaviour of human beings either acting as individuals, in mobs, groups, corporations, societies, institutions, or nations.

You and I are Satan when we fail to make moral choices. I remember seeing a chart on the classroom wall showing development in understanding vocabulary. It was something like the following:

WORD USED CHILD'S CONCEPT
DEVELOPED ADULT CONCEPT

Angel	Ghostly type of being with a white dress and wings	Any method whereby God communicates with humans- e.g. dreams, vision, messenger, voice of conscience
Devil	Creature with horns, tail and trident who lives in Hell	personification of evil, death, pain, suffering, and every kind of absence of life. Symbol for all evil
Sin or Evil	Being bad or Naughty	Whatever opposes the creative, life-giving activity and love of God
Hell	A hot place underground	Absence of God, a sphere of Evil, frustration, sterility, pain And death
Satan	Same as the devil	A Hebrew notion personifying All that prompts and leads Towards evil.
Heaven	A place in the sky	Presence of God, perfection.

If God created human beings in His image, then He enables us to eat of the tree of the knowledge of good and evil. If you and I now know the difference between those two, then the choice is yours and mine.

THE JUDGEMENT OF GOD: DOES SUFFERING STILL CONTINUE?

I could not dismiss Hell and Satan, however, before examining the role of God's Judgement. Is God's judgement the same as Hell?

All religions deal with punishment for evil. For Jews and Muslims there is Hell; for Christians there is either a Hell, Purgatory or Cessation; and for large numbers of Hindus, Buddhists and Shintoists there is reincarnated punishment.

The **Old Testament** is full of coming judgement, especially in the prophetic and apocalyptic writings. The Day of the Lord, The Day of His Judgement, The Day, were all references to the coming Judgement of God. Cities would fall in that Day.

The coming catastrophe was seen by the early Christians to be fulfilled in the breaking of God into history and dying on a cross. Christ, the Messiah, was the judgement.

Jesus mentioned "judgement" on numerous occasions. Sheep would be separated from goats – one lot to be with God and the other to be judged.

Much of Jesus' teaching concerns punishment. He mentions millstones around necks, sending to the inferno of Gehenna, outer darkness where there is gnashing of teeth, sending to prison until all debts are paid, and a Broad Way that leads to destruction.

Paul says that we are all to appear before the judgement seat of Christ, and The book of **Revelation** deals with a lake of burning fire into which the dragon, Satan, the devil and all his angels are to be cast.

WHY JUDGEMENT?

Human beings are judged for the evil they do, or in theological language "for their sins."

I do not like to use the word "sin" very much. It is only a Biblical word in that it occurs so frequently in the King James' translation of the **Bible.**

In the **Old Testament** there are twelve different Hebrew words translated "sin". They vary in meaning from "wickedness" or "confusion" to "failing" and "distortion".

Some words, literally meaning "lying", "breach of trust", "disobedience", "injustice", "negligence", "guilt", "vanity", "trouble", and "rebellion", are unfortunately merely translated as "sin".

Furthermore, in the **New Testament** are another eleven words also simply translated "sin". The Greek, *Hamartia and harmetema occur 175 times.* They literally mean "falling short" or "missing the mark" or failing to live up to God's ideal.

Other Greek words translated as "sin" literally mean "rejecting the standard", "unrighteousness", "lawlessness", "impiety", "transgression", "to stumble", "to deprave", "disobedience", "lust" and "debt".

It seems a pity that the correct translations are so rarely given - just a blanket word, "sin".

Jesus condemned people for specific reasons. Some of them are as follows:

1. Refusing to use the gifts, abilities or talents they have been given; or as another writer puts it: "He that knoweth to do good and doeth it not – to him it is sin."

2. Refusal to alleviate human need. Jesus told of Dives who ignored a beggar, Lazarus; and also, of naked, hungry and homeless outcasts who were ignored by so called "religious" people (**Matthew** 25 KJV).

3. Leading others astray. "Causing little ones to stumble" (**Matthew** 8:37 KJV).

4. Hypocrisy. "Profession without practice" is the old saying (**Matthew** 7:21- 27 KJV).

5. Inappropriate daily actions. "Every idle word which men speak – they shall give account at the judgement" (**Matthew** 12:37 KJV).

6. Refusal to accept God's salvation in Christ. Jesus' teaching is couched in invitations and commands that demand a response (**Like** 9:26).

7. Materialism and wealth gathering. Jesus told the story of a rich fool who made plans to increase his wealth, but had no time for others or for God (**Luke** 12).

8. Refusal to repent. "Unless you repent you will likewise perish" (**Luke** 13:1-5 KJV).

9. Religious Self-Righteousness. Jesus condemned the loveless legalism of the Pharisees of his day for using man-made rules and regulations above those of God.

Unfortunately, much modern Christianity is also full of rules, regulations and hypocrisy.

Christians have difficulty in answering the questions raised about future retribution. How does God punish the wicked and ungodly?

Broadly, I discovered three main interpretations given by different groups of Christians to these questions

1. Punishment in Hell

    This has already been examined. Hell is separation from God. It is insisting on one's own selfishness, thus separating from one's neighbours through hatred, anger or greed. It is loneliness and isolation. That is the death of the soul. Traditional concepts seem to me to be too dualistic. If God sent sinners to Hell, then His victory on the Cross is a kind of Pyrrhic victory. I cannot reconcile the traditional teaching on Hell with the teaching of God's love and grace in sending Christ to Calvary. As the word "Hell" comes from Gehenna, the Valley of Hinnom, I take it to be a symbol. Certainly, I cannot believe that the love and grace of God are limited only to this life. Eternal Hell is totally disproportional – 1 to 90 years of life for a few years, compared with an eternity of torture.

2. Conditioned Immortality

    Many evangelical Christians believe that human beings do not have a soul. They believe there is no such thing as immortality. Death means oblivion, total and complete cessation of existence. The Puritan, Edward White, claimed that humans were created immortal but lost their immortality at Eden. These Christians see immortality as a gift from God. "The wages of sin is death; but the gift of God is eternal life through Jesus Christ" (Romans 6:23 KJV). That is why Christians believe in the resurrection. Only believers, or those chosen by God for their love to him, will be resurrected at the Judgement Day, for Jesus Christ has "abolished death" and "brought life and immortality to light through the gospel" (**2 Timothy** 1:10 KJV). Immortality or eternal existence is applied in **The Bible** only to God. He alone is "immortal, invisible, the only wise God" (**1 Timothy** 1:17 KJV). In his explanation of the resurrection, Paul claims to show a mystery when "this mortal shall put on immortality" (**1 Corinthians** 15:54 KJV). He also mentions the "righteous judgement of God; who will render to every man according to his deeds: to them who by patient continuance in well doing seek for glory and honour, immortality and eternal life" (**Romans** 2:6 KJV). Paul clearly sees immortality as an attribute of God, given only to His children.

3. Ultimate Restoration

    As a young teacher I attended a short course at Sheffield University on "The Cappadocian Fathers of the fourth Century," one being Gregory of Nyssa who believed

God would save everyone. He based his belief on three premises:

a.   God's character is love, grace and wisdom. He is not vengeful or vindictive, but gracious, loving and merciful.

b.   The Nature of evil is negative, to be removed. God, in Christ, will overcome all evil, so eventually only good will remain.

c.   The Nature of Punishment is remedial. God uses punishment to discipline and reform the sinner as part of his redemption.

Origen, who believed that even Satan would be saved, proposed a similar view. God will triumph over all evil.

Origen believed references to the fires of hell were visions of purification. He quotes **Malachi** 3:2: "Who will be able to endure the Day of the Lord? Who will survive when he appears? He will be like strong soap, like a fire that refines metal. He will come to judge like one who refines and purifies" (KJV).

Origin passionately taught that Hell was a purifying experience, not eternal, but transient.

Many scriptures also teach that "all mankind" will be saved.

Paul wrote, "As in Adam all die so also in Christ shall all be made alive" (I **Corinthians** 15:22 KJV).

In addition, John states that Christ is the means by which our sins are forgiven "and not only ours but also ... the sins of the whole world" (I **John** 2:2 KJV).

Even in his condemnation of Jew and Gentile in the early part of **Romans**, Paul also explains that as Adam's one sin condemned all mankind, "so by the righteousness of one (Jesus) the free gift came upon all men unto the justification of life" (**Romans** 5:18 KJV).

Of these three interpretations of God's judgement, it seemed to me that the second most fully accounts for God's love and Justice.

God does not hate, but He is saddened and will judge each of us. We can love and serve him, or go our own way. We can choose to lie, steal, cheat, bully or fail to live decent or caring lives.

Do evil people just cease to exist and that's the end? To take an extreme situation - Is Adolf Hitler or Pol Pot now in Heaven; or have they ceased to exist?

A further problem concerns the timing of judgement. Those who believe in a literal judgement almost always think of it as a future event, yet there is no agreement as to when that might be.

The questions remain unanswered. Are the dead judged immediately after dying? Is the soul immortal or does it cease to exist? Do human beings even have souls? Or is belief in the soul purely a Greek concept handed down from Plato? Is there an intermediate period of prolonged "sleep"? Does death from the body mean to be "present with the Lord"? Or is the resurrection to take place in some future aeon of time? These are questions that philosophers and theologians have discussed over the centuries with no agreement.

There are those who believe that judgement occurs now, in the individual heart and life. The Gospel according to **John** suggests that judgement may be present. "He who believes on him that sent me", said Jesus, "has eternal life and shall not be condemned but is passed from death to life...The hour is coming and now is when the dead shall hear the voice of the son of God" (**John** 5:24 KJV).

It seems to me that judgement may be remedial and reforming in its nature. If some prefer the loneliness and isolation of separation from God and companions, then perhaps God may leave them "asleep" in peace.

Laurence Ellis in, **Heaven and Hell**, expressed Hell in this way:

> "Hell is your own choice, or, sometimes, your neighbours... seeing alone what you did as a mob... the fall that comes after your pride...letting your parents down...envying someone else's lot...seeing time slipping away... the hurt look in someone's eye... war, in its waste and futility... seeing yourself through someone else's eyes," while "Heaven comes as a gift, to be accepted, not pursued."

IS HEAVEN A REAL PLACE?

Heaven is a symbol for the spectacular, awe-inspiring, new life promised in the **Bible**. Some call it the state or experience of perfection. Almost no details are given in the **Bible** of the future-life.

Jesus promised, "Great is your reward in heaven," and urged his listeners to "lay up treasure in heaven." He spoke much about the "Kingdom of Heaven," but not as some future place.

Jesus' first recorded words, "The time is fulfilled, and the kingdom of God is at hand; repent ye, and believe the Gospel" (**Mark** 1:15 KJV), referred to the reign of God on earth, in the hearts of believers.

When a Jewish ruler asked Jesus how to obtain eternal life, he replied, "No one can enter the Kingdom of God unless he is born again" (**John** 3:3 NIV).

Using proverbs and puzzling parables, Jesus taught his followers the how, what and why of the Kingdom.

God rules His Kingdom through the Messiah in justice, peace and stability.

His kingdom is a spiritual conquest of the hearts and lives of men and women. It is extended through personal relationships between God and individuals, offered to "all nations" (**Matthew** 28:18-19 NIV).

We pray, "Thy kingdom come; Thy will be done on earth as it is in heaven." As God's will is acted upon, so the kingdom of heaven is extended in the hearts of believers.

In his account of suffering, Paul considers suffering "not worthy to be compared with the glory that shall be revealed" (**Romans** 8:18 KJV).

His optimistic view of future glory is summarised in his letter to Corinth: "No eye has seen, no ear has heard, no mind has conceived what God has prepared for those who love him, but God has revealed it to us by his Spirit" (**1 Corinthians** 2:9-10 NIV).

Most concepts of Heaven come from John's **Revelation**, a book full of grotesque and awesome symbols. Great white thrones in the sky, elders playing harps, millions of angels praising God and the Lamb with seven eyes are among some of these symbols.

An innumerable multitude "with robes washed" and "made white in the blood of the Lamb...serve God day and night in His temple" (**Revelation** 7:13-15 NIV). Hunger and thirst are no more, for the Lamb feeds his people, gives them living water and "wipes away every tear from their eyes." (17 GNB).

John has taken these words straight from **Isaiah** 49, where the prophet predicts the glorious Day of the Lord.

The greatest insight into the afterlife seems to come from John's symbolic use of Jerusalem, dressed as a Bride descending onto a new earth containing no sea (**Revelation** 21).

Tears, death, mourning, crying and pain will cease as the old order of things disappears (verse 4). The picture of a city dressed in a bridal gown, continues. The heavenly Jerusalem, shining with the brilliance of God, is described in symbolic Christian and Jewish terms.

There are twelve jewels, gates, walls, and foundations. The dimensions, 12,000 *stadion* (144,000 furlongs in the

Authorised Version) for the city, and 144 cubits for the height of the walls cannot be taken literally. They are combinations of twelve, the number of Hebrew tribes and apostles.

Finally, John ends his apocalyptic vision by reference to the original Garden of Eden.

The new Eden is the city paradise. A river flows through the main street (a wonderful vision to those struggling to survive in desert conditions on Patmos).

The tree of life from **Genesis** now bears twelve different crops each month - fruit "for the healing of the nations."

It could not be more appropriate for this finale of John's to close his visions of horrors, trials, dangers and persecutions of the church.

In symbolic language, he expounds the blessed state of the righteous at the end of time.

I discovered some vital truths about heaven from my studies.

1. The word heaven means "above the earth." Normally it refers to the sky or the universe. In **Luke** 15:18, "I have sinned against heaven," simply means sinning against God. The idea of something being "up" or "higher" indicates quality and superiority. We speak of those "over us," "going up in the world," being promoted to the "top of the class," or going to "a high school." Each expression illustrates the concept of superiority or excellence. In terms of spiritual values, heaven is supreme, surpassing any other

existence, more desirable, exalted and grand. It is the abode of God and His Son, the Christ who sits at His right hand.

2. The **Bible** never reveals any place embodying heaven. In fact, no such place as Heaven is even mentioned. According to the inspired writers of Scripture, the entire universe will be heaven. The new heaven and new earth refer to a new world order, for the old heaven and earth are "passed away."

3. Such a new world order will be free from evil and its consequences. No more tears, sorrow, death, crying, pain or curse. Those who enter the presence of God will live in full joy and happiness. Jesus reflected this in his parables. He spoke three times of joy in heaven over sinners repenting (**Luke** 15), of marriage feasts and banqueting scenes (**Matthew** 8:11)

4. The biblical writers have stretched language to its limits as they attempt to describe the indescribable. Beauty, holiness and joy – paradise indeed. Such perfection is rightly identified with a holy, clean, fresh, unspoilt virgin "bride adorned for her husband" (**Revelation** 21:2).

5. Every symbol, every metaphor, every allusion of wonder and grandeur, point beyond a place to a person. Heaven is the presence of God. It is the relationship with God that is "water to the thirsty; rest to the weary; health to the sick; light to the blind; security to those under threat" as **The Lion**

Handbook of Christian Belief so eloquently states it. "Eternity will not exhaust the constantly expanding wonder of exploring God himself." That is heaven!

6. Heaven is the dwelling place of God. That is why we pray, "Our Father who is in heaven." But God does not live in a special place. God is omnipresent. He is everywhere. Unlike us, he is not limited by natural phenomena. He is a spiritual being who controls both within and outside of His creation.

7. Christianity does not make much of heaven. It emphasises the resurrection. Numerous **Biblical** writers mention the resurrection. Probably, the greatest exponent of the resurrection was Paul. He shows that Christ rose from death according to the **Old Testament** and the testimony of eye witnesses (**I Corinthians** 15). He shows how the resurrected body will be "incorruptible" (verse 42), "glorious" and "powerful" (43), "spiritual" (44) and like Christ's own resurrection body (45 and 50).

Perhaps such concepts are beyond human comprehension. I am convinced, however, that the God who so loved the world that He gave His only Son to die at Calvary, is indeed the God of grace and mercy.

He who commands us to love Him with heart, soul, mind and strength, and our neighbours as ourselves, will certainly have something more wonderful than punishment in the traditional Hell of fundamentalist and medieval thought.

The world was made for a purpose – that people like you and me might know, love and live in joyous relationship with One who prefers to be called, "Our Father" in an exciting new order called, "Heaven."

Chapter 31

Pain is God's Gift

Joni Eareckson Tada, a paraplegic who broke her neck over fifty years ago, was paralysed from her shoulders down, undergoing years of agonizing pain in which she sought help to commit suicide.

Now she is a Christian author, radio host, and founder of Joni and Friends, an organization "accelerating Christian ministry in the disability community". She is in a wheelchair, attended by others for her daily needs.

She says, "Sometimes, all you can do is cry…Rant and rave if you must, scream and yell. It's good to experience the depth of your pain and, like that seed which falls into the ground and dies, experience that kind of Good Friday trauma – so that when the resurrection occurs it makes our joy all the more meaningful." (Quoted from Colin Duriez, "Talking Point" **Crusade Magazine**).

"My life is made much richer by my injuries," said Simon Weston on "Simon's War," (U.K. TV) in April, 1999.

He had suffered 64% burns with 80% of his body carrying the scars, since an Argentinean bomb destroyed the Sir Galahad troop-ship off the Falkland Islands.

Now, following five years of skin grafting, he suffers from cramps and phantom pains and severe itching caused by profuse sweating.

Simon is now married, takes part in numerous fund-raising activities for burns' victims, and has a family of his own.

Simon explained to Lynda Lee-Potter in the **Daily Mail** (3 April, 1999), "It might sound crass, but I feel that being burnt and injured has been positive for me. I've been allowed to do so much. I've achieved a level of happiness and contentment that I might not have achieved otherwise."

In her book, **The Blessings of Illness:** (Lakeland), Basilea Schlink suggests that illness and pain bring special temptations to self-pity and ingratitude. Certain benefits may come from suffering, and it may be essential to overcome self-pity.

Regrettably, however, I cannot accept her premise that we must accept our suffering "with love and thanksgiving" or that illness, suffering and pain are "ordered specially for you, by your Lord and God."

Illness, suffering and pain are to be fought tooth and nail. Research, medical advances and improved patient care are all at the forefront of the battle.

WHAT IS PAIN?

Pain is a mystery. There do not seem to be "pain sensors" as such.

Nerve endings can detect touch and pressure. Some Nerves that transmit sensations such as tingling, tickling, smoothness, roughness, or sexual excitement seem to come into play only when needed.

Some researchers see crying, laughing and gasping in pain as a natural class of "repeated exhalatory vocalisation," laughter apparently containing an element of emotional pain.

Tickling may also be considered a bondage torture, bringing about uncontrollable laughter usually on someone who is helpless.

In "The Perception of Pain" (**Scientific American**: February 1961) Ronald Melzack details experiments showing that pain is not always perceived after an injury, even when a victim is fully conscious and alert.

Each of us responds to pain in a unique fashion. Studies in childbirth indicate that pain may not be perceived in other cultures.

Fear in older women increases the amount of pain felt in Western labour, whereas women in tobacco fields may give birth and continue working afterwards, leaving their husbands to groan in agony in para-sympathy with their wives!

Doctor Grantley Dick-Read witnessed local women in northern Kenya calmly giving birth. In his book, **Childbirth**

without Fear, he suggests that the pain of childbirth in Western society is caused primarily by "fear, tension and ignorance."

In an experiment with electric shocks, reported by Hans and Michael Eysenck (**Mind Watching**: Michael Joseph Ltd), patients could tolerate only 350 micro volts before giving up in pain. Given a placebo (a sugar pill) and told that it would cause heart-pounding, increased breathing and hand trembling as normal, patients not only reported less pain, but also could endure up to 1,450 micro volts of current.

Another experiment gave dental patients a button to press when their discomfort became unbearable. Although the button did nothing, the patients with the button could tolerate far greater pain than patients without one.

One other study with a bizarre outcome, reported in the book, **Mind Watching**, consisted in giving sugar pills (placebos) to insomniacs.

Some were told the pills would help them relax, while the others were informed that the pills would wake them up and actually arouse them.

Those given the information that the pills would arouse them fell asleep 20% faster than previously, while those informed that they had been given relaxants took 40% longer than usual to fall asleep.

Perhaps, concluded the researchers, the patients were inclined to worry more if they were expecting to relax!

It has also been discovered that differences in pain thresholds occur between Italians and Jews on the one hand and Northern Europeans on the other.

Italian and Jewish women cried out in pain, expecting sympathy when a "painful" electric current was passed through them.

The Northern Europeans and "Old American Stock women" in the experiment suggested that the current was merely "warm." Such women seemed stoical and suffered in silence, suggested Professor of Anatomy, J.R. Young, University College, London (**Programs of the Brain**: Oxford).

Jamie Barr, Britain's strongest man, pulled a seventy-ton Air Malta Jet over a set distance for one minute in 1999.

On being interviewed on television, he explained, "I start with pain. Half way there is more pain, then lots of pain, and even more pain at the end." Yet his intense pain did not stop him.

In another television interview with a marine training sergeant, it was stated that one object of survival training is "to enable soldiers to control pain and suffering to the edge." As marine recruits were forced to perform excessive numbers of press-ups, the Sergeant would shout, "Can you handle the pain?" When the recruits responded in obvious agony with, "Yes, Sergeant," he repeated his question more loudly and received even louder affirmations.

During the second world war, Henry K Beecher of Harvard Medical School noticed that only a third of severely wounded soldiers required morphine to relieve their pain, whereas over eighty percent of civilian wounded seemed in severe pain and pleaded for pain killing drugs.

The soldiers were not in shock, nor were they unable to feel pain, for they complained as vigorously as other men at poor injections.

Beecher suggested there is no simple direct relationship between the injuries per se and the pain experienced.

He suggested that the soldiers were influenced far more by the significance of the wound, the sense of relief and thankfulness at escaping alive from the battlefield, mixed with euphoria, thus feeling less pain.

The civilian casualties, on the other hand, saw their wounds as calamities that left them depressed.

Simon Weston was concerned only to ask "Is my wedding tackle still OK?" An affirmative answer made him sigh with relief.

Prize-fighters, wrestlers, football players and athletes can sustain severe injuries without being aware of being hurt.

It seems that pain, like all perceptions is "subjective, individual and modified by degrees of attention, emotional states and the conditioning influences of past experience" suggests W.K Livingstone ("**What is Pain?**")

My father may have "gone to hell and beyond", yet he survived. He came both to accept and forget the degree of pain through which he had passed.

We often talked about his experiences, and how he returned to driving his car, walking and even cooking his meals afterwards.

THE FUNCTION OF PAIN

Pain must play a part in free choice for animals as well as humans. Bacteria and predators rid the planet of sick, maimed, aged and dead creatures, so that any pain is temporary or terminal.

God is not cruel or callous in His creation. Pain serves a useful function. It is a positive gift from God. It is a sensor to warn of danger. It is the signal that something biologically harmful is happening, and makes us examine ourselves.

Two authorities on pain claim it is God's greatest gift to his creation.

Dr Paul Brand of the Leprosy Mission is quoted by Philip Yancy as saying: "Thank God for inventing pain! I don't think He could have done a better job. It's beautiful" (**Where is God When it Hurts?** Pickering and Inglis).

Pain "is perhaps the paragon of creative genius," states Philip Yancy.

Why do they think pain is such a gift? Both Dr. Brand and Philip Yancy have written a number of books extolling pain's virtue. They point to three vital truths.

1. The nervous system and the millions of nerve endings that detect danger, save us from harm. We stop walking on a broken leg because it hurts. We stop eating food when we feel stomach pain. We pull our hand from the fire instantly. Pain is a brilliant warning system.

2. Unfortunately, there are people who feel no pain. Children born without the ability to feel pain, often receive extensive burns and bruising. They regularly bite their tongues or inside cheeks while chewing food. Inability to feel pain is the main cause of accidents and disfigurement in lepers who may pick up containers holding boiling water without any feeling.

3. Pain is also associated with pleasure. Pain can be essential in the enjoyment of our richest experiences. The same nerve endings that produce pain also produce the pleasure of sex. The pain of over-hot water in a bath can be exhilarating as one gradually enters and slips under the water.

Doctor Richard Croft, who served for five years with The Leprosy Mission in Bangladesh, explains the danger caused by loss of pain in leprosy. Nerve damage caused by the Mycobacterium leprae spreads steadily causing anaesthetic skin patches, and sense loss in both hands and feet. "Even the eye surface may lose sensation so the sufferer can't feel if he gets sand in his eye." (**"Newday: Leprosy – the Facts"**: The Leprosy Mission, January 2001).

Feeling no pain, leprosy victims are so much more prone to ulceration, broken bones, skin damage and other problems just because they feel nothing!

When I worked as a chiropodist, I treated twenty or more patients suffering from peripheral neuropathy, a diabetes-related disease that affects the nerve endings in the feet so that sufferers may not be aware of touch, temperature, pain, vibration and position.

Since being diagnosed as diabetic, myself, I have annual foot sensation tests, and am already aware of sensation loss in both feet. Naturally, I check my bath water by hand, and ensure the correct footwear to protect my feet, especially when walking on the beach.

The entire pain mechanism is so complex and sophisticated it seems to be designed to warn creation of dangers that could easily destroy it. Those without pain are to be pitied. Pain is truly God's gift.

No one answers the question, "Where is God when it Hurts?" better than Philip Yancey. This is how he summarises the role of God in the midst of pain.

"He has been there from the beginning, designing a pain system that still, in the midst of a fallen, rebellious world, bears the stamp of His genius and equips us for life on this planet.

He has watched us reflect His image, carving out great works of art, launching mighty adventures, living out this earth in a mixture of pain and pleasure when the two so closely coalesce they sometimes become almost indistinguishable.

He has used pain, even in its grossest forms, to teach us, asking us to let it turn us to Him. He has stooped to conquer...He has allied Himself with the poor and suffering, establishing a kingdom tilted in their favour...He has promised supernatural strength to nourish our spirit, even if our physical suffering goes unrelieved.

He has joined us. He has hurt and bled and cried and suffered. He has dignified for all time those who suffer by sharing their pain.

He is with us now, ministering to us through His Spirit and through members of His body who are commissioned to bear us up and relieve our suffering for the sake of the head..."

Chapter 32

My Problem Solved?

At last I have reached the end of my journey of discovery. Of course, there are still unanswered questions. I cannot begin to comprehend the mind of the creator.

Yet, I have come to believe that God does exist, that He is revealed in the suffering, abandonment, death and resurrection of Jesus of Nazareth, the Messiah predicted from past ages.

I have come to understand just a little, but enough to assure me that God is not incompetent. He is all knowing, all understanding, and all powerful.

Yet, He has limited His power by giving His creation free will – the freedom to be itself.

He has chosen to enter the human world of suffering, abandonment and death through the cross on which His "only Son" experienced human agony and shame.

He has developed an amazingly sophisticated defence mechanism that enables bodies to fight disease, although He has programmed death and decay into His creation.

He has provided a pain mechanism that is amazingly sophisticated in itself.

In fact, there is nothing simple in His creation. Almost all creation is beyond human understanding – more and more is being discovered daily and new questions only reveal human ignorance.

The mind of a supernatural mathematician who controls the forces of gravity, electromagnetism and the nucleus shows the unsurpassed genius of omnipotence - words fail even in this.

As shown, God has created a world which is amazingly different from all known others, on which creatures can live and survive.

We are the correct distance from the Sun, our tilt enables North and South to have seasons, where crops can grow in areas where it would be impossible if both poles were at right-angles to the Sun.

The Moon prevents us from going closer to the Sun, as it rotates around the Earth.

Hydrogen and Oxygen are sufficient to provide seas, water and the Ozone Layer, which keeps all life healthy and able to survive.

The whole Universe appears to be made in such a way that everything seems to be able to recreate itself; thus, enabling life to create and develop itself.

"Acts of God" are shown to be normal aspects of a world with seas, mountains, deserts, tropical forests and different landscapes in which winds that encircle the globe develop strength and forces essential for breaking rocks and developing nutrient soils.

The heat inside the Earth is crucial for life. Untold millions of species live around the volcanic eruptions under the seabed.

Volcanoes on land surface produce minerals in rock formations, which are broken down by water and winds into fertile soil, full of microscopic life necessary for insects and the subsequent food chain.

The amazing DNA and RNA in all living cells still show how ignorant we are about the astounding wonders that researchers and scientists are just beginning to discover.

As already shown, pain and suffering has always been a mystery.

Yet, hopefully, I have shown that pain is essential in assisting life to avoid dangers, and is also the result of genetic accidents, alcohol or drug taking, social problems like pollution, malnutrition, war or oppression caused by people rather than God.

In a living world in which all creatures have choices, animals that hunt to kill, parasites that lay eggs, bacteria that seeks to multiply in warm cells or eat dead and dying tissue, shows a clear balance of nature.

Yet this all-powerful God has not only revealed total competence in the Universe, but through His union "in Christ" He is revealed as loving, gracious and concerned for His creation.

Uniquely, He understands our suffering and pain, for He has entered into our existence, and experienced it for Himself.

The pain and suffering that God has endured is an amazing proof that the Christian God is passionate and loving.

He is not an omniscient being who knows everything, for He has deliberately given free choices to all living creatures, which has limited His knowledge of the future by deliberate choice.

Remember, without danger, there is no freedom!

God did not cause my father's suffering. It was human error and inadequate thermal cut-out devices on the electric blanket. Perhaps my anger should initially have been directed at the blanket manufacturer or the staff responsible for my father's operation.

My father's agony and pain was finally overcome. The hospital board paid compensation. His pain was alleviated by human kindness, human skill and surgery, by the use of drugs – all acquired by people made in God's image; people who chose to help the sick and suffering. Doctors, nurses, physiotherapists, pharmacists, volunteer car drivers, ministers, friends and family, and hospital visitors all played their parts.

His healing came through human means, but I believe it came also through the amazingly sophisticated healing processes in the human body that are part of the creative process of a competent God. Now, I have been drawn closer in my relationship with God. I can only, like Job, stand in awe, and express my own love in worship, adoration and praise.

I find that I can now trust the Creator of the Universe, who knows what He is doing.

He comes to His created beings and is willing to listen to their cries. There is a total intimacy with those who know Him as "Our Father in Heaven."

I am sure my own earthly father is without suffering in a new heavenly world that answers the questions of the present. There I hope to meet my father and discover no more pain or tears. We hope we will share in God's glory for, as Paul of Tarsus proclaims, "We shall see Him face to face."

Then we shall have an eternity to discover the answers to our ultimate questions.

Indeed, the best is yet to be!

Notes and Bibliography

NOTES

1. It is worth noting that in verses such as Genesis 24:2 'Abraham said... 'Put thy hand under my thigh' the two sides to an agreement are in fact taking hold of each other's testicles – a rather graphic (and trusting) way of sealing an agreement which actually gives us the word, "testament".

2. Virgin births were among the oldest and most common elements of ancient myths. Alexander has a virgin birth; Augustus Caesar was born of a virgin. No one could be a god unless one of the great gods had impregnated his mother. Jesus was part of God, Himself, and was born of Mary. He is called "Son of Man" and "Son of God" in Scripture. His virgin birth is recorded by four Gospel writers, by Mary, "who kept these things in her heart", and by his own numerous miracles.

3. **Halley's Bible Handbook** originally saw the vision of 'locusts with women's hair' (9:8) as predicting the rise

of Mohammed who led his troops from Arabia (the land of the locust) with their long (women's) hair swirling behind them. Others have interpreted the Great Red Dragon (12:3) as Soviet Russia, while Sun Myung Moon, who founded the Unification Church in South Korea, claims the Red Dragon to be North Korea and the woman clothed with the sun and the moon (12:1) to be his own mother, hence 'Sun' and 'Moon' in his own name.

4. **Acts** 9:1-19, 22:6-16, and 26:12-18 each tell a story of the conversion of Saul, later known as the Apostle Paul.

BIBLIOGRAPHY

1. **Universe** (Richard Joseph) **The Book of Job** with an Introduction by Louis de Bernieres
2. (Cannon Books) Anthony Kemp. **Witchcraft and Paganism Today** (Brockhampton Press)
3. **The Book of Job** with an introduction by Louis de Bernieres (Canongate Books Ltd)
4. **Great Disasters** (Readers Digest)
5. Basil Booth. **Earthshock.** (Dent)
6. A. H Strong. **Systematic Theology** (Pickering and Inglis Ltd)
7. Geoff Walters. Why **Do Christians Find it Hard to Grieve?** (Paternoster Press)
8. Jamieson, Fausset and Brown. **Commentary on the Old and New Testaments** (Marshall, Morgan and Scott)

9. Margaret B Crook. **The Cruel God** (Beacon Press)

10. Stan Telchin. **Betrayed** (Marshall, Morgan and Scott)

11. David Day. 'Jeremiah: Speaking for God in a Time of Crisis' **Bible Biographies** (Intervarsity Press)

12. Bernard Ramm. **Protestant Christian Evidences** (Moody Press)

13. John Stott. **The Cross of Christ** (Intervarsity Press)

14. Richard Wurmbrand. **Where Christ Still Suffers:** (Marshall Pickering)

15. J B Phillips. **The Book of Revelation.** (Geoffrey Bles Ltd)

16. John Stott. **What Christ Thinks of the Church** (Lutterworth)

17. William Barclay. **The Revelation of John: Volume 2** (Saint Andrew Press)

18. Paul Davies. **God and the New Physics** (Pelican)

19. Fred Hoyle. **The Intelligent Universe** (Richard Joseph)

20. Sir John Houghton ('**A God Big Enough**' Real Science: Real Faith)

21. Roy Peacock. ('**Credibility and Credo**' in Real Science: Real Faith)

22. JND Anderson. **Evidence for the Resurrection.** (Intervarsity Press)

23. Robert Boyd. **Can God be known?** (Intervarsity Press)

24. Patrick Moore. **The Great Universe** (CMP Publishing)

25. William Irwin Thompson. **The Time Falling Bodies Take to Light.** (Riding/Hutchinson & Co)

26. G. Jantzen. **God's World, God's Body.** (Dalton, Longman and Todd)

27. Andrew Pinset. **Physics World** (June 2000)

28. Bob Ogly. **In the Wake of the Hurricane**. (Froglets Publications)

29. E.K. Victor Pearce: **Evidence for Truth: Science**. (Eagle Publishing)

30. "The Nucleotide Sequence of a Viral DNA" **Scientific American,** Dec. 1977.

31. **Diabetes Wellness Letter**, March 2001

32. Richard Dawkins. Preface to **The Selfish Gene** (Oxford)

33. David Wilkinson. **God, The Big Bang and Stephen Hawking** (Monarch)

34. Harold Kushner. **When Bad Things Happen to Good People** (Pan Books)

35. Richard Harris. **Evidence for the Love of God**. (Mowbray)

36. **Animal Rights and Ways**. (Hodder and Stoughton)

37. David Howell. **Healing and Wholeness in the New Testament** (Crowhurst Occasional Paper)

38. Dennis Wheatley. **The Devil and All His Works** (Peerage Books)

39. Paul Enns. **Moody Handbook of Theology** Page 292 (Moody Press)

40. Sigmund Freud. 'The Anatomy of the Mental Personality, Lecture XXI, in **New Introductory Lectures on Psychoanalysis** (Norton 1964)

41. Leon Morris, **Revelation: Tyndale New Testament Commentary** (Intervarsity Press)

42. Paul S Fiddies. **Past Event and Present Salvation** (Darton, Longman and Todd)

43. Quoted by Colin Duriez in 'Talking Point' (**Crusade Magazine**)

44. Basilea Schlink **The Blessings of Illness** (Lakeland)

45. Ronald Melzak. '**The Perception of Pain**' (Scientific American: February 1961)

46. Hans and Michael Eysenck. **Mind Watching** (Michael Joseph Ltd)

47. J R Young. **Programs of the Brain** (Oxford) 52. Quoted by Philip Yancy.

48. **Where is God When it Hurts?** (Oxford)

49. Newday: **Leprosy – the Facts** (The Leprosy Mission, January 2001)

50. Rev. Nick Jowett. 'Street Credibility' in **The Observer** (7 July 2002) taken from the internet 'Guardian unlimited site'

51. Paul Davies **God and the New Physics** (Pelican)

About the Author

eoffrey E L Bennett is author of **Why Does God Not Answer Prayer? Can a Christian be gay?** And **How Does God Guide?** By Credo Research Publishing.

He has also written five romantic novels under the pen name of Olive Youngly.

The Kids Book of Weather, Kids Book of Rocks, and **Kids Book of Oceans are also from Geoffrey.**

Geoffrey served in the Royal Army Medical Corps for three years, including a two-year period on active service in Malaya.

He graduated from the University of Regina, Canada, (with Great Distinction), where he studied English, Philosophy, Anthropology, and Geography.

In addition, he obtained the Fellowship Degree from the College of Preceptors, London; holds the University of London Certificate of Proficiency in Religious Knowledge; the University of London Teacher's Certificate in History and Divinity (with Merit): and received the Biblical Studies Diploma (with Distinction) from All Nations Bible College.

Following early retirement as Head of Religious Studies at a UK grammar school, Geoffrey was accepted for the Baptist ministry. He served as Chaplain's Assistant for six years, counseling, offering the sacraments, conducting regular hospital worship, and providing spiritual guidance for staff and patients at the William Harvey Hospital, Ashford, Kent.

Married with two sons, he has been a popular speaker and ecumenical Bible Teacher and preacher in Methodist and Brethren Assemblies in Malaysia and Singapore; in Mennonite, Baptist and the United Churches of Canada; and in Baptist, Methodist, Brethren, Pentecostal, Anglican, and Free Churches in Britain.

Christine, Geoffrey's wife, was in a Nursing Home with paralysis and vascular-dementia caused by two brain-tumours and died recently; while Geoffrey is Diabetic (on insulin) and has heart disease and Cancer.

He has just retired as an Associate Tutor at the University of Sussex, UK, with the "Carers and Service Users Network" in the Social Work department.

Now remarried to Diane, he enjoys retirement in Southern England, and is Chairman of an Inter-church Men's Coffee Morning, which meets monthly.